Determinants of Public Interest Cable Communications Policies

Stephen C. Godek

University Press of America, Inc.
Lanham • New York • London

Copyright © 1996 by
University Press of America,® Inc.
4720 Boston Way
Lanham, Maryland 20706

3 Henrietta Street
London, WC2E 8LU England

Library of Congress Cataloging-in-Publication Data

Godek, Stephen C.
Determinants of public interest cable communications policies /
Stephen C. Godek.
p.   cm.
Includes bibliographical references and index.
1. Telecommunication policy--United States. 2. Cable television--
United States. 3. Communication--Social aspects--United States. I.
Title.
HE7781.G593   1995   384.55'51 --dc20   95-39228 CIP

ISBN 0-7618-0158-8 (cloth : alk: ppr.)

⊖™The paper used in this publication meets the minimum
requirements of American National Standard for information
Sciences—Permanence of Paper for Printed Library Materials,

Contents

List of Tables and Figures

Acknowledgements

I owe my first debt of gratitude to Doris Graber, who, as my dissertation advisor, encouraged me to apply my interest in communication policies to an examination of cable communications when I as casting about for a dissertation topic. Chronologically, my next debt must be paid to Denese Wecker as well as to my other students, as well as colleagues, at California State University who helped me with data collection and coding while I was teaching and finishing the first incarnation of this book as my dissertation. During that time I was also graciously helped by comments from colleagues, including, Paul Schmidt, at Cal State, Long Beach, and Kas Kalba, of Kalba Bowen Associates.

For typing the first complete draft of the dissertation and forgiving me for forgetting her birthday during the process, my wife, Merrilee, deserves more thanks than I can give.

I would feel that I've been remiss if I were to fail to mention two anonymous reviewers (one from another press, the other secured through the good offices of Doris Graber) whose criticisms were trenchant but encouraging enough to make finishing this project seem possible. If either of your should get the opportunity to read this book, I hope you will recognize who you are and understand that I genuinely appreciated your efforts to make this book the best it could be.

At the College of Wooster, special thanks go to Stan Hales, vice president of academic affairs (and acting president, at the time of this writing), and Yvonne Williams and Susan Figge, successive deans of the faculty, who had enough confidence in me to provide essential funds for getting this work published. Dijana Plestina, chair of the political science department at Wooster, gently pushed me to do the things necessary to get this into print, and for that I will be forever grateful.

Finally, to Michele Harris, Julie Kirsch, and Helen Hudson, at University Press of America, I offer my thanks for keeping this project alive even after I thought it had died too often to be resuscitated.

According to custom, and with the utmost fairness, I hold anyone other than myself blameless for any errors, conceptual or mechanical, that still may afflict this book.

Chapter 1

Problems in Cable Communication Policy

The coaxial cable as a communications medium has had (and continues to have) its advocates and adversaries. From an inauspicious beginning as an extension of the broadcasting system in the United States, the cable system has come to be recognized as an independent medium capable of carrying not only broadcast programs but a great variety of other forms of information and entertainment as well. It has been seen by some as a means of realizing the seemingly contradictory goals of programming diversity and localism which the Federal Communications Commission has long held for the broadcast system.[1] In addition, the relatively unlimited number of channels and potential for two-way communications on "the cable" have been touted as means by which citizens could finally "talk back" to both their televisions and their governments as well as receive services providing for their security and convenience.[2]

But the "blue sky" promises of cable enthusiasts have not gone unanswered by cable's critics. As soon as large scale deployment of cable technologies appeared feasible, critics in the broadcasting and common carrier industries began to warn of the deleterious effects of cable's unfair competitive advantage on the existing media of communication.[3] Beyond these criticisms, which were motivated by economic interests, many have questioned the wisdom of emphasizing the development of a subscription-supported medium as likely to aggravate the information gap which already exists between rich and poor.[4] Still others see cable's two-way potential as an invader of privacy and an instrument of mass manipulation bringing us a large step closer to the dystopias of authors like George Orwell and Aldous Huxley.[5]

Arguments on both sides of the cable issue merely serve to emphasize the importance of careful analysis before policy decisions affecting the development of communications technologies like cable can be made. The basic question we must ask is how new technologies can be organized to operate in the public's interests. This question, when applied to any new technology is problematic for two reasons: First, technological innovations are often accompanied by claims about their potential usefulness which remain untested until relatively new applications have been widely implemented. Although cable systems have become so commonplace as to convince many that the industry has reached a mature stage, we remain largely uncertain about the practical uses to which the medium can be put. Hence we are unsure of where the real public interests in cable lie and, consequently, what standards we should apply to assessing societal attempts to organize the application of this technology. Second, despite the explosion of cable franchising during the late 1970s and early 1980s, we have very little generalizable knowledge about the factors which affect policies regarding uses of the cable medium. This problem is, of course, closely related to the difficulty in specifying public interests in this area or in any issue area. Without a clearly articulated consensus on the standards for applying cable technology to the fulfillment of public interests, it is difficult to determine what cable policies we should be trying to implement. Yet, even within a consensus about the potential value of deploying cable communication systems, we have little knowledge about how this potential can be realized.

The research upon which this book is based was motivated by an interest in these two problems, and the book will address them in turn. First, in this chapter and the next, we shall examine the nature of public interests with regard to cable communications policies. From this examination we draw out at least a preliminary understanding of the dimensions of public interests in cable. These dimensions, diversity, localism, and interactive capability will provide the structure for a review of research findings regarding the potential of cable to serve or promote public interests in the communities in which systems are built. We shall then review explanations for the current shape of cable communications policies and empirically examine the validity of these explanations. Since the explanations are not mutually exclusive, we will examine tests of potential syntheses which contain elements of each explanation in statistical models of the determinants of cable communications policies, with particular emphasis on those policies with the greatest potential for serving the interests of communities in which cable systems operate.

Public Interests and Cable Technologies

The concept of public interest, regardless of the policy area involved, is enveloped in controversy. Although the concept found widespread application in both the theoretical formulations of political science and in the justifications of a variety of policy actions, an argument has been waged for some time over its usefulness. Basically, the argument revolves around the concrete applicability of the term as a standard for public decisions. Methodological individualism and a concern for the empirical accessibility of concepts have led many political scientists and economists to argue that the concept of public interest, as applied to any collectivity, can be reasonably understood as nothing more than the sum of individual private interests of the members of a community.[6] This conception focuses on the definition of "interests" as preferences held by individuals. As attributes of individuals, interests are held to be observable only in the demand for various actions as revealed in the willingness of individuals to overtly consent to, or pay for, those actions or their consequences. As such, the concept of a public interest which overrides the private interests of individuals as a justification for policy has been treated, at best, as an unobservable (and therefore unscientific) fiction, or, worse, as a value-laden rationalization for the imposition of the preferences of a segment of society on the society as a whole.

I will assume an alternative position which treats public interests as objectively identifiable grounds for policy by focusing on the motive force of interests as guides to action, rather than the preference interpretation of the term. In this view, any action which is reasonably likely to produce some good, or, conversely, avoid some harm, to a community is considered to be in the public interest.[7] The usefulness of this conception in empirical research turns on the ability to identify and reasonably assess the potential for positive and negative effects of various actions. Once the potential outcomes of various actions have been assessed can we begin to see the dimensions of public interest in any particular situation. The nature of these outcomes depend upon the technical capacities for action available to any individual, organization, or community, and, upon the constraints affecting the organization of actions to employ those capabilities. The problem of designing a policy to promote the implementation of cable communications technologies in the public's interest is largely one of understanding and manipulating the technical, legal-political, and economic constraints within which efforts to organize cable systems take place.

In order to understand the dimensions of the public interest in cable communication systems then, we must begin with a review of the technological structure of a typical cable system. The general principle underlying an cable system is a "communications tree", a network with includes: 1. A central transmission point (the "head end"), 2. A branching network of coaxial cables, amplifiers, and switching devices reaching out from the head end to, 3. various peripheral devices such as television receivers, computer terminals, printers or facsimile machines, and other automatons which may be controlled by electrical impulse.

The head end of a cable system will normally have facilities to receive signals (e.g., an antenna, microwave station, and/or satellite dish) and to transmit those signals over the cable network to the peripheral devices located in the system's area of operation. Alternatively, the head end must have facilities for the production or reproduction of other media of communication or information storage or retrieval (e.g., film or videotape cameras and replay equipment). Thus the central transmitting station (head end) may send programs from various sources, including other media, and/or the cable system's local production unit out to the peripheral devices in the community it serves.

Transmissions from the head end are carried to peripheral devices via coaxial cables which may be strung on poles or run underground. Usually existing utility poles (e.g., telephone poles) or underground conduits (e.g., those used for electric power lines) are used. The cable network usually consists of a "trunk" line which runs through the service area, a number of "feeder" lines which carry the signals from the trunk to the areas served, and "drop" lines which connect individual sites or peripheral devices to the feeder lines. Since electronic signals transmitted via coaxial cable are degraded in proportion to the distance they must travel, all but the smallest cable systems include amplifiers to maintain the quality of the signal over longer distances.

The channel capacity of cable systems far exceeds that of the broadcast media in any locale. A single-cable system may carry twenty separate channels of information. Deployment of multiple cable systems makes channel capacity technically unlimited. This release from the constraints on the number of communications channels available to a community is especially important when we consider that information may flow two ways on the same cable system. Even if only one-way transmissions are made on the system, the channel capacity makes possible a diversity of information sources which cannot be approached by broadcast media.

The combination of the relatively limited area which may be served by cable lines and this large channel capacity makes cable an ideal medium for the transmission of locally originated programming. The capacity for local origination was one of the first non-broadcast uses of cable systems. Local origination of cable programs may include automated channels, live programs originated in studios at the head end or at remote facilities connected to the head end, and "canned" programs on film, tape, or other information storage medium. The issue of local origination of cable programming is also related to the potential access of individual citizens or groups to channels of a truly local community-oriented medium.[8] This is what has made cable a unique instrument for promoting localism in our mass communication system.

Finally, a cable network may include switching devices located at various points which permit signals to be sent from peripheral devices "upstream" to the head end. Thus a cable system is potentially a two-way medium of communication and information which has distinctly different technical capabilities from broadcast systems (one-way, from transmitter to viewer or listener) and telephone-telegraph systems (point-to-point interactive communication systems). The interactive character of cable communications may be applied to remote program origination sites with direct interconnection by cable between remote sites and between each site and the head end.[9]

Perhaps the most important aspect of cable technologies is the wide variety of peripheral devices to which cables may be connected. Practically any form of electronic information processing device may be wired to a cable system. Thus, although cable communications have been generally equated with cable television, cable systems can provide a wide variety of non-broadcast programs and services such as centralized burglar and fire alarm systems, automatic utility billing, electronic credit and banking transactions, public bulletin boards,[10] polling of cable subscribers,[11] meetings conducted with various degrees of participant interaction,[12] and a variety of "on-demand" services in which subscribers control the content and timing of their use of information or entertainment services.[13]

Cable communication systems have come to be identified with improved television reception and an increased number of video programming channels, but their potential uses are limited only by decisions concerning the investment of resources in particular configurations of technical facilities. These decisions constitute public policies regarding the development and use of available communications technologies. Decisions about the technologies deployed in a given system define the limits on uses of cable communications until technical innovations and the organization of resources in a given community permit a change in the system's configuration. The most important constraints on the application of cable technologies, however, are not technical but political and economic in nature.

History and Political Economy of the Cable Industry

The cable communications industry in the United States began during the late 1940s and early 1950s as an adjunct of the television broadcasting system. Cable systems were first constructed in rural areas where distance from broadcasting stations or terrain prevented clear reception of television signals. The pioneers of the industry were typically small business people who constructed cable systems primarily to stimulate demand for television receivers. The systems themselves were relatively simple, consisting of a strategically placed antenna from which nearby television signals were re-transmitted to subscribers via coaxial cables. Later some systems began to interconnect using microwave and satellite networks which brought the possibility of not only clear reception of the closest television stations but also reception of more distant signals.

By the 1960s the success of these small cable operators had begun to attract larger investors who began to put together groups, or multiple system ownerships (MSOs). This industrialization was accompanied by a wave of "blue sky" promises about the unlimited potential of cable technologies. A period of overselling cable ensued as operators began to recognize the profits likely to be generated when cable penetrated large, densely populated urban markets. The aggressive marketing efforts of early cable industrialists prompted broadcasters to seek regulatory protection of their primary markets from competition with cable.

From 1963 to 1985 regulatory policy affecting the development of the cable industry was made in a three-tiered system in which federal, state, and local governments were all involved. At the national level, regulation by the Federal Communications Commission began in 1963 and was upheld by the Supreme Court in 1968.[14] The earliest federal regulations affecting cable system operations were formulated in response to the demands of over-the-air broadcasters that the F.C.C. protect their markets from encroachment by the emerging cable industry. During this phase of federal regulation, the Commission imposed severe restrictions on signal carriage, mandating carriage of all local VHF and UHF television signals and forbidding carriage of distant signals from stations which might compete with local broadcast outlets.[15] Between 1968 and 1972 the F.C.C. put a freeze on the development of new cable systems in the top 100 television markets. In addition, F.C.C. rules limited the interconnection of cable systems, forbade ownership of cable systems by common carriers, and prohibited pay channel operations. This protection slowed the growth of the cable industry in the late 'sixties.

Nevertheless, by 1970 a phase of consolidation in the industry had begun and very large MSOs began to appear. In 1972, the basis for federal regulation shifted from the protection of broadcasting interests by prohibiting certain types of cable services to the imposition of a requirement that cable systems positively address the development of their potential for serving public interests. In a 1972 *Report and Order*,[16] the Commission required that all cable systems serving more than 3,500 subscribers provide the equivalent of twenty television channels and a technical capability for non-voice return (two-way) communications by 1986. These systems were also required to provide "access" channels for public, educational, government, and leased channel uses where there was a demand for them, and to meet fairness, equal time, gambling, and obscenity requirements in locally originated programs. Although implementation of the 1972 *Report and Order* was lax, the rules generated a great deal of opposition from the cable industry which saw them as extensions of the F.C.C.'s attempt to protect broadcasters from competition. Despite these regulations and despite the contraction of capital markets in the national economy, cable firms were able to continue their expansion through the mid-seventies by offering an increasing variety of services to subscribers and using the strong cash flows generated by subscriptions and local advertising to attract investments from banks, insurance companies, and other corporations hungry for cash.

By 1975 the Commission's rationale for involvement in cable regulation had shifted away from protecting broadcasting and toward the promotion of the cable industry. The shift was further emphasized by a number of court rulings invalidating F.C.C. regulatory decisions in the areas of pay programming[17] and access requirements.[18] In the late 'seventies, the expansion of the cable industry had become a boom of major proportions fueled by the availability of satellite transmissions and the piece-meal deregulation of various aspects of cable operations.[19] These made cable a viable alternative to traditional television services even in the largest broadcast markets, and a period of aggressive bidding for franchises in the largest U.S. cities began. Despite the setback to the industry's development caused by the recession of 1981-82, cable penetration of urban markets was practically complete by the late 'eighties.

More recently, the F.C.C.'s move toward total deregulation of the cable industry has been legislatively sanctioned in the Cable Communications Policy Act of 1984, which took effect in December of that year. The act ended the three-tiered structure of cable regulation by pre-empting regulatory authority for the federal government and formally deregulating many aspects of cable system operations.[20]

The deregulation effected by the Cable Communications Act of 1984 had three important effects. First, provisions in the Act allowing for looser controls on the ownership of cable systems promoted consolidation and concentration of ownership in the industry. The four- and eight-firm concentration ratios for the cable industry by 1995 were 28% and 35% respectively. Furthermore, the largest MSOs have been acquiring each other as antitrust policies have been relaxed through the 1980s and 1990s. [21] The increase in cable rates in the late 1980s was a second and related effect. Although it probably cannot be solely attributed to the increased concentration of ownership in the cable industry, the ownership of systems by a smaller proportion of the firms in the industry constituted a reduction in competition that had relatively predictable effects on prices, at least until other technologies (e.g., direct satellite) diffused to the point where they represented realistic alternatives to cable. Finally, the Act, by both mandating public access and government channels and limiting the authority of local franchisors to introduce new demands into their franchise requirements had the effect of freezing innovation in the industry, as cable service packages became standardized and systems came under the ownership of fewer and larger MSOs.

Although concentration of ownership in the cable industry and reduction in innovative programming packages might have been good reasons for reconsidering the wisdom of deregulation, the demand for re-regulating the cable industry appears to have been fed primarily by concern over rising cable subscription rates. Ironically, this emphasis on rates over service packages or monopoly concerns was an indication of the maturation of the cable industry which had fueled the earlier demand for deregulation. Whether the cable industry had actually entered a mature phase of its development by the early 1980s may have been questionable, but it appears that after deregulation maturity came rapidly to the industry as product became standardized and investment stabilized. However, despite this maturity, which had been claimed as the justification for deregulating the industry, consumer concerns focussed on rising cable rates eventually generated a political demand to rescind the deregulation of the industry and reintroduce controls on rates. By the early 1990s this demand led to the passage of the Cable Communications Consumer Protection Act of 1992 which Congress passed over President Bush's veto and which amended the Cable Communications Act of 1984 reintroducing some controls on rate increases.

By the mid-1990s, the deregulatory urge had received an unexpected boost from the defeat of the Democratic majorities in both houses of the Congress. It appears that the new Communications Act, a long overdue revision of the original Communications Act of 1934, will include provisions once again removing regulatory constraints on cable rates, this time with a sounder justification in the argument that the industry is mature and competitive. In fact, the cable industry has joined the telephone and broadcasting industries in seeking the shape this legislation to their advantage in the face of potential competition from satellite and computer communications.

Until the passage of the Cable Communications Act of 1984, cable regulation at the state level had varied greatly from state to state. While 43 states enacted some form of legislation affecting cable systems, only 11 set up permanent regulatory agencies to deal specifically with cable communications.[22] Typically, state laws affecting cable involved provisions regarding theft of service (29 states) or franchising authority (22 states). Most states granted franchising authority to local governments; only 5 states pre-empted this authority for themselves.[23]

In terms of relative restrictiveness, the states could be roughly ranked into several categories. The least restrictive cable regulations were in states which enacted no legislation or only protective regulations (e.g., laws regarding theft of cable services, tax and licensing exemptions, etc.). At the opposite end of the scale would be states which enacted legislation restricting the activities of cable firms (e.g., establishing construction or technical requirements over and above those imposed by the F.C.C., constraining channel use, regulating rates, etc.) or establishing comprehensive cable regulations under special cable regulatory agencies or existing public utility commissions. Between these poles would fall states which enacted a balance of protective and restrictive laws.

The post-1975 tendency toward deregulation of cable at the federal level was reflected in some states as well. In the late 1970s, the states with independent cable regulatory agencies revised franchising standards for local governments in a deregulatory direction. Connecticutt, which had previously limited the duration of certificates of public convenience and necessity to a maximum of 15 years, moved in 1979 to require perpetual franchises. In California, the most heavily cabled state, the state legislature, in May, 1982, extended a bill, originally passed in 1979, allowing cable system operators to unilaterally deregulate rates under certain conditions.

At the level of individual cable systems, the predominant regulatory mechanism affecting cable policies has been local franchising. Although federal and state laws acted as general constraints, the franchise has been (and under the Cable Communications Act of 1984 continued to be) the basic policy document of any cable system. The franchise is basically a contract between the cable system's owner and the local government responsible for controlling rights-of-way under its jurisdiction. In it, policies regarding the ownership structure of the system, services to be provided, rates charged, and other terms under which the system will operate are specified.

Local franchising of cable systems has been justified by a variety of arguments. First, cable systems are usually local monopolies. Overlapping service areas and direct competition for subscribers by existing systems is rare. Therefore, households must subscribe to the local cable system or forego its services entirely. Furthermore, once a television receiver has been connected to the cable system it can no longer receive normal over-the-air broadcasts unless it is disconnected and switched to its own antenna. Consequently, there is some concern that the cable operator, holding an exclusive franchise in a service area, may be able to exercise monopoly power and extract surplus profits by charging excessively high rates or offering inferior service. Although the extent to which cable operators can actually exercise this monopoly power is unclear,[23] many local governments have relied upon this possibility to justify their jurisdiction in franchising matters. A related argument for local franchising and regulation has been made on the basis of the similarity of cable systems to public utilities which are regulated on the grounds that they are local monopolies.

A more stable argument for local regulation stems from the necessity for cable operators to use public rights-of-way (utility poles, underground ducts, streets and easements) to provide cable services to subscribers. Ever since the earliest cable systems in the late '40s and early '50s, local governments have looked upon the franchise as a contract for the use of rights-of-way under their control.

Aside from the legal arguments supporting local franchising, there is also a significant argument based on the economic efficiency of such an arrangement. Franchising authority represents a mechanism for reducing contract costs for both providers and consumers of cable communication services. By contracting with a system operator to provide cable services in a given area, local governments aggregate the interests (and demands) of constituents who will be the ultimate consumers of those services. This eliminates for the operator the prohibitive expense of negotiating separate contracts with each subscriber and allows for the packaging of a single set of services capable of attracting subscribers within the franchise area. At the same time, the franchising agency, by acting as a purchasing agent for the community it represents, reduces the information costs to subscribers by undertaking the search for a system configuration and service package that will satisfy its constituents' demands and interests. Since the contract costs of purely competitive development of cable systems would be prohibitive, the franchising arrangement is not only a more efficient form of organization for operators and the communities of subscribers, it is practically necessary if cable systems are to be built at all.

Early in the history of the cable industry's development, granting a franchise was considered a relatively unproblematic, *pro forma* function with franchises going to operators who met the barest minimum of requirements. As the industry developed, however, franchisors exercised increasing authority in both franchise negotiations and post-franchise regulation of cable systems. There are two reasons for the increased intervention by local governments: 1. As the potential for providing non-broadcast services via cable systems was realized, local governments began to self-consciously perceive themselves as purchasing agents, bargaining with franchise applicants for the mix of services and rates which would best serve their conception of their constituents' interests. Thus there was an increasing tendency for expanded service and lower, or controlled, rates to be incorporated as conditions for granting cable franchises; and, 2. An important aspect of franchise negotiations is the franchise fee paid by the cable operator to the franchising agency. Several methods of payment have been used, but the main types of payments have been either fixed annual fees or a percentage of the system's gross income. Local governments beset with a deepening fiscal crisis have found cable systems more and more attractive as revenue sources and have tended to require a percentage of gross revenues as a franchising fee.[25]

Despite increasing sophistication on the part of local officials dealing with franchise bidders and a tendency on the part of these officials to view requirements related to channel capacities, access, and content related issues as important to choice of a franchisee, possibilities for local regulation were somewhat hampered by Supreme Court decisions and the passage of the Cable Communications Act of 1984. In *CCI vs. Boulder, Col.*[26] the court ruled that cities may be violating anti-trust laws by regulating cable franchises. Although the ruling was not expected to have a major impact on local franchising authority, Cynthia Pols, legislative counsel for the National League of Cities has pointed out that "It (would) have a chilling effect in the sense that it (would) create probably more doubt in the minds of city officials than there should legitimately be."[27] Indeed, concern for the confusion brought about by the piece-meal judicial and administrative dismantling of the existing regulatory structure affecting cable brought negotiators from the League of Cities together with representatives of the cable industry in the formulation and passage of the Cable Act of 1984.

With the passage in December, 1984, of the *National Cable Communications Policy Act*, the cable industry entered a new era. The primary effect of the act was to officially sanction the deregulation of the cable industry which had been going on in the F.C.C. and in the courts for ten years. The Act was a response by the Congress to an increasingly vocal demand by the cable industry for relief from the regulatory burdens which were placed on cable operators by the tripartite system of federal, state, and local regulations which had evolved. The Act pre-empts regulatory authority over cable operations for the federal government and then effectively deregulates most aspects of the industry at that level. In a compromise that neutralized the opposition to the Act by local governments (which give up authority to regulate subscription rates), local franchising authority was retained and guidelines for the franchising process were established. Rules requiring local access programming were also included, but the primary intent of the act was to remove most of the formal constraints that had come to be seen as impediments to the development of the cable industry erected by all three levels of government.

Over the next decades three trends in the industry appear likely to continue: 1. The concentration of ownership in the industry; 2. The slow expansion of services provided by cable systems; and, 3. The continued penetration of large urban markets.

The most salient economic fact about the cable industry is that the enterprise is highly capital-intensive. The construction of a cable system is an extremely expensive project. The average cost of wiring a community in 1982 was estimated at $600 to $800 per household. This means that an average system built in the mid-1980s would involve construction costs between $11 and $15 million. Furthermore, the cable industry's need for capital investment is not likely to slacken even after total penetration of available U.S. markets because the upgrading of older systems and addition of new technologies (e.g., fiber optic cables) may require extensive rebuilding of systems well into the twenty-first century.

This appetite for capital has a number of implications for the future of the industry. First, as in other capital-intensive enterprises, there is a strong incentive for the concentration of ownership in the industry as a whole. Both economies of scale and the relative advantages of larger firms in capital markets are at work here and a trend toward oligopolization of the industry appears inevitable in the absence of vigorously enforced anti-trust regulation.[28]

Second, although a number of observers have pointed to the similarities between the cable and utility industries as a justification for public control, it is highly improbable that local governments will be willing to assume the responsibility for building cable systems themselves. Nor is it likely that municipalities will take over the operation of existing systems. Once a system is built, investors have strong claims against public takeover. Thus public ownership and control of cable systems, which is currently very rare, is not likely to become more common.

Third, despite the tax advantages of carrying the kind of debt involved in building a cable system, cable operators must look to the ultimate profitability of their systems. This means that they will need to attract and maintain subscriber bases sufficient to generate advertising revenues capable of covering their operating expenses and eventually retiring their debt. This dependence on subscriptions may act as a force for innovation in the development of new services and cable-related technologies but it will also emphasize the "private good" aspects of cable services. Individual subscribers are likely to be unwilling to subsidize the costs of community uses of cable and operators are therefore not likely to emphasize these uses in their attempts to attract customers. Also related to the profitability of the cable enterprise, is the need to minimize operating expenses such as payrolls and programming costs. Taken together with the need to attract subscribers, this implies that cable system operators will be likely to prefer automated and/or satellite fed programming to locally originated programs. It may also imply a preference for offering leased channels if operators can avoid identification as utilities subject to strict regulation of content. At any rate, the mix of forces impelling innovative applications of cable technologies, while continuing to operate in favor of expanding the diversity cable services offered to subscribers, are likely to do so at a relatively slow pace.

Finally, one major effect of the Cable Policy Act of 1984 was to open up for cable penetration the large urban markets which had been protected for broadcasting stations by the bulk of federal regulations. Thus this penetration is likely to continue until saturation of the potential cable markets nationwide is practically complete. By 1994 with 90% of U.S. homes with televisions passed by cable systems, the industry has already come very near to complete saturation. Thus future development of the cable industry is likely to be driven more by the effects of other communication technologies that are likely to compete with cable for consumer acceptance.

The Functions of Regulation

Even this brief review of the history of cable regulation should be sufficient to illustrate the complexity of the system of cable regulation in the pre-1984 period and the confusion at all levels of government regarding cable communication systems.   Although the Cable Communications Policy Acts of 1984 and its amendment in 1992 have reduced this confusion, a number of questions regarding cable regulation cannot be answered by legislative action.   Although the Act of 1984 authorized a wholesale deregulation of the cable industry and the Act of 1992 established federal authority to regulate cable subscription rates, these Acts did not address deeper questions. Assuming that the decision to locate responsibility for the implementation of cable technology in the hands of private firms is irrevocable, what is the appropriate function of government as an agent of the public interest in this area?   How can we ensure the proper consideration of communities' goals in the private calculations which determine cable policies?   Essentially, we must ask how regulatory policies may be employed to induce private firms to provide public goods.

In order to answer this question, it will be helpful to step back from the case of cable communications and consider the concept of regulation more generally.   We may then attempt to apply our general analysis to the specific problems of cable communications with greater confidence than the history of policy in this area is likely to inspire.

Articulation errors are failures to meet demands for desired outcomes of organizational actions.   The failure to produce enough of a particular good to satisfy the consumers of that good and the production of more of a good than will be consumed are both forms of articulation error; so is the suboptimal provision of some public good.   This type of error is caused by the inability of an organization to respond to rapid changes either the supply of its resources, including available technologies, or in the demand for its products or services.

Control errors involve the ability of organizations to unilaterally impose undesirable outcomes on other organizations, consumers, or the public.   This kind of an error is a result of suboptimization, that is, the tendency of any subunit of an organization to emphasize its particular goals over those of the parent organization or of society as a whole. When this tendency is unchecked, the suboptimizing organization is likely to commit control errors in the attempt to defend itself against the uncertainty of its environment.   The notion of monopoly power in economic theory is based on the possibility that a single supplier of a good may commit control errors by either undersupplying the market or overcharging for the good.

As long as organizational errors remain marginal, i.e., within the margins set by a shifting social consensus, an organization will retain its legitimacy as an autonomous actor in society.   However, when social errors exceed the current margins of acceptable risk, or when societal acceptance of a given level of error changes, the organization is likely to be faced with a demand that it submit to external controls, i.e., regulation.

John T. Scholz has developed a typology of functions of regulatory policy based, in part, on the capability of firms to avoid social errors.[29] Scholz points out that most research on public regulation has assumed that firms are highly capable organizations and that the rationale for regulation in specific industries depends upon the congruence of corporate incentives with public goals. In industries in which corporate incentives reinforce motivation to behave in a socially responsible fashion, regulation can be justified only to preserve markets as the most efficient means of organizing social activity. If, however, corporate incentives motivate socially undesirable behaviors, government should intervene to the extent that it can manipulate the motivation of the firm to act in a responsible fashion. This may be done by punishing undesirable behaviors (as in criminal sanctions or taxes on pollution creating activities) or by rewarding more desirable behaviors (e.g., tax subsidies for environmental clean-up efforts of polluters).

Scholz suggests that two more functions of regulation be added to this schema in order to handle the cases of firms with more limited capabilities of error avoidance. When firms exhibit limited capabilities but a relatively high level of agreement between corporate and public goals exists, he suggests that regulation be directed at increasing the reliability of firms by creating public systems of error detection and correction to augment those of the firms themselves. When low capability is combined with disagreement between corporate and public goals, regulation should be aimed at enhancing the adaptability of firms to public concerns. Consequently regulatory agencies must be ready to shift their functions, focusing on reliability or motivation (or both) as the regulated firms' capabilities or corporate incentives change.

Thus the functions of regulatory policy may be arrayed in a two-by-two matrix defined by the capabilities of firms in regulated industries and the congruence of corporate and public goals. (See Table 1.1, below) Furthermore, this typology may be related to the types of social errors as follows. By definition, firms with high levels of capability will minimize articulation errors, bringing them to within an acceptable margin as long as corporate incentives coincide with public goals. If corporate incentives diverge significantly from public goals, control errors are likely to occur unless some agency acts to enhance the motivation of firms to act in the public interest.

In cases where firms are less capable, both articulation errors and control errors are possible. However, as long as incentives with the firms reinforce public goals, regulation may focus on reducing articulation errors. When both corporate capabilities and congruence between corporate and public goals are low, control errors become more probable while articulation errors may also tend to exceed acceptable margins. In this case, a regulatory agency must attempt to facilitate corporate learning processes which will allow the firms in a regulated industry to develop either the capabilities or the motivation to bring social errors to within acceptable margins.

Using this typology of regulatory functions, developments in the regulation of the cable industry may be interpreted as rational responses of regulatory agents to changes in the cable industry based on their perceptions of the appropriate functions of regulation under different circumstances. The apparent shifting of federal policy, in particular, may be explained as the response of the F.C.C. to the exigencies of regulating activities in an industry marked by both low capabilities and a wide divergence between corporate and public goals. In addition, the societal definition of acceptable errors in the area of cable communications has been changing, making the apparent inconsistencies at all levels of policy-making practically unavoidable.

TABLE 1.1
APPRPORIATE FUNCTIONS
FOR REGULATORY POLICY

Capability of Firms

		HIGH	LOW
Congruence of Firms' Incentives and Public Goals	HIGH	Preserve Markets	Ensure Reliability
	LOW	Ensure Motivation	Ensure Adaptability

Adapted from Scholz (1981)

Perceived as adjuncts of the television broadcasting system, the earliest cable systems were considered unlikely sources of social errors in the provision of a comprehensive national broadcasting service. Indeed, market forces, in the form of the demand for television in areas poorly served by broadcast stations, brought these cable systems into existence. When the goal of localism was threatened by the microwave interconnection of cable systems, the F.C.C. moved to regulate cable systems in order to preserve local broadcast markets from competition with potentially attractive distant signals. Although the Commission may have been mistaken about the congruence of corporate incentives in the broadcasting industry and public goals of diversity and localism, it was reasonably committed to broadcasting as the technology of choice for achieving these goals and moved to protect broadcast markets.

The next change in F.C.C. policy regarding cable reflected the shift in the public's perception of cable technologies which occurred during the late 1960s and early 1970s. As cable began to take on the character of an independent medium capable of carrying both traditional (broadcast) television signals and newer, more diverse broadcast and non-broadcast services, the F.C.C. moved to ensure adequate motivation for cable operators to provide greater channel capacities, local originations, access channels, and two-way capabilities by requiring them as conditions for granting the certificates of compliance necessary to carry broadcast signals, the "bread and butter" of cable services. Simultaneously, the Commission was attempting to ensure the reliability of cable services through the imposition of technical standards and preserve broadcast markets through signal carriage rules.

During the early 'seventies there was also an apparent shift in the approach of state governments to cable regulation. Prior to that time, activity had been sporadic, lacking any consistent commitment to state regulatory functions. However, between 1973 and 1978 most of the state laws related to regulating cable operations were enacted. These laws tended to deal much more consistently with issues involving the reliability and motivation of cable operators. An inspection of state laws affecting cable communication systems reveals that states which enacted cable related laws between 1973 and 1978 were primarily concerned with reliability issues like complaints, construction standards, forfeitures, landlord-tenant relationships, liability, and safety. The motivation of cable operators to consider public interests was addressed in laws covering educational uses, ownership, rates, and franchising authority.

If regulatory activities through the mid-'70s can be interpreted as reasonably addressing the adaptability of cable communications enterprises to public interests, the more recent movement at all levels to deregulate cable must be attributed to a perception on the part of policy- makers that the cable industry has moved into a "mature" phase in which both the capabilities and motivation of cable firms warrant action only to preserve the operation of markets for communication services. The impression of cable firms as capable actors is apparent in the Federal Communications Commission's justifications for its deregulatory decisions, in the character of state laws enacted since 1978, and in the Cable Act of 1984.

In effect, the actions at higher levels of government had, until 1984, recognized local responsibility for performing the regulatory function of ensuring adaptability of the cable operator to public interests as defined at the community level. However, the direction of regulatory policy suggested by the *Boulder* decision and some of the provisions of the *Cable Communications Policy Act* removed much of the regulatory authority of local agencies and replaced it with an exclusive federal jurisdiction that provides for minimal, mostly market-preserving, regulatory functions. By the late 1980s, cable rates increased by about three times the general rate of inflation. More importantly, rates charged for basic cable services which constitute a minimum price for cable, for the first time exceeded rates for premium services and the complaints of consumers regarding this increase generated a strong political demand for reregulation that was clearly based on the perception of these increases as evidence of the occurrence of a control error in which cable monopolies were violating the public interest in reasonable prices for cable services. As a result, attention was shifted from the types and quality of cable services to prices and the industry was ostensibly re-regulated in the Cable Communications and Consumer Protection Act of 1992. Although this Act may have brought decreased rates for both basic and premium cable services[30], the change in the political climate in the U.S. Congress symbolized by the Republican majorities achieved in the 1994 mid-term elections and the ascendance of a commitment to deregulated markets as the most appropriate policy response to almost any issue have allowed for a shift back to treating the cable industry as both capable and motivated to act in the public interest.

During these latest gyrations in basic policy premises, attention to the public interest potential of cable programming policies has receded and an almost exclusive concern for the rates charged for what are assumed to be standardized cable service packages has dominated policy discussion. Built into this assumption is the perception that cable is both a mature industry and one which faces meaningful competition from newer broadband communications technologies (e.g, satellite, low-power broadcasting, computer networks). One of the basic questions I shall address is whether the cable industry has ever actually entered a "mature" phase characterized by high levels of capability and congruence of industry incentives with the interests of communities served by cable firms. It is the thesis of this book that, while the industry has shown signs of being able to respond to demands for an increasing number of channels, the cable market does not allocate the available channels to the uses for which cable is uniquely suited as an instrument of localism to promote interests of the communities in which cable systems operate. The current perception of the maturity of the cable industry is based on an exclusive reliance upon channel capacity as the standard of the industry's level of capability and of rates as an indicator or the congruence of cable firm's goals with public interests. Furthermore, evidence regarding the rate-making behaviors of cable firms has been overlooked in favor of a presumed superiority of the market as a device for setting efficient prices. Thus, while the cable industry may be displaying the maturity necessary to assure fulfillment of the goal of diversity (at least at a superficial level), the real diversity of uses of cable as a local and interactive medium of communication remains dependent upon public intervention promoting those uses.

Before we examine the argument supporting this thesis, we will develop an understanding of what community interests might have been served by cable communications systems. As we have seen in this chapter, the technological capacities of cable systems appear to make them ideal instruments for promoting diverse, local, and interactive communications within cabled communities. In the next chapter we will turn to the task of assessing the technical capabilities of cable systems to serve interests in diversity, localism, and interactive services. We will then examine the determinants of policies which promote these interests.

---

1 FCC policies affecting cable systems are described and analyzed in Smith(1970), Sloan Commission (1971), Seiden(1972), LeDuc (1973,1976), Baer, et. al.. (1974), Hollowell(1975,1977, 1980), Ross, Owen and Braeutigam (1978), Krasnow and Longley (1978), Shapiro(1980,1981), Cole(1981) and Stein(1985).

2 The potential of interactive cable is discussed in Steiner(1972), Pool(1973), Page(1973), Veith(1976), and Schoenberger(1979). See, also, works cited in chapter 2.

3 An excellent summary of the economic literature generated by this controversy is found in Park(1972).

4 Strasser(n.d.), Laudon(1977), Sackman(1971), and Kay(1978) all make this argument.

5 Steiner(1972), Laudon(1977), Hollowell(1980).

[6]   Schubert(1960) reviewed the concept of "public interest" and reached this conclusion.

[7]   7. Flathman(1966); See, also, Linblom's (1977) concept of "volitions" for a similar derivation of the distinction between preferences and motivating interests.

[8]   Othmer(1973), Ksobiech(1975), Wurtzel(1975), Bretz(1975), Doty(1975), Wenner(1975), Topper and Wilson(1976) and others cited in Chapter 2.

[9]   Burns and Elton(1978), Moss(1978a), Chapters 2 and 3.

[10]   Sabbah(1985), Ash(1984), Scott(1978), Schoenberger(1979).

[11]   Campbell(1974), Laudon(1977) Ch. 2, Schoenberger(1979), Sackman(1971).

[12]   Pool(1973), Laudon(1977), Baldwin(1978), Moss(1978a).

[13]   Pool(1973), Cable Television Information Center(1974).

[14]   *U.S. v. Southwestern Cable Co.*, 392 U.S. 157. See, also, Cantor and Cantor(1986) for a brief synopsis of the history of cable regulation in the United States.

[15]   Seiden(1972) reviews the history of federal policy through 1972.

[16]   Federal Communications Commission, "Cable Television Report and Order," 37 *Fed.Reg.* 3252(1972).

[17]   *Home Box Office v. F.C.C.*, 567 F. 2d 9 (1977) cert. denied, 434 U.S. 829 (1977).

[18]   *F.C.C. v. Midwest Video Corp.*, 440 U.S. 689 (1979). See, also, Nimelman(1982) for a comment on the impact of Supreme Court deregulatory decisions on the cable industry.

[19]   FCC deregulation is reviewed in Stein(1985), Wiley and Neustadt(1982), Cole(1981), and Shapiro(1980).

[20]   Cable Communications Policy Act of 1984, Public Law 98-549, 98 STAT. 2779, 47 U.S.C. 609 note, October 30, 1984.

[22]   Alaska, Connecticutt, Hawaii, Massachusetts, Minnesota, Nevada, New Jersey, New York, Rhode Island, and Vermont.

[23]   Alaska, Connecticutt, Hawaii, Rhode Island, and Vermont.

[24]   Posner(1980).

[25]   Seiden (1972 and 1965).

[26]   *Community Communications Co., Inc. v. City of Boulder, Col., et al.*. No. 80-1350, Jan. 13, 1982; 456 U.S. 1001(1982).

[27]   *Los Angeles Times*, January 19, 1982.

[28]   Sabbah(1985), Salmons(1984), Howard(1981).

[29]   Scholz(1981).

[30]   The actual impact of the reregulation under the Cable Communications and Consumer Protection Act of 1992 is difficult to determine. Although both basic and premium service rates have declined industrywide since passage of

the Act, changes in the rate structures of many of the largest MSOs have made determination of whether rates have gone up or down practically impossible. See, Crandall (1994).

Chapter 2

Public Interests and Cable Communications

The potential benefits of cable communication technologies have been proclaimed in the popular press and in official studies since the early 1970s.[1] Although the medium was originally conceived as an adjunct to television designed to serve viewers in areas where broadcast signals could not be transmitted, cable system developers and observers quickly recognized the wide variety of broadcast and non-broadcast services that can be provided via coaxial cable.[2] Despite the promise of the early "blue sky" claims, most of cable's potential has remained unrealized. During the 'seventies, cable technologies began a steady process of diffusion from the hinterlands into cities already well served by broadcast television channels. By the mid-seventies, unbounded optimism began to be replaced by a somewhat pessimistic acceptance of cable systems as providers of essentially private services, i.e., traditional broadcast programming spiced with occasional movies or sports events made available at extra cost to subscribers willing to pay for them. The development of local origination and non-broadcast services originally seen as essential for cable penetration of urban broadcast markets did not proceed apace. Instead cable entrepreneurs relied upon improved reception and the importation of distant broadcast signals to attract subscribers. More recently, satellite and pay cable networks have contributed to a resurgence of interest in cable in urban markets. Yet, even with these developments, the original promise of cable technology has barely begun to be fulfilled.

Anne Branscomb, described the state of cable development in 1974 by depicting the cable industry as oversold, overregulated, and undercapitalized.[3] The "blue sky" claims of early boosters were so named because they represented unrealistic expectations about cable's potential given the legal and economic constraints under which the cable industry operated.

However, the legal and economic environment of the cable industry has not remained static. Since 1974, the Federal Communications Commission has been steadily dismantling the regulatory framework established in its 1972 Report and Order. Now, with the *de jure* deregulation of the industry in the form of the Cable Communications Policy Act of 1984, the old blue sky claims about the capabilities of cable communications systems have been translated mostly into promises of unbounded diversity of programming. Now these promises are coming from large well-capitalized multiple system organizations (MSOs) with access to the economic resources needed to undertake the expense involved in realizing the technical capabilities of the medium.

Remarkably, neither the claims of cable promoters nor the caveats of more sober observers of the industry have tended to be well supported by systematic and comprehensive research. As a result, the debate over the social impacts of cable communications development has consisted largely of speculation about the implications of cable technologies. In this chapter, I shall examine widely scattered evidence relevant to assessing the realistic potential of cable technologies to serve public interests. Public interest in cable development is considered to lie along three dimensions:

1. The potential for increasing the diversity of information channels available to individual households and communities;

2. The potential for augmenting the autonomy of communities by providing local communications services; and,

3. The potential for integrating community structures through interactive services available with cable technologies.

The focus of this review of the evidence on cable's social impacts is at the level of the local community. This seems to be the most useful level for evaluation of the medium because cable communications systems are, by nature, uniquely suited to local applications. Furthermore, although federal law now pre-empts much local regulatory authority, this is the level at which social policy defining cable as a provider of collective goods is most likely to be made. The continued use of local franchising to assure decentralized decisions regarding the configurations of individual systems and the interests of even the largest multiple system organizations in developing service packages capable of attracting subscribers at the level of individual communities both ensure this will be the case. Finally, the community level will be emphasized because the diversity and localism of cable services as well as the interactive capability of a cable system have some of the characteristics of impure public goods and joint products.[4]

The benefits of diversity, localism, and interactive capabilities are neither fully appropriable nor perfectly divisible since franchises generally stipulate that community services be offered as a part of a system's basic service package, available to all subscribers. They should therefore be examined in terms of their impact beyond the level of the individual subscriber.

Diversity

The diversity of information available to individuals is considered essential to a working democracy. Theoretically, issues can only be democratically defined in a free "marketplace of ideas" from which truth (and wise policy) arises out of the competition of diverse opinions. On this point democratic theory directly reflects the classical economic assumption that a competitive market depends upon the participation of a large number of producers and consumers. *Ceteris paribus* the larger the number of producers in the market, the more likely the market mechanism will operate efficiently. Official policy regarding the mass media in the U.S. has tended to apply the economic analogy without reservation--the goal of information diversity implies a preference for maximizing the number of ideas which can be communicated in public. Until very recently, this goal has been more or less consistently restated in Federal Communication Commission policies limiting cross-ownership of mass media and promoting program balance in broadcasting. Much of the excitement in public debate about the potentials of cable communication systems has been related to the possibility that this family of technologies might afford an opportunity to increase the number of available communication channels beyond the limits set by the scarcity of radio frequency spectrum space.

If we accept, for the moment, the ideal of unconstrained diversity, the first question we may wish to ask is whether the development of cable systems has, in fact, expanded the number of channels available to the public. The answer to this question is a very qualified yes. Data on the channel capacities of cable systems do indicate a general trend toward increasing channel capacities. (See Table 2.1, below.) The percentage of systems operating with a capacity of 13 or more channels increased from 1% in 1969 to 74% in 1985. During that same period, systems with five or less channels have decreased from 27% of operating system to approximately 1%. After a brief drop in the proportion of systems with more 13 or more channels following the deregulation by the NCCA of 1984, channel capacities have expanded with over 80% of systems currently in operation having at least a 13 channel capacity.

TABLE 2.1
CHANNEL CAPACITIES OF U.S. CABLE SYSTEMS, 1969-1994
(percentage in each category)

Number of Channels	Year											
	1969	1970	1971	1972	1973	1974	1975	1976	1977	1978	1979	1981
13+	1	4	6	13	16	18	21	23	25	26	29	38
6-12	72	74	77	73	73	71	71	72	71	70	67	57
5	24	20	15	10	10	10	6	5	4	3	3	2
<5	3	3	2	2	2	1	1	*	*	*	*	*
N=	2160	2362	2460	2774	2986	3159	3378	3704	3901	3985	4163	4637

Number of Channels	Year										
	1983	1984	1985	1986	1987	1988	1989	1990	1991	1993	1994
13+	51	57	74	68	70	71	76	76	76	83	83
6-12	40	34	23	23	20	17	13	11	9	6	6
5	1	1	1	1	*	*	*	*	*	*	*
<5	*	*	*	*	*	*	*	*	*	*	*
N=	5748	6400	7546	7546	7836	8413	9010	9612	10,704	11,160	11,216

*indicates less than 1% in category. Totals may not add to 100% due to non-reporting or rounding.
Source: *TV Factbook*, various years.

However, the overall statistics on channel capacities tell us little about the effective increase in the diversity of communication channels available to the public. Channel capacity does not represent the number of channels actually in use. Furthermore, the figures in Table 2.1 do not contain information about the distinct dimensions of diversity which may be identified. We will now deal with each of these problems in turn.

The question of channel use involves two aspects: First, we may ask how many of the available channels on cable systems carry programming. If the availability of more communication channels is not put to use by filling those channels with information, the argument for maximizing diversity in democratic theory is surely empty. Second, to what extent has expanded availability of cable programs affected usage patterns of cable subscribers? If available information is not used by individuals, increased availability cannot be effectively translated into democratic participation. Depending upon the answer to these two questions the justification for a policy of encouraging information diversity may fall in the face of obstacles imposed by limitation on the human capacity for processing information and the potentially dire consequences of information overload.

Figures on the channel utilization for a sample of 417 cable systems in operation in the United States as of September, 1979, indicate that, on the average, 26% of available channels remained unused.[5] In the subsample of 121 cities with over 10,000 population the percentage of idle channels was slightly lower (21%) in 1979 and declined to 17% in 1985. In addition, most of the channels that were in use were devoted to carriage of broadcast television signals. Thus, despite the trend toward greater channel capacities, the diversity of programming available to cable subscribers remains more limited than simple examination of channel capacities would suggest.

The use of cable channels by viewers has been examined in a number of studies conducted in the U.S. and Canada. These studies indicate that the introduction of a more diverse menu of television programming by cable systems has had little effect on the number of channels actually used by viewers.

Comparing broadcast and cable viewers in five U.S. broadcast markets, Agostino found that individuals tended to watch only 3 to 5 channels on a regular basis.[6] The number of channels watched increased only slightly as the availability of channels increased. Heavy television viewers tended to watch more channels than light viewers. For household groups, channel use ranged from three to six channels with the presence of children being associated with a more even distribution of viewing time across channels. On the whole, broadcast market differences appeared to influence the number of channels used more than the availability of more channels on cable. This was probably due to the concentration on viewing programs of network affiliates by both cable and broadcast viewers. The dependence on networks appears to have declined as more cable channels on more systems have attracted viewers away from broadcast programming.[7]

Similarity of broadcast and cable viewing patterns in Canada was also reported by Babe, who found that the only difference between Canadian cable and broadcast viewers was that the former tended to watch slightly less Canadian programming due to the availability of American television channels on Canadian cable systems.[8]

Despite the negligible effects of the increased availability of channels on the use of channels, Babe did suggest that cable viewers might be more discriminating in the choice of programs. This suggestion has been examined in research conducted by Leo Jeffres.[9] Jeffres has reported that the five additional channels made available by the introduction of cable in a Minnesota community provided more redundancy than variety in programming, but hypothesized that the availability of extra channels would lead to increased selectivity in the viewing choices of cable subscribers. While increased selectivity was not evident in the decisions to initiate viewing sessions, it did appear in decisions about continued viewing. Jeffres suggests that this pattern may have been less selective about turning on a cable channel simply because cable was a new phenomenon. However, viewers did appear to be more selective about continued viewing because of the availability of a more diverse set of viewing options.

Taken together, the findings on the availability and use of extra channels carried on cable systems might lead to the conclusion that the ideal of unconstrained diversity is unrealistic as a goal for communications policy. These findings echo those of earlier research on media competition and use which indicated that the total resources devoted to mass media consumption tend to remain relatively constant after a certain point. This may mean that the diversity of communications channels used by individuals is limited by human capacities for acquiring and processing information. It does not mean that the ideal of diversity must be scrapped, but only that the wholesale application of the market analogy is improper. Rather, given the limited human capacity for handling information, the diversity of messages carried over available channels becomes all the more important. It may therefore be useful to shift our focus from raw numbers of channels used to a finer discrimination of the dimensions of the concept of diversity.

Referring to the F.C.C. policy of encouraging communications diversity, Levin has distinguished three distinct dimensions of the concept.[10] First, we may speak of the diversity of sources available. Levin defines "sources diversity" in terms of the ownership of television stations within a given broadcast market. This dimension of diversity is the object of federal policies discouraging cross- ownership and encouraging local ownership of media. Second, Levin refers to "programming diversity" which he further subdivides into "types diversity" (the number of separate program types, e.g., comedy, drama, news, sports, etc.) and "options diversity" (the number of different programs available regardless of their type). Levin further distinguishes between horizontal diversity, which refers to the program types or options available in a given time slot, and vertical diversity, which refers to the types or options available over the course of a day. Although information on types and options diversity on cable channels in not available, the broader dimensions of sources and programming diversity can be used to organize the findings of a number of studies relevant to cable policy questions.

How do cable systems fare with regard to the diversity of their ownership and control, the equivalent of Levin's notion of sources diversity? Though the relationship between ownership and control is ambiguous, data on the ownership of cable systems tend to suggest that diversity of sources may be more an ideal that a reality. Table 2.2 (below) shows the trends in categories of owners of U.S. cable systems operating between 1972 and 1984. The largest category of owners is broadcasters, who have maintained a stable ownership of about one-third of all cable systems throughout the period. Despite the avowed policy of the F.C.C. discouraging cross-media ownership, practically all systems have been at least partially owned by firms with interests in other communications industries. Data from the 1979 sample of operating systems indicate that 59% of all systems were at least partially owned by firms with other interests, most in communication-related firms. The percentage of systems in cities with over 10,000 population was 75% in 1979 and increased to 82% by 1985. Furthermore, 75% of all systems and 87% of systems in the larger cities were wholly owned by multiple system organizations (MSOs) in 1979. Among larger cities, the proportion of systems owned by MSOs increased to 91% in 1985.

Of course, ownership may not be effectively translated into control. This is especially true in the U.S. cable industry since owners and managers of cable systems overwhelmingly tend to see the systems simply as bundles of channels for carrying programming produced by other sources. This may make sources diversity in cable industry seem to be a secondary consideration in formulating policy. Nevertheless,

TABLE 2.2
OWNERSHIP OF U.S. CABLE SYSTEMS, 1972-1984
(Percentage in each category)

Category of Ownership	Year										
	1972	1973	1974	1975	1976	1977	1978	1979	1981	1983	1984
Broadcasters	38	35	37	32	32	30	30	33	38	28	32
Newspapers	6	10	15	14	13	12	13	13	16	16	18
Publishers	3	7	7	7	13	13	11	11	12	10	9
TV Prod/Dist	8	20	23	23	20	20	18	18	21	27	20
Theaters	3	4	5	9	8	8	4	4	3	2	2
Telephone Co.'s	2	2	4	2	2	2	2	3	2	4	5
Communities	3	3	3	3	3	3	3	2	3	1	2
TV manufactures	na	11	19	19	12	11	5	7	12	20	26
Others	*	*	*	*	*	*	*	*	na	na	na
N=	2839	3032	3190	3405	3715	3911	3997	4180	4637	5748	6400

*rounds to less than 1 percent

Source: *TV Factbook*, various years

the owners of cable systems are in a position to control the sources which will be carried on their systems. Therefore, it is necessary to consider this dimension at some point in the policy process, particularly since there has been a tendency toward concentration of ownership in the industry.

A more basic dimension of diversity is programming diversity. In fact this dimension might be considered a measure of the effects of the concentration of ownership. The ultimate standard for evaluating communications policy in a democratic society must be the variety of messages available to the public. The availability of a wide range of programs, especially of different types, is the precondition for the effective exercise of consumer sovereignty in the market for ideas.

The issue of programming diversity raises two related questions: First, how many different types of programming have been madeavailable on cable systems. Second, what level of demand exists for various types of programming?

The potential variety of cable programming services is stressed by Goldman, who lists 117 types of services which could be made available on cable.[11] Since most systems (98% in 1979) carry all three broadcast television networks, a rough measure of the diversity of programming available may be found in the types on non-broadcast services listed in Table 2.3 (below). The mean number of broadcast television channels carried by all systems operating in 1979 was about eight. In larger cities this number was approximately 10. 90% of all systems (and of systems in the cities with more than 10,000 population) carried between four and twelve channels of broadcast programming. By 1985 90% of the systems in larger cities carried between 8 and 15 broadcast channels. Despite the increases in channel capacity, this necessarily leaves fewer channels to carry the types of non-broadcast services which represent the full diversity of programming possible with cable. Added to the "must carry" rule for local broadcast stations is the explosion of cable services that became available by satellite in the 1980s. Together the availability of broadcast and satellite programming help to explain the relatively large perecentages of systems carry no locally originated programming.

Aside from the broad trend toward less local origination, Table 2.3 suggests that the requirements for carrying access channels, which were reaffirmed in the 1984 Act, may have had some effect. However, one should note that the increase in public and educational access channels is coincident with the decline in local live originations, suggesting that systems have tended to shift the burden of actually producing local programming to the communities they serve. This is, of course, consonant with the oft-expressed preference of system operators to be treated merely as providers of communication channels and is not

TABLE 2.3:
FORMAT AND CONTENT OF CABLE ORIGINATIONS, 1969-1990
(Percentage in each category)

Format/ Content	Year																	
	1969	1971	1973	1975	1976	1977	1978	1979	1981	1983	1984	1986	1987	1988	1989	1990	1991	1993
No Originations	62	54	37	37	35	34	34	33	34	41	45	47	48	52	55	57	60	58
Automated	36	57	55	61	62	63	62	64	63	57	51	47	46	43	40	39	36	35
Time/weather	35	47	53	58	60	60	60	61	60	50	44	38	36	34	31	29	27	24
News ticker	4	6	10	12	14	15	16	18	19	16	13	10	9	7	6	6	5	4
Stock ticker	1	1	4	6	6	7	8	8	10	8	7	6	5	4	4	3	3	2
Sports ticker	na	na	1	3	4	5	6	6	7	6	4	3	3	2	2	2	1	1
Message wheel	na	na	6	9	11	10	9	10	10	8	13	14	15	15	17	20	20	20
Emergency alert	1	na	1	2	na	na	2	3	4	6	4	6	6	6	6	7	7	7
Non-automated	12	20	25	28	28	28	26	28	30	28	28	32	32	29	28	28	26	31
Local live	9	na	19	19	17	17	17	17	16	13	10	10	10	10	10	9	9	10
School Channel	na	na	na	3	5	6	6	8	11	13	13	13	13	13	13	13	13	14
Public access	na	na	1	1	3	5	5	7	10	13	15	16	17	17	17	16	16	18
Advertising	na	2	8	9	8	7	2	1	na	12	14	20	21	21	21	21	21	25
N=	2300	2578	3032	3405	3715	3911	3997	4180	4637	5748	6400	7546	7836	8413	9010	9612	10702	11160

*indicates less than 1 percent
Source: *TV Factbook*, various years

necessarily problematic from a policy perspective as long as production support is provided to ensure the widest use of the access channels available. Also apparent in the table and related to the availability of both broadcast and cable network programming discussed above is the decline in automated originations that has occurred since 1980.

Given the findings on the limited number of channels used by individuals discussed above, the most important question about cable programming diversity may be the demand for the types of program which could be made available. Studies dealing with this question fall into two main categories based on their approach to determining demand:

1. Surveys examining the intentions to use different types of services if they were to be made available; and,

2. Surveys of the use of various types of service which have been carried by existing cable systems.

Summarizing the results of a number of surveys of the first type, Goldman concluded that the services most preferred by potential cable subscribers were entertainment, civic functions, and programs devoted to developing special skills. On the average, between half and two-thirds of subscribers surveyed would purchase these types of services.[12] Goldman also identified a secondary cluster of services including education, banking, government information, and visitation on interactive cable channels. Two-fifths to one-half of the respondents in the eight surveys reviewed said they would purchase these types of services. Focusing on political uses of cable programming, Kaid, *et. al.*, found that about two-thirds of their random sample of residents of multi-unit dwellings in Norman, Oklahoma, would use live coverage of legislative sessions at least sometimes. Over 80% said they would use channels dedicated to candidates for public office.[13] Similar demands for government and political programming were found in surveys in Reading, Pennsylvania, and Reston, Virginia.[14]

The results of fifteen separate surveys of the intended use of cable services are compiled in Table 2.4 (below). Although there is little consistency in the precise questions used and programming types covered, the overall picture suggested by these data indicate that, despite a strong preference for entertainment, there is a potentially strong demand for a variety of other services as well. This conclusion is further supported by findings from surveys of actual use of available cable services. Table 2.5 (p. 35) presents a summary of findings from nine surveys conducted in six separate communities (five in the U.S. and one in Sweden). As might be expected, figures on the actual use of available services are somewhat lower than those on intended use of possible services. Also the great preference for broadcast television

TABLE 2.4
PROJECTED NON-BROADCAST PROGRAM PREFERENCES, VARIOUS COMMUNITIES, 1973-79
(Percentage of respondents reporting that they would use each type of programming, if available)

Programming Type	Community/State/Year(s)/(N)										
	LA Ca 1973 (197)	Columbus In 1975 (200)	Reston Va 1975 (200)	LA Ca 1977 (325)	SD Ca 1977 (500)	Sacramento Ca 1977 (400)	Reading Pa 1976 1976 1977 1977 (50)(351)(344)	Norman Ok 1977 (220)	MainCo. Ca 1978 (626)	Lincoln Ne 1978 ()	R.Worth Tx. 1979 (200)
Education	39	81			64	63			46	71	28
Shopping	20				39	39			25		19
Entertainment	47	74			68	72			66		70
Medical	29				45	40	87		27		24
Banking	13			21	56	59	75		50		37
Civic	27				73	74	79		62		57
Visit	38				64	54	59		47		50
Print	21										
Government	26		85		56	61	81 75 72 58	68	63		
Skill	51				66	76			64		47
Mail	34			24							
Job	16				39	33			28		28
Local News		81	58								
Sports		58									
Arts		61									
Consumer Ed	94	94	94			73	86 62				

Table 2.5
Frequency of Use of Available Cable Services,
Various Communities, 1972-77

Type of Service	Times used/week 4 +	1 - 3	<1	Community, Year (N)
Distant TV stations	62	25	13	Woodland Hills, Ca., 1976 (204)
Automated services				
Weather	28	41	31	"
Sports	21	24	55	"
News	19	37	44	"
Community Information	15	43	42	"
Financial Information	2	12	86	"
Local Origination	21	38	41	Kiruna, Sweden, 1975 (437)
	At least Once		Never	
Local Origination	59		41	Reston, Va., 1975 (200)
Local Origination	45		55	" (100)
Public Access	48		52	Columbus, In., 1975 (44)
Public Access	28		72	" (102)
	At Least Occasionally		Seldom or Never	
Public Access Interactive	25		75	N.Y., N.Y., 1975 (250)
Public Access Interactive	20		80	Reading, Pa., 1976 (406)
Public Access	26		74	" (50)

Sources: Kaplan (1978); Commission on Radio and Television in Education (Sweden, 1975); Topper and Wilson (1976); Ksobiech (1975); Othmer (1973); Moss (1978)

programming is apparent in the use of distant television signals, but non-broadcast services do appear able to attract significant audiences. Over 50% of the respondents in a survey conducted in Woodland, California reported regular use (at least once per week) of automated weather, news, and community information channels.[15] Local origination channels appear to be about as popular as automated services,[16] and even public access channels, which have been plagued by problems related to production quality and scheduling appear to be able to attract about one-fourth of those questioned as at least occasional viewers.[17]

In the broadest sense, cable systems in the U.S. have been tending toward the fulfillment of the promise of diversity. This is important since channel capacities of cable systems are direct measures of their adaptability to local communications needs. However, the actual progress in adapting cable systems to public interests must be measured in terms of the fit between services actually offered and local needs. Thus far cable system owners and managers have interpreted these needs primarily in terms of the demand for services as measured by the willingness of individuals to pay for them. Consequently, available channels have been filled mainly with broadcast programming essentially similar to that available off the air. In reviewing the evidence from studies discussed in this section it is important to keep in mind that a more appropriate measure of communication needs is the expectation that given service will be useful to individuals or households regardless of their willingness to buy the cable package specifically for that service. By this measure, it appears that cable systems in the U.S. have not lived up to their promise.

Finally, the findings in the studies reviewed above suggest that diversity cannot be treated as an end in itself. Rather, diversity is an instrumental value. Its importance lies in the fact that it is a precondition for realizing cable's other potentials as a local and interactive medium. If the programming available on cable systems does not meet local needs, the diversity of program types available will be of little importance since most of the programs will go without being used.

Localism

Along with diversity, a major goal of communications policies in the U.S. has been to ensure a commitment to local service. Broadcasting has proven ill-suited for accomplishing this goal. Cable, on the other hand, is a quintessentially local medium. Consequently, cable has been seen by many persons as a solution to the problems of providing communities with local telecommunications services.

The basic problems which arise with regard to localism in cable policy revolve around two issues: ownership/control of cable systems by local elements and access to use of the medium. Some observers argue that genuine community autonomy requires local ownership of cable systems.[18]   Others hold that ownership is less important than access.[19] We shall therefore treat these as two basic dimensions of localism.

We have already reviewed some data on the ownership of cable systems which have indicated a tendency toward centralization in the industry. The concentration of ownership of cable systems has been accompanied by an increased degree of ownership by non-local interests. According to data derived from the sample of all systems operating in 1979, about 37% of all U.S. cable systems were wholly or partially owned by individuals or corporations outside of the states in which the systems operated. In the subsample of larger cities this proportion of out-of- state ownership of systems was about 50% in 1979 and rose to approximately 71% by 1985. Although these data do not directly measure genuine localism of ownership, they do indicate a tendency on the part of smaller MSOs combining smaller systems to operate only within a single state while ownership of larger systems has become increasingly cosmopolitan. Relatively few (2%, see Table 2.2, above) systems are owned by municipalities or subscriber co-ops. More common are partnerships in which local residents hold a percentage of cable system ownership. It is not clear how effectively these kinds of partnerships promote local autonomy, particularly since local shareholders characteristically hold less than 50% interests in their systems (the modal share is 20%). The practice of offering a minority share of ownership in return for support in franchise bargaining has come to be somewhat pejoratively identified by such terms as "rent a local citizen" in the cable industry. On the whole then, it appears that autonomy of ownership at the level of the community is rare.

Regardless of ownership structure, the benefits of locally produced programming are clear. Lucas and Possner have found that regular viewing of local television news sources was related to knowledge about local issues.[20] In terms of perceived need for and use of available local information sources, the demand for local programming appears strong (see Tables 2.4 and 2.5 above). Surveys also indicate that subscribers evaluate local information programs favorably where they are available.[21] In one survey conducted in Sweden, a plurality (39%) of viewers of local cable channel reported that it had provided the best coverage of a local miners' conflict. Seventy percent thought that the local channel was successful at discussing local questions and sixty-five percent thought it was successful at including persons with local connections.[22] Ksobiech reported that a majority of cable subscribers and forty-four percent of non-subscribers familiar with the public access channel in Columbus, Indiana, thought the service was valuable enough to deserve public funding.[23] Nor is appreciation of the value of local channels limited to viewers. Producers in New

York[24], Toronto[25], and a nation-wide survey tended to evaluate their experience with using public access channels positively.[26]

Yet local programming and access in the U.S. have had a difficult history, and the problems involved in realizing localism are common elsewhere as well.[27] Klaver, reporting on a demonstration project involving local participation in cable system management in six Dutch municipalities, concluded that while members of the communities showed some interest in locally originated programs, they did not tend to become actively involved in managing the local channels. Rather, most of the work of planning and producing local programs was done by experienced professionals at the local radio stations.[28] A possible key variable in determining the extent of participation by local "amateurs" was the structure established to mediate and encourage such participation. Klaver points out that direct individual membership in the local planning councils (called representative cultural institutions) was associated with greater involvement in local programming decisions by non-professionals than indirect involvement through local organizations. Perhaps the closest American analog to the Dutch representative cultural institutions are Connecticut's mandated cable advisory boards. However, the responsibility of these boards is limited to oversight of local cable system management. The boards do not become directly involved in production.[29]

Another country which has grappled with the problem of localism in cable programming is Canada. As early as 1970, Feldman reported a variety of locally originated programs on Canadian cable systems.[30] Systems carried from 20 to 60 locally originated programs per week. At the time, the Canadian Radio and Television Commission (CRTC) was pursuing a policy of encouraging local origination which held system operators primarily responsible for the content and most local programs were produced by the cable systems' staffs and supported by advertising sold on the community channel. By the mid-1970s, however, the CRTC came around full circle to a position which proposed to forbid operator control of locally originated programs. Instead Canadian cable systems have developed what Sparkes has called a "facilitator" role for the operators.[31] This requires them to provide up to 10% of the system's revenues to supply studios, equipment, and professional staffs to assist users of the community channels. In addition, the system operators may act as initiators of local program production groups and are responsible for scheduling the use of the community channels.[32] They cannot, however, act as independent program producers supported by the sale of advertising.

In the United States, the policy regarding local programming has also shifted away from an earlier support for local origination by cable system operators. The bias in this country has been to treat cable systems as carriers rather than originators of local programming. Since 1974, U.S. policy has called for operators to set aside channels for community access and provide only basic production capabilities for the use of local individuals, groups, and/or institutions seeking to produce cable programs. Access channels generally fall into four types: educational access channels, government access channels, public access channels, and leased access channels. In this system, primary responsibility for ensuring the localism of cable programming rests with the communities. Operators are essentially removed from any programming responsibility. While this approach most clearly divorces ownership from the control of locally produced programming, it has also led to funding problems. Without the kind of internal subsidy that supports Canadian local originations, users of U.S. access channels must seek outside funding for program production[33] or produce program of inferior quality.[34] As a result, cable policy in the U.S. has not developed a strong access component.[35] According to surveys conducted by the National Cable Television Association (NCTA), the number of systems with public access channels has increased from 175 in 1974 to 252 in 1980.[36] Over the same period, the number of educational access systems increased from 328 to 409. Although corresponding numbers of systems reporting carriage of public and educational access channels in 1994 were... the increase in both cases is roughly proportional to the increase in the total number of systems in operation over the period. The 1980 NCTA figures are actually lower than the numbers of municipalities reporting that their cable franchises required educational and public access channels in a 1974 survey conducted by the International City Managers' Association.[37] In the sample of 121 cities with over 10,000 population, 58% of the systems carried access channels in 1979. This proportion also decreased to 54% by 1985.

Why has access been so unsuccessful? Some observers have suggested that access channels, especially public access channels, have been unable to attract audiences because of poor production quality.[38] However, surveys asking people familiar with public access programming about the importance of production values have indicated that viewers are generally not bothered by poor quality.[39] A more common problem for potential viewers has been the difficulty in finding out about the access channel and its program schedule[40], but the most important obstacle to local access programming appears to be the funding of productions.[41]

Despite these obstacles, and despite the dismal record of access policy in the U.S. cable industry, the studies cited above, as a whole, and a variety of case studies of successful attempts at local origination and access support the argument that locally originated programming on cable is a desirable policy goal.[42]   The major obstacle to implementing this goal in more cable systems in the U.S. has been the general unwillingness of system operators to assume more of the expense of producing local programs. In most cases the need for local programming has not been translated into a willingness to subscribe to cable service solely for its local component, but, as with the diversity of information, the community's need for local programming cannot be adequately measured by this standard of profitability.

Local programming requires a great deal of support. First, it requires the cooperation of cable system operators.   The Canadian experience in this area suggests the importance of this variable, at least in the short run, to get local programming efforts underway. Second, local programming requires careful planning, especially in terms of scheduling and promotion. The most common viewer complaint about local programming services has been the lack of advance notification of programs available on community channels. Finally, the success of local programming appears to depend heavily on the active involvement of the community in both production of programs and management of the local channels. A part of the success of local channels is the extent to which they can be integrated into the pre-existing networks of communication in a community.

Interactive Capabilities

The most impressive potential of cable technology is its capability for two-way communication. Indeed, it is interactive capability which makes cable a medium of communication and not simply another bundle of channels for the one-way transmission of information. The potential importance of interactive capability is suggested by the variety of uses to which this capability can be applied.[43] Lemelstrich has categorized these uses under four main objectives for the development of two-way cable technologies: 1. Commercial services; 2. Educational services; 3. Social facilitation; and, 4. Participatory democracy. Problems relevant to the formulation of policy regarding interactive capabilities arise from the necessity of meeting these objectives within a set of constraints identified by Lemelstrich as: 1. The state of available technologies, including both hardware (production and storage equipment, terminals, etc.) and software (programs guiding the use of the available hardware); 2. Human nature, including the physiological and psychological characteristics of users which limit the applicability of technological capabilities; 3. Limited economic resources to support the application of two-way technologies; and, 4. Political resistance from individuals and groups that have a stake in the pre-existing networks of communication in the community.[44] Policy research in this area must therefore take the general form of an examination of how these constraints affect the possibility and effects of applying interactive cable to the achievement of any particular objective.

The technical requirements for a variety of two-way services have been outlined elsewhere and a detailed discussion of research on technical aspects of two-way applications is beyond the scope of this chapter.[45] We shall focus instead on research which addresses the social, economic and political aspects of two-way cable.

Sheridan provides evidence that computer assisted feedback on a cable network can be used to sustain useful dialogues within small groups. Participants in experiments conducted at the Massachusetts Institute of Technology (MIT) found that carefully planned interactive "meetings" could be helpful for opening issues for group consideration and allowing participation in group decisions. The group sessions were relatively efficient, handling an average of 20 questions per hour while following a sequence of steps similar to the Delphi technique for obtaining consensus among a group of experts.[46]

While the MIT experiments were limited to small groups of anonymous participants, more generalizable evidence of the applicability of two-way cable to community-oriented problems has been provided by an ambitious series of experiments funded by the National Science Foundation.[47] Projects conducted in three separate communities explored a variety of questions about the applicability and effectiveness of interactive cable.

The Rockford Two-way Cable Project focused on in-service training for fire fighters and found significant differences between traditional classroom and television training programs and a computer assisted two-way cable course which favored the cable method.[48] Specifically, interactive cable instruction was found to be more effective than comparable one-way television for conveying cognitive information.[49] The interactive cable course was also more favorably evaluated by participants than one-way television and considered at least as good as live instruction in a classroom setting. Significantly, the cost of two-way cable training was lower than either autotutorial or lecture methods. Although the cable training program was more expensive than ordinary television, the system of automated cable lessons was more efficient for record keeping and progress evaluation of trainees.

Two sets of experiments conducted in Spartanburg, S.C., on the effectiveness of two-way channels for adult in-home education found that both classroom and two-way cable methods of preparing for high school equivalency exams and learning principles of child development were effective. However, these experiments found no significant difference between the methods.[50] The researchers suggested that this form of two-way educational service be left to commercial development since the convenience of the two-way cable method was the only difference found between it and traditional techniques.

Results of an experiment examining the utility of cable for in-service training of day care workers in Spartanburg were even less encouraging.[51] This experiment involved a comparison of one and two-way child care television workshops with a control group of child care centers without workshops. While both treatment groups showed cognitive gains, the one-way group's gains were greater than the two-way group. Although participants reported workshops were more interesting with the interaction than without, there was no difference in either attendance or attrition rates between the treatment groups. In economic terms, the workshops began to break even with about 40 to 50 participants and the two-way cable workshops only became economically attractive as the number of participants increased beyond that range.

Taken together, the Rockford and Spartanburg experiments indicate that the usefulness of two-way cable for skills training programs may depend upon the specific skills involved. They also support a conclusion that two-way cable training programs are most feasible where the numbers of participants involved are likely to be large enough to make the use of cable cost effective.

A final set of experiments focused on the social and political effects of interactive public access programming.[52] These experiments involved the establishment and operation of neighborhood communication centers (NCCs) to serve senior citizens in Reading, Pennsylvania. One of the aims of the Reading project was to determine the potential for involving senior citizens in the operation and programming of a community access channel by employing two-way cable to connect the NCCs. Interaction between centers was augmented by phone-ins from home viewers on the community access channel. The findings of this project represent the most dramatic evidence of the value of two-way cable to the public. With the involvement of seniors and cooperation of local government agencies, the NCCs successfully used their two-way capabilities to generate interest and increase awareness of both the public access channel and available social services for seniors. Although the uptake of social services was not appreciably increased, participation by both seniors and home viewers did increase measurably. An analysis of the style and content of interactions observable on the programs indicated that both in-center and home viewers became more sophisticated in the use of two-way programming to become informed about local government and politics. Both seniors and public officials tended to evaluate the activities of the NCCs favorably (although appointed officials were considerably less enthusiastic than were elected officials). Elected officials found the system particularly useful for receiving input and allowing interaction with their constituents. Furthermore, over time it appears that this opportunity for citizen-official interaction led to increased responsiveness on the part of officials. As the Reading project proceeded, the participants in NCC programs became increasingly assertive and more willing to request and give information and opinions.

Perhaps the most convincing indication of the satisfaction of the community with the project was the willingness to continue the experiment as a regular part of the Berks County Cable system. After funding for the project ended, members of the senior citizen community actively sought grants and engaged in other fund-raising activities in support of Berks Community TV, a local non-profit corporation set up to manage the cable system's community access activities. These activities have continued through 1985.

The success of the Reading project may have been a function of the fact that the criterion for evaluating the effectiveness of the NCCs was system-oriented rather than narrowly goal-oriented. The major purpose of the project was not to evaluate the extent to which two-way cable could effectively and efficiently be used to meet a specific goal as it was in the Rockford and Spartanburg projects. The objective in Reading was to establish the NCCs as an ongoing system. The goals toward which the system would work were specifically left for the participants in the public access project to determine. The result was the establishment of a project with the public actively involved in production and management and therefore responsible for setting the criteria by which the effectiveness of the system would be measured.

Summary and Conclusions

Probably the most important conclusion which may be derived from this review of the research on cable's public interest dimensions is that our understanding of exactly how cable technology can be applied to public interests is tantalizing but incomplete. Given the evidence reviewed here there appear to be grounds for expecting cable communication systems to provide the diversity of programs necessary to meet community needs. Although a large number of cable viewers may not venture far from the comfort of familiar broadcast television programming, the demand for specifically local programs and the potential for the design of interactive community information systems are great enough to justify greater use of the expanding channel capacities of American cable systems. Yet, with the exception of a few experimental demonstration projects, few efforts have been made to carefully assess the impact of the full range of potential cable services on community interests. Most of the research we have examined has focused on limited measures of effects on individual subscribers. This emphasis is undoubtedly valuable for informing decisions about the commercial development of cable systems, but it is inadequate to guide public policies which affect commercial development. What is needed then is more emphasis on an examination of the impact of cable services on whole community systems.

Despite the shortcomings of the available research, several conclusions relevant to community interest policies for the application of cable are possible. First, with regard to the federal role in regulating the cable industry, the findings suggest that policies encouraging the use of cable channels to carry a diverse set of program types are appropriate. Along with its responsibility to assure a baseline level of technical reliability, the federal government must be concerned with ensuring the adaptability of cable systems to the specific needs of the communities in which they operate. To this end the general policy of requiring a minimum channel capacity and access channels has been basically sound. Within the broad framework set by these policies, local communities should be encouraged to work out cable policies which will serve unique local interests.

Second, future research on cable applications should be directed at assessing the needs and possibilities for organization of cable systems in individual communities. The uniqueness of local policies must be based on information about community needs gathered on a case by case basis. The general questions which may be adapted to these kinds of assessments include:

1. What are the types of local programming which will best serve the community's interests? There is an apparent need for local news and information across communities, but beyond that the specific types of programs likely to meet local needs vary from community to community.

2. What organizational forms should local cable activities take? It is clear that the involvement of members of the community in management and programming of local channels is a key element in the success of those channels. Whether the involvement is better directed and supported by a local origination model of by a pure access model is

probably best answered at the local level. The success of the Canadian experience with a hybrid "facilitator" model suggests that there is a broad range of intermediate possibilities between these two poles. The assignment of specific responsibilities among the cable system operator, local government, and the general community must therefore be made on the basis of an accurate understanding of the local availability and distribution of economic and political resources.

3. What kinds of interactive programs are most useful to the community? Clearly, not all interactive services can or should be applied by public decision. Furthermore, it is probable that services which can be most efficiently provided via two-way cable in one community would be better provided by other media in another. The conditions which affect the uses of cable services cannot be well understood until a wider variety of experimental and demonstration projects have been carried out and evaluated. Until that time relatively limited case studies are the only way of identifying the general conditions determining the utility of specific cable services.

Finally, one thing made clear by the existing research findings is the importance of local involvement in cable decision-making. Though cable can be a "participatory technology," it is not capable of stimulating participation unless members of the community are already organized for involvement in cable policy bargaining. The medium cannot provide a technological fix for a lethargic democracy. Its potential for facilitating dialogue within an active community is limited only by the willingness of the community to use that potential.

---

[1] Sloan Commission(1971), McKenna(1974).

[2] Marchese(1972), Steiner(1972), Carpenter-Huffman(1974).

[3] Branscomb(1975).

[4] Loehr and Sandler(1978).

[5] Figures from three samples of communities with cable systems are reported throughout the remainder of this book. All were derived from a systematic sample of 10% of all systems operating in 1979 described in Godek(1983). For a longitudinal analysis, all cities in this basic sample with 10,000 population or greater (in 1979) were included in a panel (N=121) which was reanalyzed in 1985. The number of communities in the panel sample was reduced to 107 by missing data on several key variables used in the analyses reported in Chapters 5 and 6, below.

[6] Agostino(1974).

[7] In recent years Nielsen and Arbitron rating figures indicate a significant diversion of viewers from network programming by cable, as well as other video technologies (tape, disk, and satellite transmission). See, also, Hurwitz(1980), Wines(1981).

[8] Sabbah(1985), Stoller(1982), Babe(1975). Hill and Dyer(1981) report that the availability of distant stations had a similar effect on patterns of local news viewing in the U.S. with an estimated 30 percent of those watching news on cable using distant stations.

[9] Jeffres(1978,1976).

[10] Levin(1980).

[11] Goldman(1979), Ash(1984), Sutherland(1982).

[12] Goldman(1979).

[13] Kaid, *et al.*(1978).

[14] Moss, *et al.*(1978), Topper and Wilson(1976).

[15] Kaplan(1978).

[16] Commission on Radio and Television in Education, Sweden(1975), Topper and Wilson(1976).

[17] Doty(1975), Othmer(1972), Ksobiech(1975).

[18] Noam(1982), MacKenna(1981), Jacobsen(1977), Jeffres(1975), Pool(1973).

[19] Wenner(1975).

[20] Lucas and Possner(1975).

[21] Commission on Radio and Television in Education, Sweden(1976), Topper and Wilson(1976), Ksobiech(1975), Othmer(1973).

[22] Commission on Radio and Television in Education, Sweden(1976).

[23] Ksobiech(1975).

[24] Othmer(1973).

[25] Sparkes(1979).

[26] Bednarczyk(1977).

[27] Commission on Radio and Television in Education, Sweden(1976), Klaver(1975), Feldman(1970), Sparkes(1976).

[28] Klaver(1975).

[29] Connecticutt State Commission on Educational and Informational Uses of Cable TV(1975).

[30] Feldman(1970).

[31] Sparkes(1976).

[32] Forbes and Layng(1978).

[33] Bednarczyk(1977).

[34] Wenner(1975).

[35] Rood(1977), Wenner(1975).

[36] National Cable Television Association(1974, 1980).

[37] Borko(1974).

[38] Wenner(1975), Doty(1975).

[39] Othmer(1973), Commission on Radio and Television in Education, Sweden(1976).

[40] Othmer(1973), Wenner(1976), Sparkes(1979).

[41] Wenner(1975), Bednarczyk(1977), Lippke(1975), International Institute of Communication(1977).

[42] Feldman(1970), Moss(1978), Carpenter-Huffman(1974), National Cable Television Association(1974a).

[43] Goldman(1979), Pool(1975), Mandelbaum(1972), Lucas and Yin(1973).

[44] Lemelstrich(1974).

[45] Lemelstrich(1974), Pool(1973), Carpenter-Huffman(1974), Boetz(1983).

[46] Sheridan, in Pool(1973).

[47] Brownstein(1978).

[48] Baldwin, *et al.*(1978a, 1978b,1978c).

[49] Baldwin(1978b).

[50] Lucas, *et al.*(1979).

[51] Berryman, *et al.*(1979).

[52] Sheehan and Ammon(1986).

Chapter 3

Explanations For Cable Community Interest Policies: Three Pure Types

The review of research findings in the previous chapter makes two points very clear: 1., despite uncertainty about how cable can be most usefully employed in any given community, the potential for the use of cable systems in the public interest is great. The benefits provided by the diversity, localism and interactive capabilities of cable make them genuine public goods. 2., because this potential for public goods is often subordinated to the commercial development of cable, there is a wide variation in the extent to which cable systems have furthered public interests in cable development. To the extent that public interest dimensions of cable policy remain undeveloped, cable firms may be said to be committing social errors which warrant regulatory action by the public sector.

In this chapter we shall turn to the question of how this variation in public interest uses of cable has been and can be explained. This question goes to the heart of cable policy. If we can understand the factors or conditions which are conducive to minimizing cable firms' social errors it may be possible to rationally approach the formulation of regulatory policies for the cable industry. Although the problem of developing public interest uses of cable has been recognized since the potential uses of the medium were first recognized, the availability of public interest services has never led to a widely accepted theory to guide cable policy. Rather, at least three general types of explanations for cable policies have been offered. We may refer to these types as the pluralist, economic and stratification explanations. In this chapter I review the basic structure of these "proto-theories" as they have been presented in the literature on cable policy-making. The aim of this review is to identify important concepts and list propositions which can be reduced to causal models describing the arguments made in each type of explanation. As we shall see, the explanations are not mutually exclusive. Indeed, they are most often found in combined form in the work of social scientists, journalists, and cable activists who have addressed the questions of explaining the variation in cable systems' programming commitments.

The Pluralist Explanation

Throughout the history of cable development political analysts and journalists have suggested that the potential of the medium to serve public interests would be realized only if citizens were organized for participation in the process of franchising.[1] Implicit in the argument of these observers is an essentially pluralistic political model of cable system policy-making in which policy is viewed as the product of organized groups interacting in a bargaining process. This model suggests that the institutionalization of citizen participation would be the primary determinant of cable system policies affecting the interests of individuals and communities in which cable technologies are deployed.

The logic supporting the pluralists' model of cable policy-making is based on a set of assumptions about the nature of the cable medium and about the various actors involved in pre-franchise negotiations and cable system operation.

Pluralist explanations of cable service policies usually involve an implicit assumption that cable is primarily a public service technology.[2] The potential applications of cable in providing diverse communications services with strong local and interactive components becomes *per se* an appropriate goal for cable policy.[3] However, advocates of the pluralistic model of cable policy-making also assume that the types of cable services most often viewed as community benefits would be poorly understood by a public accustomed to thinking of cable as just another form of broadcast television.[4] A third implicit assumption in pluralist explanations is that cable system operators are likely to be unwilling to offer potentially beneficial services since these services are costly to provide and unlikely to be demanded by individual subscribers.[5] Some kind of public organization is therefore considered necessary to obtain public interest cable services. Finally, the pluralistic model often assumes that existing public agencies will not exert pressure on cable operators to provide services in the public interest unless they are faced with an organized demand to do so by their constituents.[6] At best, well-intentioned public officials responsible for franchising and regulating cable operations could not be expected to understand the public interest potential of cable any better than the public they represent.[7] At worst, officials may be viewed as exclusively self-interested individuals easily Two basic problems tend to be foremost in pluralist explanation of cable service policies: 1. How can the genuine public interests of a community be reliably identified? and, 2. Once recognized, How can these interests be effectively served by cable policy-making processes? influenced by the blandishments of rich and often unscrupulous cable system owners.[8]

According to pluralist arguments, the solution to the first problem depends upon recognizing the group nature of politics. Genuine community interests will be reflected in the formation of groups which articulate demands for cable services.[9] The organization of community groups demanding access channels or community ownership of a cable system, for example, would constitute *prima facie* evidence that those issues involve the legitimate interests of the community. If groups do not organize around an issue, the pluralists argue that the preferences of citizens for that particular policy are weak and, therefore, can not be called genuine community interests. Alternatively, if the citizens fail to become aware of the nature of their true interests in those issues it may be necessary for small groups of concerned citizens to act as vanguard in disseminating information about cable.

Regarding the problem of the responsiveness of policy to public interests, pluralists have characteristically emphasized the importance of establishing formal procedures designed to keep cable policy-making open to group demands.[10] Community ascertainment surveys[11], public hearings[12], and other forms of public participation in franchising and regulating[13] cable systems have all been suggested as means of accomplishing this end. Within the broad limits set by procedures designed to maintain the openness of the cable decision-making process, the pluralist argument relies on competition among groups representing different interests to ensure that cable policies faithfully serve public interests. In any case, only highly organized groups of informed citizens are seen as capable of both informing the public about the value of cable technologies and exerting the pressure on both operators and officials required to implement policies which serve public interests.

Although the role of governments in the pluralist model is largely limited to balancing conflicting interests by maintaining an open decision-making process, authors supporting the pluralist explanation have concentrated on two main policy implications of their model. First, some form of public regulation of the cable enterprise is viewed as necessary. Some system of cable regulation is generally accepted as given. Within this system, the various levels of government are held responsible for informing the public of its potential interests in cable policy and encouraging a maximum amount of public involvement in public sector policy deliberations. This responsibility for informing the public also implies a responsibility of officials at each level to inform themselves and one another about the realistic potential of cable as a public service technology. Second, governments at each level are expected to respond to publicly expressed demands regarding cable service policies by using the weight of their authority as franchisors and/or regulators of the cable industry to negotiate with cable operators for the provision of public interest services.

While the pluralistic argument is often prescriptive in tone, a purely explanatory model is implied by its emphasis on the institutionalization of public involvement in cable policy making. First, the core hypothesis of this explanation is that the level of institutionalization of public participation in cable policy making is an immediate cause of cable policies serving public interests. Second, prior research on political participation suggests that an important set of antecedent variables in determining the level of institutionalized participation in a community includes a variety of community characteristics including size, diversity and socio-economic status.[14] Thus the causal chain diagrammed in Figure 3.1 (below) may be used to summarize the pluralistic explanation. First, community characteristics like the size of the community, the diversity of its members, and their socio-economic status act together to determine the level at which participation is likely to become institutionalized. Institutionalized participation then shapes cable service policies within the constraints set by federal and state regulation of cable firms. In addition, both federal and state regulation can affect the extend to which local participation is institutionalized.

Despite the appeal of the pluralist argument it suffers from both prescriptive and explanatory inadequacies. As a prescriptive theory the pluralist explanation of cable policy is subject to a variety of criticisms. First, the organization of groups within a community may not reflect genuine public interests. What Mancur Olson described as the "public goods" and "free rider" problems may operate to ensure that the most general public interests will not be effectively organized. Interests which are organized are therefore likely to be "special" rather than "general" in character. It is precisely this argument which has been leveled against community groups aspiring to become involved in cable franchising and operations.[15] Compounding the problem of potential unrepresentativeness of groups in the political process is the inherent bias built into the procedural solutions to political problems.[16] Groups which manage to prevail on procedural questions may be able

Figure 3.1
The Pluralist Model

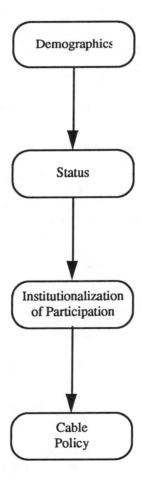

to effectively prevent the future entry of new demands into the decision-making process. The result of the pluralist emphasis on procedures may then be profoundly conservative. First, in order to approach an ideal of fairness, an attempt may be made to delay cable decisions long enough to evaluate the potential impact of a variety of procedural institutions for public participation. However, because of problems related to the evaluation of participatory programs[17] it is likely that there can never be enough time to evaluate all possible procedures in a dynamic environment. As a result a decision on a cable franchise is either postponed indefinitely or the matter is prematurely closed. Second, the institutionalization of participation necessarily reflects a mobilization of bias in the community at a point in time. in a dynamic environment like that of the cable industry, such a crystallization of issues almost certainly works against the introduction of new items of demands into the policy-making agenda. In effect, then, institutionalization of participation may work against changes in the cable policy agenda necessary to respond to changes in cable technology.

While these and other criticisms of pluralism as a prescriptive model for policy-making can be applied to the area of cable communications policy, our major interest here is the adequacy of pluralism as a descriptive and explanatory model.

Empirically, neither institutionalized public participation, in general, nor involvement in cable policy-making, in particular, has shown up as a strong candidate for explaining policy outcomes.[18] There is little variation in the organization of cable systems. Most cable systems[19] are commercial ventures owned and operated by various business interests with little explicit involvement by the public in policy-making. The 2.1 percent of U.S. systems operating in 1981 under community (usually local government) or subscriber ownership provides little room for examining variation in public involvement at the highest levels of cable policy-making. Second, the most common form of direct citizen involvement in which the cable firm offers a percentage of ownership (usually 20 percent) to local individuals or institutions has been used by the cable industry mainly as a cooptive mechanism to build support for proposed cable systems. Even the industry's terminology for these arrangements, "rent-a-citizen" and "rent-an-institution" reflect the superficial character of this form of participation.

Recognition of the arbitrary nature of empirically workable definitions of participation has led some to eschew efforts to construct general models of participatory processes in cable policy-making and to concentrate on phenomenological "thick description" of participation and policy-making in single communities. Observers of citizen participation, examining case studies of individual communities, cannot fail to be impressed, sometimes overwhelmed, by the variety of forms participation in cable policy-making has taken. Aside from the very rare cases of direct public or community ownership of the cable system, communities have been involved in franchising and regulating cable operations through a variety of organized community groups, advisory boards,[20] public access facilitator groups,[21] as well as through quasi-governmental and governmental mechanisms derived from the local government's role as franchisor for cable systems.[22] In addition, some cable system operators and franchising agents have undertaken to ascertain the needs for particular cable services, thus introducing still another avenue for public participation,[23] albeit an indirect one. Faced with this bewildering array of modes of participation some observers have forsaken any attempt to construct general models in favor of historical-descriptive case studies which treat each cable-community system as a *sui generis* phenomenon qualitatively different from any other situation.[24] The attempt to overcome the problem of restricted variation in public participation brings us to the diametrically opposite problem of infinite variation which makes each case of participation seem unique. In such a case, the independent variable, participation, may vary, at least qualitatively, but the dependent variable, policy, is relatively constant. We can, therefore, draw no conclusions about the impact of participation on policy.[25]

The pluralist model is also deficient as a basis for evaluating the procedures established to ensure wider participation. Without agreement on the nature of participatory activities, standards for evaluating these activities are difficult to design.[26] In general, should participatory procedures be judged by the feelings they induce in participants (e.g., satisfaction with the fairness of a decision-making process) or by the policies which result from citizen involvement? Should the criterion for successful participation be civic involvement or individual benefit? Should procedures promote direct involvement of citizens or representation of their interests in policy-making?

The lack of agreement over the answers to these questions when they are applied to cable communications policies introduces a definite circularity in pluralistically guided analyses of the impact of participation on policy outcomes. Without agreeing on the nature of genuine participation we cannot evaluate procedures designed to promote it. However, without acceptable standards for evaluating participatory institutions we must remain uncertain about the true nature of participation. Thus our poor understanding of the concept of participation leads pluralist explanations into a paradox.

The Economic Explanation

Economic explanations of cable service policies begin with assumptions which are very different from those underlying the pluralist model.[27] A primary source of disagreement between proponents of these two types of explanation is the difference in their understanding of the nature of the cable medium itself. While the pluralist explanation tends to view cable in terms of its public interest potential, economic explanations assume that cable is a consumer technology useful for providing households with essentially private services like an expanded choice of entertainment programming or pay channels carrying non-broadcast programming. These are essentially private goods. They may be purchased or foregone depending upon the individual household's ability and willingness to pay for them without affecting the welfare of others. Under this assumption, the most efficient means for distributing cable benefits is a competitive market mechanism. Thus the competitive market model may be read into economic explanations of cable policies. As providers of private goods, cable systems are most appropriately developed by commercial enterprise with a minimum of government intervention in the decision-making activities of cable firms.

The concerns which provide the impetus for pluralist explanation are not problematic for proponents of the economic approach. In particular, economic explanations assume that cable consumers (subscribers) are adequately informed about cable's potential for improving their welfare and can therefore maintain their sovereignty in market arrangements. The genuine interests of the community are assumed to be limited to those preferences effectively expressed in the context of the market for cable services. These interests are measured by the willingness to pay for preferred services.

In a pure market system, cable operators seek to attract subscribers by offering the services most desired at a price which will maximize their profits. Firms providing cable services respond to demands from the market according to their ability to do so. In the terminology introduced in Chapter One, successful cable firms are those which avoid articulation errors and supply the services demanded by the largest number of consumers at prices those consumers are willing to pay. Only capable firms survive in a competitive market.

Finally, government action of any type is viewed with suspicion. Proponents of economic explanations tend to see public intervention in markets as a costly and inefficient means of organizing the provision of social welfare. It involves either complicated analysis of individual desires or arbitrarily imposed goals for social activities.[28] Government action, beyond the protection of property and markets is assumed to be inefficient. Two problems motivate economic analyses of cable policies: 1. How can the viability of cable firms be assured in the market for cable services, and, 2. How can government involvement in the decisions of cable firms through franchising and regulation of cable systems be minimized?

Analysts applying economic explanations for cable service policies tend to emphasize the viability of cable firms as businesses in explaining variation in the types of services provided in different communities. The expensive extras most often seen as public interest cable policies are most likely to be provided by the economic organizations with the slack resources needed to absorb the costs these policies entail. This argument mirrors that of Wolf[29] with regard to broadcast news programming. In effect, this theory implies that the representation of public interests depends upon the benevolence of large organizations capable of employing economies of scale or with diversified interests in other industries that allow them to underwrite the costs of public interest cable policies. This benevolence can also be explained in terms consistent with the assumption of rational self-interest as the primary motive for economic behavior. Large corporations may be expected to offer public interest cable services in order to increase the demand for cable services in lucrative urban markets already well served by broadcast television stations.[30] In some cases, investments in cable systems may be used as tax shelters and write-offs to protect profits earned in other activities.[31] Finally, corporations may need the kind of public relations advantage investments in public interest cable policies could provide.[32]

Factors most often included in economic explanations for cable public interest policies refer primarily to the capital needs and profitability of cable operations, including the sensitivity of cable firms to the general availability of capital in the economy and the need to attract subscribers in order to justify investments in relatively expensive non-broadcast services. In any case, the active involvement of citizens in policy-making is largely irrelevant in economic explanations of public interest cable policies.

Related to the concern for firms' profit-making potential is a concern about the "over-regulation" of the industry which is seen as hindering efficient development by imposing overly restrictive constraints on the managers and operators of cable systems. In particular, regulation is seen as an evil which arbitrarily increases prices by limiting entry or imposing demands for services for which there is

no real market.[33] In addition, government intervention is criticized for:
1. fostering oligopoly by favoring large existing firms over smaller, newer ones;[34] 2. retarding or preventing innovations by imposing unnecessary costs on the development of new products and services;[35] and/or 3. arbitrarily limiting consumer choice by imposing authoritative mechanisms in place of markets.[36]

These concerns are usually translated into two general types of policy prescriptions. First, if community interest services are accepted as a legitimate policy goal for cable development, the economic explanation suggests that this goal can best be attained by promoting the development of cable systems by the most profitable multiple system organizations. By taking advantage of economies of scale available to larger firms they are most likely to be able to cross-subsidize local origination, access, and interactive services where these services are demanded.[37] Alternatively, the burden of subsidizing these services must be assumed either by subscribers in the form of higher rates or by public expenditure to underwrite the extra expense assumed by operators who provide public interest services.[38] Since neither higher rates nor public expenditures to support cable operations are politically palatable to franchisors, most franchises granted in recent years have gone to larger, well-established multiple system organizations.[39]

Among cable systems run by smaller independent operators, economic explanations point to the importance of low costs to offset the expense of public interest services. Thus low franchise fees, low wages and salaries, and low construction costs are considered conditions likely to facilitate community interest service policies. The impact of this suggestion on public policy may be seen in policies which limit the fees charged by local franchisors,[40] establish pole rights for cable construction (especially at low rents),[41] and limit community interest service requirements to systems above a certain size.[42]

Of course, these prescriptions assume that there are public interests at stake in any cable service policy package. Many proponents of the economic explanation will not concede this point. Rather, they hold to a strong form of the assumption of cable's private-good nature. according to these proponents, variation in cable service policies is simply a function of demand and a (non-random) disturbance caused by government intervention. If there is no genuine demand for public interest services, government intervention requiring such services is arbitrary. It is also inefficient since the drain of providing public services for which subscribers will not pay diverts resources from the improvement of cable services for which there is a willingness to pay.

If there is a genuine demand for public interest services and the current distribution of these services is not optimal, the obvious solution is to remove government intervention and allow the market to efficiently allocate them. In any case, deregulation of the cable industry appears desirable. Consequently, the economic explanation is part of the justification for the deregulatory movement in the cable industry and in state and federal governments.

The explanatory model which lies at the heart of economic explanations for cable service variation is diagrammed in Figure 3.2 (below). The primary determinants of service policies are cable system level characteristics defined by each system's unique costs and income. System characteristics are, in turn, defined by three influences: 1. the characteristics of the markets in which the system operates, especially their relative competitiveness; 2. the characteristics of the firm which owns the cable system plant, particularly its ability to attract capital investors; and, 3. the nature of the regulatory environment in which the system operates. Due to policies of grandfathering and otherwise waiving regulatory requirements, the regulations under which systems operate vary widely across, and even within levels of government. This unpredictability of the regulatory environment is, in fact, one of the major policy problems addressed by the proponents of economic explanations.

The economic explanation has somewhat stronger empirical support than the pluralist model. Experience in the broadcast industry indicates that public interest programming and services are considered expensive services which are more likely to be provided by larger stations owned by larger firms in more competitive markets, than by smaller firms in less competitive markets.[43] Likewise, local origination, access, and interactive cable services are expensive options compared to the retransmission of broadcast signals and pay services.[44] There is also some evidence that regulation, in particular rate regulation by state and local agencies, retards innovation and expansion of cable services.[45]

Despite this support, the economic explanation is also subject to a variety of criticisms. First, like any market model, the economic explanation for public interest cable policies may be criticized for the failure of observable cable markets to meet the assumptions of pure competition.[46] In particular, three assumptions appear especially questionable: 1. the assumption of individual competence and perfect information; 2. the assumption that transactions are cost-free; and, 3. the assumption that there are large numbers of producers and consumers capable of entering and leaving the market for cable services without cost.

**Figure 3.2
The Economic Model**

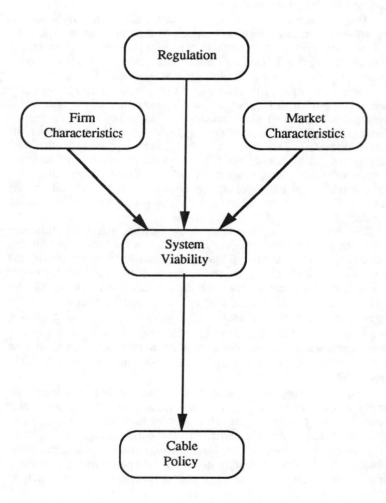

A basic assumption of any competitive market model is that individuals in the market are endowed with perfect information and are fully competent to identify transactions which will result in improvements in their own welfare. Only under this assumption can individuals bargain as equals and agree upon prices for goods or services which reflect the true preferences of both buyers and sellers. Without the capability to correctly identify true preferences among a full range of alternative cable service packages, efficiency pricing of these packages is impossible. If the consumer is not informed and competent, consumer sovereignty is lost and the seller may arbitrarily impose high prices for any level of service, thus bringing about a net loss in consumer welfare. If the seller of cable services cannot adequately identify demand, articulation errors caused by his/her uncertainty will lead either to underproduction of demanded services and a failure to satisfy consumers, or to their overproduction which drains the producer's profit and, in the extreme, leads to an unwillingness to provide any level of the demanded services without public subsidy.

The more serious of these two problems, incompetence of consumers, appears to describe the situation in the cable industry. Individual consumers have relatively little knowledge about cable system technologies and capabilities beyond the retransmission of television signals and pay services providing movies and sports programming. Furthermore, local officials assuming the roles of purchasing agents for their communities are often no more informed than their constituencies, as pluralists have correctly pointed out.

Of course, problems caused by incompetence may be overcome with time. Consumers may ultimately learn to accurately calculate their benefits from alternative packages of cable services. When the consumers of cable services (individual households or community representatives) can shift their purchases of service packages freely among all available suppliers, increasing consumer sophistication would ultimately lead to a matching of preferences with the capabilities of a particular firm. However, the nature of the cable enterprise makes other adjustments to new consumer knowledge difficult and costly.

The transaction costs involved in the purchase of cable system services include information costs (associated with overcoming the problems of incompetence discussed above), bargaining costs, and enforcement costs. Since cable service packages are not homogeneous products, information costs incurred by consumers looking for a particular service package are high. In addition, the cost to community representatives of determining the mix of services to require as a condition of granting a franchise can be considerable, especially if they make an honest effort to ascertain community needs before settling on franchise requirements. To these costs must be added the costs of bargaining with potential operators and compensating any displaced operators for their investment in the existing cable plant and programming contracts when suppliers of cable services need to be changed. Finally, the cost of enforcing new franchise requirements must be taken into account. These costs may include expensive upgrading of the system's plant or programming capabilities (as in the addition of more channels or two-way channels). As a result, cable franchises tend to be relatively long-term contracts and freedom of movement in the cable market is significantly restricted once the franchise is granted. This restriction on freedom of movement is even more obvious for the consumer, who is faced with a local monopoly supplier of cable service, and for the community which must live up to its part of the franchise even if operators sell out their interests in the community's system. Thus, although consumer incompetence may be overcome, another obstacle to the efficiency of pure competition is the high transaction cost involved in the decision to install a cable system with any particular physical or programming configuration.

Whether or not the market model is sensitive to the violation of the assumptions of individual competence and cost-free transactions, it appears likely that cable systems will continue to operate as franchised monopolies. Government intervention in the operations of the cable market is likely at three points, even if a pure market model is held up as an ideal by public policy-makers: First, the incentives for cable system operators to collude is very strong, and becomes stronger as cable penetrates more of its potential urban markets. Second, government may become involved in cable contract negotiations in much the same way that it is involved in the negotiation of labor contracts, setting standards and overseeing the conduct of cable consumer-operator relations. Finally, regulation of cable is likely to be necessary in order for local governments to exercise their authority over public rights-of-way (the original justification for the earliest cases of public regulation of cable). Add to these opportunities for government intervention the strong tendency for cable systems toward conditions conducive to natural monopolies (i.e., capital intensiveness and significant economies of scale) and it appears that the market model underlying economic explanations of community service cable policies may be technically inappropriate for application in the cable industry.

Technical problems aside, there are two other criticisms of markets which may be applied in the case of cable communications that make the economic model questionable as a prescriptive model for public policy.

First, the economic explanation for community service policies assumes that welfare may be maximized through voluntary transactions between producers and consumers. For private goods, a market may be able to attain allocative efficiency. However, the most important community interest cable services are, by definition, collective goods. This raises the possibility that cable communications will require action to overcome the "public goods" problem defined by Mancur Olson, i.e., the disincentive to individual contributions to the provision of a collective good. If communities are to be organized to provide themselves with community-oriented cable services, they must rely on: 1. coercion (in effect, taxing either operators or subscribers to support local and interactive services); 2. the provision of a by-product private good that will attract support for the provision of community services; or, 3. a federated group structure in which incentives to contribute to the provision of community-oriented services come from small groups within each community.[47]

The fact that citizens' groups presenting demands for community service cable policies have tended to rely on coalitional forms of organization may represent the attempt by these groups to respond to the public goods dilemma in cable communications policy. A variety of special interest groups within a community, each hoping to derive some benefit from the use of a particular cable service may be able to organize sufficient support for community-oriented cable service policies that may benefit all of the groups as well as unorganized interests in the community. To the extent that this occurs, the economic explanation for community service policies begins to shade over into pluralist arguments and becomes subject to the criticisms discussed in the previous section of this chapter. More importantly, the federated group strategy remains weak as long as primary responsibility for managing cable organization rests with a commercial operator. No amount of support from outside of the cable firm is likely to produce those services when other services generate greater profits for the firm.

The role of the operator as a commercial actor also limits the applicability of the by-product solution to the public good problem in cable communications. Although it is conceivable that system operators could attract support for community interest services by tying these services to some private good, e.g., entertainment programming, it is unrealistic to assume that a collective benefit would take priority over profit as a goal for cable system operators.

It appears, then, that the public goods dilemma of cable service policies is likely to be resolved only by the use of some form of coercive authority. Otherwise, the likely result of any complete deregulation of cable communications would be a failure to provide an adequate level of community-oriented cable services.

The final criticism of the economic model as a normative guide for cable communications policy is the insecurity and instability likely to accompany unfettered market operations in the cable industry. Both relevant technologies and consumer preferences regarding cable services are certain to change drastically in the next twenty years. Leaving the social response to these changes to an unmanaged market would result in several perverse outcomes. First, market and technological uncertainties would make any but the most limited forms of planning practically impossible. This problem would extend beyond public planning agencies to cable firms themselves and would create strong incentives for collusion and concentration in the industry. Second, uncertainties would be likely to lead to increased speculation and misallocation of cable investments in technologies and services for which there is no demand or need. Finally, apart from the waste caused by uncertainties in the cable industry, or perhaps because of it, an unregulated market would be likely to be marked by the kind of corruption of public officials and institutions which marked the industry in the early 1970s.

While the economic model for explaining cable policy appears more descriptively accurate than the pluralistic model, it is somewhat deficient as a general theory of cable system policy-making. While large MSOs do appear to be more likely to provide public interest cable services, the economic explanation fails to illuminate the decision process by which some communities are chosen to receive such services while others are not. The slack resources of even the largest firms are ultimately limited. Consequently, some strategy for making such a choice is necessary. If the economic model were entirely sufficient to explain cable policy we might expect cable system developers in the largest MSOs to consistently offer a relatively standardized package of cable services in community after community. This package would presumably be based on some calculation of the average ability of the firm to provide the resources needed for cable services over and above the standard package of retransmitted broadcast channels required by federal regulations for a given area. However, there is no such standard package of public interest services. Rather, the large MSOs have tailored their bids for developing new systems to each community contemplating a cable franchise. Case studies of the franchising process have indicated that these criteria are determined in a bargaining process involving the representatives of the community (either public officials or citizens' groups or both) and firms interested in obtaining cable franchises. Drafting and awarding a cable franchise is a highly political process.[48] Without taking politics into account the economic model may help explain the capability of firms to provide the resources for cable services over and above the standard package of retransmitted broadcast channels required by federal regulations for a given area. To the extent that economic explanations fail to take bargaining into account, they do not illuminate the decision-making process by which cable policies are formulated.

Stratification Explanations

Clearly the differences between pluralist and economic models stem from fundamental disagreements regarding the appropriate assumptions to be made in explaining these policies. In particular, their assumptions about the nature of the cable medium and the competence of cable consumers place pluralists and economists in diametrically opposite positions. In a sense, stratificationist explanations offer a way out of the intractable opposition generated by differing assumptions.

First, stratificationist explanations involve no necessary assumptions about the nature of the cable medium. By avoiding the issue of whether cable is intrinsically a public or private good, stratificationist explanations can avoid the argument over the meaning of "public interests" in cable communications. Community service policies may be viewed as simply another set of potential cable services which communities may or may not seek to implement and which may or may not have impacts beyond the satisfaction of individual preferences.

Second, regarding the question of consumer competence, stratificationists avoid the extremes of the other types of explanation with an implicit assumption that public understanding of cable communications potential may vary from near total ignorance to enlightened sophistication both across and within communities.

While avoiding the extreme assumptions of the other two types of explanation, stratificationists rely on a more general assumption about the nature of society or the communities in which cable systems are developed. As implied by the name, stratificationist theories assume a stratified social structure through which the impact of any technology will be filtered.[49]   Whether cable technologies are consumer commodities or public interest technologies, stratificationist explanations suggest that the benefits of service policies will be distributed according to the status of the individuals or communities affected by cable system development.

Stratificationist arguments may therefore be melded to elements of either pluralist or economic explanations of cable policy. On the one hand, the socio-economic or political status of groups which become involved in the franchising process may be held to determine the particular interests to be represented in service policies. [50]   On the other, the status (especially economic status) of a community as a whole may make it more or less attractive to cable system operators. They may offer a wider range of services in high status communities than in low status communities in the hope that the community members' abilities will be matched by their willingness to pay for "extra" services.[51] In any case, stratificationist explanations hold that it is the status of the demanders of service policies which determine the actual distribution of services by cable systems.

The one element which ties the variety of stratificationist approaches into a single type of explanation for cable service policies is a common explanatory model. This model is diagrammed in Figure 3.3 (below). The stratificationist model contains the same elements at the pluralist model. Demographic factors are held to contribute to differences in the status of communities. However, instead of affecting cable policies through its impact on the institutionalization of community participation, status is treated as a common cause of variation in both institutionalization and policies. The institutionalization of participation in cable policy-making is considered extraneous to the causal chain leading to community service cable policies.

In general, stratificationist explanations emphasize status-based inequalities in the output of decision-making systems. Policy recommendations derived from these kinds of explanations depend mainly upon the ideological posture of the analyst. Conservative stratificationists tend to support deregulation and a *laissez-faire*approach to cable policy.[52] Those favoring redistributive goals are more likely to call for strengthening regulation and centralization of regulatory functions at the regional or national level.[53] There is also some support for policies which would encourage the provision of community services by offering incentives which would offset the operators' preference for higher status communities.[54] Finally, the remainder of stratificationist commentators are usually concerned with policies to assure universal service at reasonable rates within any community.[55]

Although stratificationist explanations avoid the prescriptive inadequacies of the pluralist model and offer a possible answer to the question of operators' criteria for offering community service policies, they are also subject to criticism for theoretical deficiencies. First, while there is some evidence that lower status groups are, on the whole, less willing and able to take advantage of cable and subscription television service than more affluent groups, [56] the impact of variables like income, race, or education on subscription to cable services is apparently small.[57] The weakness of the apparent relationship between measures of status and the use of cable services is especially telling in

Figure 3.3
The Stratification
Model

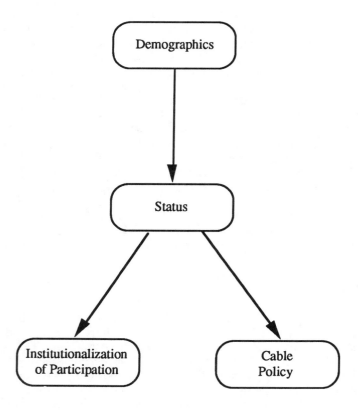

view of the counter-examples available in lower-class and minority communities which have successfully negotiated for extensive community service policies.[58]

Beyond the weakness of their empirical support, stratificationist explanations suffer from fundamental ambiguity concerning how the relationship between status and policy is to be explained. Although the forms of stratificationist explanation are relatively clear as they are outlined in Figure 3.3, in use they tend to be somewhat confounded. It is often unclear whether a given author believes status to work at the individual level or across communities.[59] Also, unless operationalized by some specific surrogate measure, the notion of status is often treated as an undifferentiated complex of characteristics which combine economic and social bases of stratification (e.g., "white middle class suburbs").[60] The only aspect of stratificationist explanations which is usually made clear is the author's ideological bias.

The most basic inadequacy of stratificationist explanations is that they confuse the possession of resources of power with the effective exercise of power in the determination of cable policies. In fact, a variety of resources may be converted into influence over cable decisions. Socio-economic status represents only one set of characteristics which may be used for this purpose. Other potential resources include mass voting power as it was used in Nashville,[61] effective organization and representation of community demands as these have been employed by video access groups,[62] and using the dependence of cable operators on subscribers in bargaining for community service packages. Even this extended list of potential power resources is not exhaustive. It is therefore unlikely that status variables could alone explain the variation in cable service packages across communities.

Summary

The three typical explanations for cable community service policy reviewed here may be related to arguments which have characterized analyses of public policy at the highest level of abstraction. These arguments have focused on two questions: 1. Who is actually responsible for making public policies? This is essentially a political question which arises in the context of a broader argument over, 2. Whether political or economic factors are the stronger determinants of public policies?

The pluralist and stratificationist explanations represent opposing viewpoints in an argument over the relative importance of socio-economic status and mass organization as power resources in society.

The argument between pluralists and elitists reached a peak in the 1960s and early 1970s in a flurry of community power studies.[63] Despite the diversity of the research published by proponents of both schools of thought, the basic argument between them remains unresolved. While the pluralist-elitist argument focuses on the political questions of who will exercise more power in determining policies, both sides tend to accept the proposition that policy-making is an essentially political process whose outcome is determined by the relative power of either status groups or interest groups in community or societal decision-making. Another, more recent argument begins with questioning the assumption that policy-making is an essentially political process. The argument over the relative importance of political and economic factors in determining policy focuses on questions about the environment within which policy makers operate and the method in which policy is actually made. This argument, like that between pluralists and elitists, has arisen in a variety of policy contexts and across all levels of policy-making. Unlike the elitist-pluralist argument (which the argument between "politics" and "economics" has largely supplanted) evidence points strongly toward the pre-eminence of economics in determining the output of policy-making systems.[64] Nevertheless, it seems unreasonable to rule out entirely the importance of political factors. Thus the competing explanations for cable service policies represent a fair characterization of our theoretical understanding of the determinants of public policy in general. A variety of plausible explanations have been offered but rarely has any one explanation been able to accrue the unique combination of empirical support and conceptual reasonableness that we tend to associate with genuine theories.

Several strategies for finding a way out of this pre-theoretical thicket are possible. First, it is possible that no single explanation can account for all of the outputs of policy-making systems either across policy areas or with regard to all dimensions of even one policy area. The explanations for cable service policies outlined here have rarely involved explicit recognition of the three dimensions of community service cable policies outlined in Chapter 2. While pluralists have tended to emphasize diversity and access, proponents of the economic explanation focus on local origination. Both "economists" and stratificationists have shown concern for pay interactive services, which may not even fit under our conception of community interest policies. However none of the literature reviewed above has systematically approached all three dimensions or the relationships among the diversity, localism and interactivity of cable services.   In this study we shall examine each as a distinct goal for public policies affecting cable.

Dimensionalizing the concept of community interest policy may provide us with a clearer picture of the impact of various factors affecting cable policies but it is unlikely to move us far beyond the current pre-theoretical arguments over precisely how cable policies are determined.   To accomplish this two approaches are possible.   First, we may take a purely synthetic approach, attempting to combine the best elements of all three types of explanation in a single model for empirical testing.   Such an approach would provide an opportunity to summarize the relative impact of factors suggested by each type of explanation and to examine the interaction of factors in determining cable policies.   Second, we may attempt to reconceptualize the cable policy-making process within the framework of political-economy or organizational theory.   In this approach we can explicitly incorporate factors and interactions among factors in a more abstract model and then test this model against available data.   In the next section we will turn our attention to the construction of such a model.   After that we will discuss strategy for constructing and comparing the "synthetic" and "organizational" models.

---

[1]   Proponents of the pluralist explanation for cable policies have included mainly political and other social scientists (except for economists), e.g., Bablitch and Thomson(1982), Baer(1974), Baer, *et al.*(1974), Carpenter-Huffman, *et al.*(1974), Ledbetter and Mendelson(1972), Marchese(1972), White(1968), and Smith(1970), and cable activists, both inside government, e.g., Minnesota Cable Communications Board(1979), Rothstein(1978), U.S. Congress(1976), and out, e.g., Young(1981), Waz(1980), Burns(1975), Tate(1971).

[2]   Reinemer(1981).   Kalba(1975) outlines the assumptions underlying three prescriptive models of cable policy-making which correspond roughly to the models discussed in this chapter.   His notion of a "local franchising" model is most closely related to the pluralist model described herein.

[3]   Carpenter-Huffman, *et al.*(1974), O'Neill and Polk(1972).   See, also, works cited in Chapter 2, especially, Wenner(1975), Topper and Wilson(1976), Goldman(1979), Pool(1973), Mandelbaum(1972), Lucas and Yin(1973), Head(1973), Marchese(1972).

[4]   Yin(1972) reported that, in Dayton, Ohio, there was "a lack of public awareness or interest in those very features of advanced cable systems which are most often associated promoted by cable technologists." (p. 296).   The problem of limited public understanding is also stressed in Head(1973), Young(1981), McKenna(1974), U.S. Congress(1976).

5 N. Johnson and Gerlack(1972), Kalba(1975), Lane(1979), L. Johnson(1975), International Institute of Communications(1977), Marchese(1972), Steiner(1972), O'Donnell, Thomas, and Gissen(1982).

6 Smith's(1972) discussion of the Nashville case makes this point painfully clear. Others who have explicitly cited the lack of public official responsiveness to public interest demands   include   Head(1973), Oppenheim(1974), Yin(1974), and Lane(1979). A particularly interesting example of a city official's complaint about the unresponsiveness of higher agencies is presented by William J. Nee, mayor of Fridley, Minnesota, who described the dampening effects of federal decisions on that towns attempt to open cable decision-making to pluralistic participation. (U.S. Congress, 1976a). See, also, analyses of local franchises in Seidman(1972), Huffman(1974), Mengel(1974).

7 Horn(1981), Ross(1973).

8 The most conspicuous case of corruption in the cable franchising process resulted in the conviction of the mayor of Johnstown, New Jersey, who was charged with accepting a bribe from Irving Kahn, president of Teleprompter, Inc., in 1971. More commonly, a strategy of quasi-legal cooptation of local officials by franchise bidders through lobbyists is involved.

9 As long as group formation is not artificially constrained by lack of awareness or official proscriptions, pluralists assume these groups will faithfully reflect true public interests.

10 Baer(1974), Kalba(1975, 1974, 1972), Model franchising procedures developed by various agencies uniformly include recommendations for open decision-making procedures. See, Baer, *et al.*(1974), Minnesota Cable Communications Board(1979), Korte(n.d.).

11 Baer(1974), Wolfsohn and Kay(1980), U.S. Congress(1976).

12 Bablitch and Thomson(1982), Mengel(1974), Baer(1974).

13 Sparkes(1975, 1974), Baukus(1976b), Jacobsen(1977).

14 May(1971), Verba and Nie(1972), Milbrath and Goel(1977).

15 The plight of the beleaguered city official, beset on all sides by special interest claims regarding cable policy, was plaintively apparent in hearings on a cable franchise for Chicago, Illinois. Presented with a demand for equal representation of local citizens' groups on the Mayor's Select Committee On Cable, Alderman Edward Vrdolyak, chair of the committee, testily asserted that the member of the appointive committee, and not citizens' groups, were the duly authorized representatives of public interests. Hearing, November 2, 1980.

16 Schattschneider(1975), Buchanan and Tullock(1974), Bachrach and Baratz(1970).

17 These problems are discussed in greater detail below.

18 Gittell, *et al.*(1980), Mazmanian and Sabatier(1980), Kamieniecki(1980), Mazmanian and Nienaber(1979), Yates(1976), O'Brien(1975).

19   98.1% as of 1984. *Television Factbook*, vol. 52, 1985.

20   Arnstein(1969), Kasperson and Breitbart(1974), Checkoway and Van Til(1978), Rosenbaum(1976).

21   Arnstein(1969).

22   Bablitch and Thomson(1982), Head(1973), Briley(1977), Baukus(1976a,b), Cleland(1976), Marchese(1972), Young(1981), Kalba(1975).

23   Carpenter-Huffman, *et al.*(1974), Rice(1980), Rice and Bednarczyk(1977), Anderson(1975).

24   Sparkes(1975, 1974), Baer(1974), Baer, *et al.*(1974), Jacobsen(1978), Jeffres(1975), Steiner(1973), Tate(1973).

25   Ayubi(1981), Wolfsohn and Kay(1980).

26   In fact, almost no analyses of representative samples of cable systems or communities have been conducted. The number of case studies which might be aggregated in order to extend the generalizability of propositions about cable policy-making is large, but differences in these qualitative descriptions limit their comparability.

27   Proponents of the economic explanation include economists, e.g., Veljanovsky and Bishop(1983), Webb(1983), Besen, *et al.*(1977), Babe(1975), Mitchell and Smiley(1974), Ross(1974), Noll, *et al.*(1973), Park(1972), Wolf(1972), Comanor and Mitchell(1971a,b), and Posner(1972, 1970), cable system operators and others in the communications industries, e.g., O'Donnell and Gissen(1982), *Broadcasting*(1980), Bernstein(1979), Smith(1979), Scott(1976), Lippke(1975), and investors in cable enterprises, e.g., Wicks(1981), Sloan(1979), Dent(1977), Committee for Economic Development(1975). The widespread acceptance of this type of explanation is reflected in the deregulatory movement at the federal and state levels of government, e.g., California Public Broadcasting Commission(1982), MacAvoy(1976), U.S. Congress(1976).

28   See, Lindblom(1977) for an excellent synopsis of the critique of "authority systems."

29   *Television Programming for News and Public Affairs*(1972), also, Williams(1955).

30   Scott(1975).

31   Early in the development of the cable industry it was a common practice to undertake the construction of a cable system, then depreciate the plant over a short period, taking advantage of tax deferrals before selling the system for a large capital gain. Although speculation and warehousing of franchises has declined with the entry of larger institutional investors into the industry, the appeal of cable investment as a tax shelter remains. Stien(1985), Sloan(1979), *Broadcasting*(1980).

32   Demonstrating a willingness to provide public interest services may yield advantages in the competition for franchises. Consequently, most major firms

have produced "information packages" for distribution to potential franchisors which tout their commitment to public service.

33 Bolick(1984), Goodman(1982), Hazlett(1982), Lippke(1975), Branscomb(1975).

34 Besen,*et al.*(1977), Ross(1974).

35 Simon(1981), Ross(1974), Posner(1970).

36 Possner(1977), Besen, *et al.*(1977), Owen, *et al.*(1974).

37 Johnson(1980), Committee for Economic Development(1975).

38 Mills and Kolsrud(1976),Branscomb(1975), White(1968).

39 Among the sample of 417 systems operating in 1979, 70% of those which began operation in 1970 or later were controlled by MSOs.

40 The Federal Communications Commission limited franchise fees to 3 percent and only in exceptional circumstances allowed rates as high as 5 percent of gross revenues.

41 Eight states (California, Connecticutt, Massachusetts, New York, Oregon, South Carolina, Tennessee, and West Virginia) have enacted pole attachment legislation. See, also, U.S. Congress(1982).

42 FCC requirements for local origination, access and two-way channels were applied only to systems with 3500 or more subscribers. In 1979 only about 26% of the systems in operation had subscriber bases that large.

43 Wolf(1972), Williams(1955).

44 McCavitt and Pringle(1986), Wiese(1984), Webb(1983), Schiller(1970), Seiden(1982), Efrein(1975), Lippke(1975), Feldman(1980), Anderson(1975), and Baer(1974) present varying estimates of production costs for local programming. Broadcast programming is basically free to cable systems after the investment in receiving equipment and cable operators and paid, usually per subscriber, for carrying other cable programming services.

45 Kalba, *et al.*(1980, 1979).

46 Lindblom(1977) also outlines the technical criticisms of market mechanisms.

47 Olson(1971).

48 Orton(1981), Bernstein(1979), Smith(1979).

49 Stratificationist explanations are the most difficult of the three types discussed here to identify with specific groups of policy analysts. Rather, elements of the stratificationist argument may be found in the work of sociologists, e.g., Mandelbaum(1972), Kalba(1975), political scientists, e.g., Prewitt(1970), Nie(1970), MacRae(1970), Pool(1973), Laudon(1977), journalists, e.g., Oppenheim(1974), Smith(1979), Wicklein(1980), and cable activists, U.S. Congress(1976a), Tate(1972).

50 This is, at least in part, a fear of some opponents of citizen groups' direct participation in franchising processes (see, for example, Laudon(1977)). It is also the cause for concern over lobbying (see, *Los Angeles Times*, August 3,

1982) and cable industry "rent-a-citizen" tactics, e.g., Bernstein(1979), Sloan(1979).

[51] *Time*(1981), *Broadcasting*(1980).

[52] Branscomb(1975).

[53] Sheehan and Ammon(1986).

[54] Oppenheim (1974); Smith (1979).

[55] White (1968).

[56] Oppenheim (1974).

[57] Noll, Peck, and McGowen (1973); Ayubi (1981); Becker and Rafaeli (1981).

[58] Baer (1974), Steiner (1972), and Kleman (1972) all discuss the experience of Dayton, Ohio. Carpenter-Huffman, *et al.* (1974) describes the activities of the Watts Communications Bureau in Los Angeles; and, Jeffries (1975), the Gary Communications Group in Gary, Indiana.

[59] Part of the confusion is attributable to the fact that service decisions are largely the responsibility of system operators who stress both the private-good, individual nature of cable services and the importance of demographics (or aggregate status) in cable market development.

[60] Smith (1979) describes the favored communities as the "white highlands." See, also, Bernstein (1979).

[61] Smith (1979) describes the use of electoral power in the case of the Nasheville, Tennessee franchise.

[62] Sparkes (1979); Carpenter-Huffman (1974).

[63] The outstanding exemplars of the opposing sides of this argument are Dahl (1961) for the pluralists and Hunter (1959) for the elitists.

[64] Savage (1980); Stonecash and Hayes (1981); Stonecash (1979); Munger (1969); Dawson and Robinson (1963)

Chapter 4

An Empirical Examination of Explanations for Cable Community Interest Policies

Using data from the sample of communities with cable systems collected for this study, we may test the adequacy of the various models of cable policy-making which have been presented thus far. First we will examine the results of tests of a series of bivariate hypotheses derived from each of the pure-type models outlined in chapter three. We will then turn to comparisons of the pluralist and stratification models and of a combined socio-political model with the economic model. This chapter, then, may be interpreted as the report of an exercise in empirical theory construction the results of which may be used in constructing a benchmark for testing an organizational model of cable policy-making which will be described in chapter five.

Bivariate Hypotheses

Before examining the models discussed in Chapter 3 as wholes, we shall focus on how the variables suggested by each explanation are related to each of the dimensions of cable community service policy. As outlined in the previous chapter, each of the explanations for cable policy variation may be associated with a number of bivariate hypotheses about the relationships between indicators of independent variables and measures of cable policy. Although our review of the empirical literature has already indicated that some synthetic alternative might be superior to any one of the pure-type explanations, it will be useful to examine these hypotheses independently using the information gathered for this study. From such an examination of the components of the theoretical models we may develop a preliminary notion of the factors which affect cable community interest policy-making. Beyond this, by focusing on bivariate hypotheses in isolation we may get some feel for the relative explanatory value of the alternative models.

Socio-Political Variables and Cable Policy: Pluralist and Stratification Explanations

Both the pluralist and the stratification models of cable policy determinants are composed of factors related to the demographic character, status of a community, and the level of institutionalization of participation by elements of the community in the cable policy-making process. Consequently the bivariate relationships suggested by each of these "socio-political" models are, for practical purposes, identical. The differences between pluralist and stratification explanations lie in the relative emphasis placed on the institutionalization of participation in each model. Consequently, comparison of the relative adequacy of these models depends upon multivariate hypotheses derived from each. We shall turn our attention to the multivariate implications of the models in the next section, and, for now, focus on the bivariate hypotheses common to both theories as well as those derived from the economic model.

Table 4.1 (below) presents estimates of the relationships between a number of indicators of general demographic characteristics and indicators of the diversity (Channel Capacity, Channel Usage), localism (Local Services, Access Channels), and interactive capability (Access Channels, Two-way Capability) of systems in the sample of 417 cable systems collected for this study.[1] Of the characteristics represented in this table, only the population size of the community shows a consistently significant relationship with cable community interest policies. Generally, the extent of commitment to community oriented policies appears to be positively related to the size of the community. Based on regression coefficients, the channel capacity of systems in operation in 1979 increased at an approximate rate of one channel for each 20,000 person increase in population (over a base of about fourteen channels). Similarly, each 30,000 increase in population adds one channel to a base of ten in use. Types of local programming increase at a rate of over one for each 200,000 in population; and weak but significant, positive monotonic relationships exist between population and the availability of access and interactive services.

These findings are consistent with both pluralist and stratification models, but may also support economic explanations of cable policy based on the characteristics of cable markets. None of the other demographic variables used in this study exhibit as strong or consistent a relationship to community interest policies as population size. On the

TABLE 4.1: RELATIONSHIP BETWEEN DEMOGRAPHIC VARIABLES AND CABLE COMMUNITY INTEREST POLICIES

	Channel Capacity	Channels in Use	Local Services	Access Channel	Two-Way Capability	(N=)
Population	b=.00005 r=.46	b=.00003 r=.42*	b=.000006 r=.36*	d=.16*	d=.21*	(412)
Median Age	b=-.31 r=-.24	b=-.11 r=-.13	b=-.04 r=-.20	d=-.12	d=-.12	(156)
Non-White Population	b=2.4 r=.05	b=4.8 r=.15	b=.45 r=.06	d=.07*	d=.07	(278)
Foreign Born	b=27.7 r=.12	b=27.9 r=.18	b=1.5 r=.04	d=.13*	d=.15*	(242)
Age Diversity†	b=16.3 r=.12	b=13.6 r=.15	b=1.8 r=.09	d=.20*	d=.19*	(184)

Independent Variables dichotomized at medians for crosstabulations from which Somer's d was computed.

    * correlation coefficient significant at $p <= .05$

    † Age diversity = $\log(1/(\%\text{over}65 + \%\text{under}18))$

whole, then, neither pluralist nor stratification theories seem strongly supported by the data examined here. However, in both models, demographic factors are considered to be the most distant from the immediate causes of cable public interest policies and may be important more for their contribution to more proximate causes than for their direct effects on policy.

Table 4.2 (below) presents findings regarding one of these factors, overall socio-economic status of the community. The pattern of relationships between indicators of community status and cable community interest policies is similar to that found in Table 4.1. Only one indicator, the median value of housing in the communities in our sample, appears to be consistently associated with all the indicators of cable policy. In this case it appears that each additional $2,000 in the median value of housing adds one channel to the systems capacity and about a $3,300 increase in the median housing value adds a channel in use, while increments of nearly $20,000 are necessary to increase the number of local programming types by one. The only other status indicator which seems to approach housing value as a correlate of cable policy is the proportion of households with two or more television receivers. Intuitively, the relationships between the proportion of multi-set households and the two indicators of diversity makes sense. Households which can find uses for more that one television set are likely to demand both more potential cable channels and more channels actually providing programming. Similarly, two-TV households may also be more likely to demand access and interactive services and, indeed, these services are more strongly related to the proportion of multi-receiver households than to any of the other indicators of community status.

Despite some problem in interpreting the statistics in Table 4.2 due to restricted sample size, it does seem clear that the diversity of cable services offered is positively related to community wealth. Although significant (at $p \leq .05$) correlations were found between most of the indicators of status and the availability of access and interactive channels, it is not so clear that status positively affects these policies. Federal regulations may be confounding our ability to infer a causal relationship. Consequently, support for pluralist and stratification models is once again quite tentative and conclusions may not be drawn until multivariate analysis is employed to test the models as wholes.

The final set of socio-political variables suggested by the pluralist model of cable policy-making may be loosely interpreted as indicators of the institutionalization of community or public participation in cable decision-making processes.   These indicators, and their estimated

TABLE 4.2: RELATIONSHIP BETWEEN COMMUNITY STATUS VARIABLES AND CABLE COMMUNITY INTEREST POLICIES

	Channel Capacity	Channels In Use	Local Services	Access Channel	Two-Way Capability	(N=)
Median Income	b=0.0002 r=.15	b=.00006 r=.15	b=.00002 r=.09	d=.11	d=.11	(249)
Income Diversity†	b=.0009 r=.16	b=.0007 r=.18	b=.0002 r=.22	d=.09	d=.11	(416)
Median Education	b=1.2 r=.20	b=.47 r=.11	b=.20 r=.22	d=.10	d=.13	(250)
Housing Value	b=.0005 r=.38	b=.0003 r=.36	b=.00006 r=.31	d=.14	d=.16	(283)
Poverty Percent	b=-.11 r=.14	b=-.08 r=.16	b=-.004 r=.04	d=-.06	d=-.01	(249)
Phone Percent	b=17.1 r=.23	b=8.4 r=.17	b=1.3 r=.12	d=.11	d=.18	(240)
One TV Percent	b=35.3 r=.35	b=10.9 r=.16	b=-2.1 r=.15	d=.05	d=.08	(417)
Two TV Percent	b=41.1 r=.46	b=18.9 r=.32	b=-4.6 r=.16	d=.33	d=.30	(119)

Independent Variables dichotomized at medians forcrosstabulations from which Somer's d was computed.

* correlation coefficient significant at $p \leq .05$

* ncome Diversity = mean income minus median income

relationships to the indicators of cable policy, are arrayed in Table 4.3 (below).

Two of these indicators, one representing federal regulations affecting the cable system and the other representing the presence or absence of a League of Women Voters chapter in the community, stand out. Both are positively related at a statistically significant level to all five indicators of public interest policies. A third variable, the proportion of system ownership in the hands of interests from outside of the state in which the system is located fails to exhibit a significant relationship only with the number of channels in use. The findings regarding federal regulation should be interpreted in light of the fact that FCC regulatory policy has specifically required systems with over 3,500 subscribers to provide a minimum twenty channel capacity, undertake local origination programming, and provide access and two-way channels. Consequently, the existence of statistically significant relationships with indicators of these policies may be interpreted more as a validation of the method by which the federal regulatory indicator was constructed than as a finding regarding the impact of federal regulation on policies.

The apparent relationship between having a League of Women Voters chapter and community interest cable policy is more intriguing. First, it could be interpreted as support for the pluralist hypothesis that community interest policies would be related to the political organization of the community. Although the Leagues themselves may not have been directly involved in cable decision-making, their existence in communities does indicate that those communities have reached a threshold of organized citizen participation in politics which may have made community involvement in the franchise process more likely. However, at least two alternative explanations for these findings are plausible: 1) the apparent impact of LWV organizations on cable policy is really an artifact of federal regulations which differentially affected larger communities where League chapters are most likely to be organized; and, 2) the apparent impact of local citizen organization is really the result of organization and cable policy both resulting from a common cause, the level of wealth in the community. Either of these alternative explanations would be consistent with a stratification theory of cable policy-making and we shall return to them for multivariate analyses.

Although the variable which measures the extent of local involvement in ownership of cable firms is a rough measure, the relationships between the percentage of cable system ownership in the hands of out-of-state investors and indicators of community interest cable policy provide the strongest support for the pluralist model. One means of institutionalizing community participation in cable policy-

TABLE 4.3: RELATIONSHIP BETWEEN INSTITUTIONALIZATION OF PARTICIPATION VARIABLES AND CABLE COMMUNITY INTEREST POLICIES

	Channel Capacity	Channels in Use	Local Services	Access Channel	Two-Way Capability	(N=)
Rate Regulation	d=.31	d=.24	d=-.00	d=.05	d=-.06	(73)
State Regulation	d=.04	d=.12	d=.03	d=.02	d=.07	(417)
F.C.C. Regulation	d=.36	d=.12	d=.19	d=.07	d=.19	(417)
LWV Chapter	d=.35	d=.41	d=.55	d=.19	d=.32	(417)
LWV members	b=.01 r=.14	b=.006 r=.10	b=.01 r=.14			(416)
Form of Local Govt	phi=.05	phi=.	C.C.=.05	phi=.09	phi=.12	(256)
Out of State Ownership	b=-.27 r=-.38	b=-.11 r=-.22	b=-.11 r=-.11	d=-.35	d=-.31	(142)

Independent Variables were dichotomized at their medians for crosstabulations from which Somer's d was computed.
* correlation coefficient significant at p<=.05

making is through local ownership of cable systems. the negative relationship between the proportion of out-of-state ownership and indicators of cable policy may be interpreted as an indication that local involvement in ownership does, indeed, increase the likelihood of having community interests represented in policy. Furthermore, there seems to be no immediately apparent reason to think that higher status communities would be differentially attractive to investors in their own states. Nor does it seem reasonable that larger communities (i.e., those affected by federal regulations) would attract more local investors than smaller communities. Consequently, even without multivariate analysis, the bivariate correlations between out-of-state ownership and less extensive commitments to public interest policies appear to support the pluralist model.

There are three other correlations in Table 4.3 which are statistically significant and deserve comment. The first is the relationship between local regulation of subscription rates and channel capacity. This moderate positive relationship could be interpreted as evidence that local involvement in cable policy-making is associated with grater potential diversity of cable programming. However, the direction of causality in this relationship is ambiguous. We cannot tell if active local regulation induced higher channel capacities or if systems with higher capacities (and therefore presumably greater attractiveness to subscribers) are particularly salient targets for local rate regulation. The last two statistically significant correlations both involve the indicator of state regulation. There are weak positive relationships between this variable and the number of channels in use and two-way capability. Although these relationships, like that between rate regulation and channel capacity, could be taken as more support for the pluralist model, the weakness of the relationships and the questionable validity of the indicator of state regulation must reduce confidence in such a conclusion.

On the whole, then the bivariate hypotheses investigated in the foregoing analyses do not unambiguously support either the pluralist or stratification models of cable policy-making. Rather, there is partial evidence supporting each model. A direct comparison of these two socio-political models will be presented after an examination of the bivariate hypotheses suggested by the economic model.

Economic Variables and Cable Policy

Whichever socio-political model proves more appropriate for describing cable policy-making in our sample of systems, we must also consider the alternative explanations offered under what I have described as the economic model. This model emphasizes the viability of the cable system as a profit-making venture as the most immediate "cause" of community interest cable policies. The viability of any system, in turn, is affected by three factors: the "regulatory burden" placed on the operation of the system, the characteristics (mainly size and solvency) of the firm which owns and operates the system, and the nature of the market within which the system operates.

We have already reviewed findings regarding the relationship of federal, state, and local regulation to cable policies in our discussion of the effects of institutionalizing community and public participation in cable policy-making. Those findings, which appear to provide some weak and ambiguous support for the role of socio-political determinants of cable policy, must also be interpreted from the perspective of the economic model. Contrary to the predictions of this model, the regulatory variables in this study are, for the most part, positively related to community interest programming policies. Local rate regulations is moderately (d = .31) but positively related to the channel capacities of the systems in our sample (at least in that subset of our sample for which information on rate regulations was available). Likewise, state regulations show weak, but again positive, relationships to usage and interactive capabilities. Finally, federal regulation, which is most often criticized by proponents of the economic model for its restrictive effects on cable policy, appears to be positively related to all three dimensions of community interest in cable policy.

We must keep in mind the infirmities of our data on regulation. Just as they did not incontrovertibly support the socio-political explanations, these data cannot be taken to unequivocally refute the economic explanation of cable policies. However, it does not seem reasonable to entirely dismiss the failure of these data to support the economic model. We must conclude that, at least with regard to arguments about the negative effects of regulation, the economic model lacks any support in these data.

Despite the negative findings on the impact of regulatory factors, Table 4.4 (below) which presents the results of analyses of hypotheses about the relationship between market characteristics and cable policies, indicates that the economic model may have some validity. The television market within which a cable system operates is related to the system's community interest policies. The negative coefficients in the table indicate that as the rank score of the television market increases (i.e., as the markets become smaller) the commitment to all three dimensions of community interest policy decreases.[2]   This conforms to the argument that competitive markets will be more likely to induce community interest cable policies than non-competitive markets. According the the regression coefficient estimates (b's) in

TABLE 4.4: RELATIONSHIP BETWEEN MARKET CHARACTERISTICS AND CABLE COMMUNITY INTEREST POLICIES

	Channel Capacity	Channels in Use	Local Services	Access Channel	Two-Way Capability	(N=)
Television Market	b=.05 r=-.38*	b=-.03 r=-.35*	b=-.997 r=-.17*	d=-.15*	d=-.20*	(207)
Percent Cabled	b=-.12 r=-.28*	b=-.08 r=-.29*	b=-.007 r=.12	d=-.16*	d=-.19*	(205)
Communities Served	b=.19 r=.09	b=.30 r=.20	b=.05 r=.14	d=-.05	d=.07	(416)
Projected Growth	b=.72 r=.24	b=.39 r=.20	b=.05 r=.12	d=.06	d=.11*	(310)

Independent Variables dichotomized at medians for crosstabulations from which Somer's d was computed.
    * correlation coefficient significant at p<=.05

Table 4.4, we could expect channel capacities to increase at a rate of about one channel for each increase of two rank scores, and usage at one channel per three rank scores. Although statistically significant, the regression coefficient associated with the number of types of local programming seems to indicate that a jump of 100 ranks is necessary to produce an extra type. This is not entirely unreasonable, given that the maximum number of types of local programming found in our sample was six. However, as a basis for prediction, the coefficient is clearly inadequate. The significance of the relationship between television market rank and local programming types, as well as access and interactive channels, may nevertheless be taken as support for the economic hypothesis.

Cable penetration of the television market in which the system operates may, at first glance, seem to contradict the importance of competition in increasing public interest commitments of cable systems. The figures clearly indicate that public interest policies diminish as the proportion of households in the market with cable increases. However this negative relationship must be interpreted in light of the fact that the most heavily cabled television markets in 1979 were those where cable was first introduced as a adjunct to the broadcasting system. In these markets subscribers are more likely to have bought cable services in order to receive the over-the-air signals denied them by the exigencies of commercial broadcasting. Competition among cable franchise bidders in such markets would therefore tend to be over prices and quality of broadcast retransmissions rather than diversity, localism and interactive capabilities. Thus the percentage of the television market with has been penetrated by cable systems may really be an inverse measure of the size of the market.[3] It should not be surprising, therefore, that the systems in our sample appear to lose just over one channel of capacity and just under one channel in use for each ten percentage point increase in cable penetration of the television market, or that access of interactive channels are negatively related to cable penetration. Nor can these findings be interpreted as a refutation of the hypotheses derived from the economic model.

The failure of the number of communities served and projected growth rate of the system to attain significant relationships with most policy indicators tells us little about the validity of the economic model. First, despite the fact that they are not statistically significant, all of the correlations indicate relationships in the expected direction. Second, the failure of our analysis to find significant relationships between the number of communities served and cable policies may be attributed to a general tendency for systems to serve more than a single community in two kinds of situations: 1) where rural communities must unite to offer a franchise likely to be profitable to the system operator; and, 2) where neighboring suburban communities unite to take advantage of the economies of scale in cable system construction.[4] In the first case we would expect few community service policies since broadcast retransmission alone could attract subscribers. In the second case we would expect significant public interest concessions from cable firms in order to capture lucrative franchises in competitive broadcast markets. The overall effect would be for systems in one situation to cancel the effects of systems in the other. Finally, the measure of projected growth is likely to be unreliable since it is based in part on the subjective assessment of the system's manager of the potential to attract subscribers in the next five years. Leaving aside any bravado which might be displayed by managers, their estimates of projected growth could be based on a number of factors including projected expansion of the system or completion of a system still under construction, upgrading of the system, addition of new services likely to attract subscribers, or simply population growth in the franchise area. Most of these factors would be related to changes in other variables which have been or shall be considered herein, but there seems to be little reason to assume that the effect of these "exogenous" variables would be to do anything but decrease the reliability of projected growth as an indicator of the nature of the market.[5]

The third factor which the economic model suggests as a precondition of system viability is the nature of the firm which owns and operated the cable system. Table 4.5 (below) displays findings relevant to the relationships between a number of firm characteristics and cable public interest policies. The primary characteristic of cable firms is whether or not the firm is a multiple system operator (MSO). Sixty-six percent of the systems in our 1979 sample were wholly owned by MSOs and 75% had part owners which were multiple system operators. Contrary to the expectation implied in the economic model, channel capacities, usage, and number of types of local programming are not significantly related to participation my MSOs in system ownership. Furthermore, neither the size of the multi-system organizations (as measured by total number of subscribers, MSOSUBS, or by number of systems in the organization, MSOSYS), nor the potential influence of MSOs (the percentage owned by an MSO weighted by its total number of subscribers) has a significant effect on the indicators of diversity and localism. Only access policies appear to be positively related to MSO participation in system ownership and here the relationships are relative weak. Although the percentage of the system owned by MSOs is significantly related to interactive

TABLE 4.5: RELATIONSHIP BETWEEN FIRM CHARACTERISTICS AND CABLE COMMUNITY INTEREST POLICIES

	Channel Capacity	Channels in Use	Local Services	Access Channel	Two-Way Capability	(N=)
MSO Percentage	b=.01 r=.07	b=.01 r=.13	b=.005 r=.20	d=.13*	d=.01*	(417)
MSO Subscribers	b=.000001 r=.04	b=.000001 r=.14	b=.0000004 r=.17	d=.13*	d=.03	(318)
MSO Systems	b=.0004 r=.00	b=.01 r=.08	b=.007 r=.24	d=.12	d=.01	(318)
MSO Influence	b=.0000007 r=.04	b=.000002 r=.14	b=.0000005 r=.18	d=.13*	d=.07	(417)
Other Interest %	b=.02 r=.11	b=.02 r=.16	b=.006 r=.29*	d=.08*	d=.04	(415)

Independent Variables dichotomized at medians for crosstabulations from which Somer's d was computed.

* correlation coefficient significant at $p <= .05$

capabilities, the correlation coefficient is practically zero due to an apparent curvilinearity of the relationship.[6]

The last indicator of firm characteristics in Table 4.5 is the percentage of the cable system owned by firms with interests in other industries. Most MSOs also hold shares in other communications firms and 58% of the systems in our sample are at least partly owned by firms with investments outside the cable industry. Over half (51.3%) are owned wholly by such diversified firms. Although the availability of capital associated with diversification does not appear to have a significant effect on either the potential (Channel Capacity) or actual (Channel Usage) diversity of cable offerings, both the number of types of local services and availability of access channels are significantly related to ownership participation by firms with non-cable investments. At least with regard to the dimension of localism of cable policy, it seems that firms with access to capital from outside the cable industry are most likely to promote community interests in their cable systems' programming policies.

The keystone of the economic model of cable policy is system viability. Systems which are better able to produce profits are, according to economic explanations, the most likely to also produce services in the interests of communities. Table 4.6 (below) presents findings relating to the effect of system viability on cable community interest policies. The table provides strong support for the economic argument. In particular, it is apparent that the size of a cable system is a key variable in understanding variations in community interest policies.

The first indicator of system size is the number of subscribers. Subscriber counts are positively and significantly related to all five indicators of policy in Table 4.6. Specifically, it appears that, in this sample of systems, we should expect an increase of one channel in system capacity for each 2,500 subscribers added to the subscriber count (over a base of just under 14 channels).Furthermore, we should expect 1 more channel in use for each 5,000 added subscribers (over a base of ten channels), and one additional type of locally originated programming (over a base of just under one channel) for each increase of 200,000 subscribers. Again, as in the case of the relationship between cable penetration and television market rank, the regression coefficient for local programming is exceptionally high. Since only about 3% of the systems in the U.S. served communities of 200,000 population or more in 1979, this regression coefficient should not be used for prediction purposes. Rather, we may interpret it as an indication that the number of local cable services offered by a system is affected by the number of cable subscribers and a number of other

TABLE 4.6
RELATIONSHIP BETWEEN SYSTEM VIABILITY
AND CABLE COMMUNITY INTEREST POLICIES

	Channel Capacity	Channels in Use	Local Services	Access Channel	TwoWay Capability	(N=)
Monthly	b=.72	b=.37	b=.12			
Rate	r=.20	r=.15	r=.23	d=.03	d=.13*	(405)
Pay	b=-.37	b=-.18	b=.003			
Rate	r=-.10	r=-.07	r=.01	d=.06	d=.15*	(145)
Base	b=.00005	b=.00003	b=.000005			
Income	r=.45*	r=.40*	r=.34*	d=.13*	d=.19*	(404)
Pay	b=.00005	b=.00006	b=.00001			
Income	r=.21	r=.40*	r=.31*	d=.13*	d=.23*	(98)
Subs.	b=.0004	b=.0002	b=.00005			
Base	r=.37*	r=.37*	r=.38*	d=.14*	d=.20*	(408)
Miles of	b=.02	b=.01	b=.003			
Plant	r=.43*	r=.43*	r=.39*	d=.17*	d=.19*	(403)
Subs.	b=.03	b=.02	b=.003			
Density	r=.23	r=.34*	r=.20	d=.10*	d=.14*	(390)
Pene-	b=-10.9	b=-6.7	b=-1.1			
tration	r=-.42*	r=-.40*	r=-.31*	d=-.11*	d=-.16*	(217)
Franchise	b=1.1	b=1.1	b=.20			
Fee	r=.24*	r=.34*	r=.30*	d=.17*	d=.14*	(261)
Age of	b=-.24	b=-.13	b=-.02			
System	r=-.34*	r=-.28*	r=-.25*	d=-.07	d=-.16*	(405)

Independent Variables dichotomized at medians for crosstabulatlions from
which Somer's d was computed.
* correlation coefficient significant at p<=.05

factors, as suggested in Chapter 2. In addition, there are relatively weak but statistically significant, positive relationships between the subscriber count and the availability of access and interactive channels.

A further indication of the importance of subscriber counts to determining public interest policies is the fact that rates charged for basic and pay-cable services are not, in themselves, related to any indicators of policy except the availability of two-way channels. However, when rates are multiplied by subscriber counts to estimate monthly incomes accruing to systems in this sample, significant relationships are found between each measure of income and all measures of community interest policy except for income from pay services and channel capacity. Both basic and pay incomes are positively related to the availability of access and two-way channels.

Finally, the size of the system's physical plant (i.e., miles of cable in the system) also appears to be positively related to the commitment to community interests. One channel in capacity appears to be added to a base of just under fourteen channels for each fifty added miles of plant; one more channel is used (over a base of about ten channels) for each 100 additional miles of plant; and one more type of locally originated programming (over a base of just less than one type) appears to be added for each 333 additional miles of cable in the system. Access and interactive channels also appear to be more likely in systems with larger physical plants.

Another variable often related to the viability of cable systems is the density of households passed by the system. As indicated in Table 4.6, this variable does appear to be positively related at the 95% confidence level to channel usage (USED) and to interactive capability (ACCESS and TWOWAY). Each increase in the density of households passed of 50 households per mile of plant appears to be associated with an increase of one channel used over a base of nine channels and the relationships to access and two-way capabilities are, again, weak but statistically significant.

Although the size of a cable system and density of households passed may be positively related to cable community interest policies, the other indicators of system viability, penetration of service area, percentage of gross income paid in franchise fees, and age of the system, all give reasons to suspend judgement on the adequacy of economic explanations.

Support for the economic model, where it can be found, appears to be somewhat stronger than support for either the pluralist or economic model. Both market characteristics and at least one set of indicators of system viability can be shown to be related to the commitment of cable systems to community interest policies. However, just as there is stronger support for some economic hypotheses, there is also stronger apparent disconfirmation of others. Although the substantive importance of the findings from bivariate analyses cannot be assessed until more complex models are constructed and tested as wholes, the findings thus far indicate that neither socio-political nor economic factors can alone account for variations in cable policy.

Pluralism or Stratification: Comparison of Multivariate Models

The bivariate hypotheses discussed in the preceding section are suggestive, but not conclusive, tests of the determinants of cable community interest policies. As we frequently had occasion to notice, many of the most important implication of our models of policy-making require multivariate analysis. In this section we shall address the first of these questions, the relative impact of social stratification and political institutionalization on the outcome of cable policy-making processes.

Before constructing a multivariate model of the socio-political determinants of cable community interests policies, each set of indicators included in Tables 4.6 through 4.13 was evaluated using the multiple indicator approach suggested by Herbert Costner.[7] The result of this evaluation was a set of socio-political indicators with two indicators of each of the basic constructs employed in both the pluralist and stratification models. Since these models differ only in causal structure, a relatively straightforward comparison of the adequacy of the models may be made by examining differing hypotheses derived from each model about the relationships between pairs of constructs under controls for other constructs employed in the models. Both models suggest that there will be a positive relationship between demographic factors like population and demographic diversity and the socio-economic status of communities. Furthermore, both suggest a similar relationship between community status and the institutionalization of community participation in decision-making. However, there are three critical hypotheses which differentiate pluralist and stratification theories:

1. the relationship between measures of institutionalization and policy indicators controlling for the effects of community status: the pluralist model suggests that this multivariate relationship will be positive since the institutionalization of participation is held to have an impact on policy which is independent of status, while the stratification model suggests that the role of status as a common cause of institutionalization and policy will cause this relationship to vanish;

2. the relationship between community status and policy under controls for the institutionalization of participation: pluralist theory

suggests that the role of institutionalization as the most proximate cause of policy will cause indicators of this relationship to approach zero while stratification theory suggests that they would be positive;

3. the relationship between demographic factors and policy controlling for the institutionalization of participation: pluralist theory again suggests that this relationship should vanish, but stratification theory asserts that it would be positive since the causal chain linking demographics, status and policy is independent of institutionalization.

Tables 4.7 through 4.9 present findings of partial correlation analyses relevant to these hypotheses. Table 4.7 (below) displays the empirical relationships between two indicators of institutionalized community participation and each of the policy indicators discussed in the previous section. Zero-order/Pearson product-moment correlation coefficients indicate that there is a significant positive relationship between League of Women Voters membership and channel capacity, usage and number of types of local services. There is also a significant negative relationship between out-of-state ownership and channel capacity, usage, access and two-way capabilities. These findings are consistent with the expectations of both socio-political models. However, examination of partial correlation coefficients reveals that the relationships between our indicators of institutionalization and cable policy are specified somewhat when controls for income diversity and median years of schooling are introduced. Controlling for status, the relationship between community political organization, represented by League of Women Voters membership, and cable policy is seriously attenuated or vanishes. However, the relationship between local ownership and cable policy is essentially unchanged. Thus this test of the first critical hypothesis appears to indicate that the pluralist model, to the extent that it emphasizes purely political forms of institutional involvement in policy-making, is inadequate in the case of cable policy. However, the stratification model, to the extent that it emphasizes status over both political and economic forms of institutionalization, is also deficient. These findings, therefore, seem to point to the need to construct a socio-political model of cable policy-making which incorporates some form of interaction of status and institutionalization in explaining cable policies.

The utility of such an "interactive" model of the effects of status and institutionalization appears to be supported by the analysis reported in Table 4.8 (below). Although zero-order correlation coefficients indicate the expected positive relationships between status and at least the three interval level indicators of policy (channel capacity, usage and number of types of local programming), the introduction of controls for political (LWVMEM) and economic (OOS%) institutionalization have mixed effects. Contrary to the expectations derived from the

TABLE 4.7
RELATIONSHIP BETWEEN SYSTEM VIABILITY
AND CABLE COMMUNITY INTEREST POLICIES

	Channel Capacity	Channels in Use	Local Services	Access Channel	TwoWay Capability	(N=)
Monthly Rate	b=.72 r=.20	b=.37 r=.15	b=.12 r=.23	d=.03	d=.13*	(405)
Pay Rate	b=-.37 r=-.10	b=-.18 r=-.07	b=.003 r=.01	d=.06	d=.15*	(145)
Base Income	b=.00005 r=.45*	b=.00003 r=.40*	b=.000005 r=.34*	d=.13*	d=.19*	(404)
Pay Income	b=.00005 r=.21	b=.00006 r=.40*	b=.00001 r=.31*	d=.13*	d=.23*	(98)
Subs. Base	b=.0004 r=.37*	b=.0002 r=.37*	b=.00005 r=.38*	d=.14*	d=.20*	(408)
Miles of Plant	b=.02 r=.43*	b=.01 r=.43*	b=.003 r=.39*	d=.17*	d=.19*	(403)
Subs. Density	b=.03 r=.23	b=.02 r=.34*	b=.003 r=.20	d=.10*	d=.14*	(390)
Pene-tration	b=-10.9 r=-.42*	b=-6.7 r=-.40*	b=-1.1 r=-.31*	d=-.11*	d=-.16*	(217)
Franchise Fee	b=1.1 r=.24*	b=1.1 r=.34*	b=.20 r=.30*	d=.17*	d=.14*	(261)
Age of System	b=-.24 r=-.34*	b=-.13 r=-.28*	b=-.02 r=-.25*	d=-.07	d=-.16*	(405)

Independent Variables dichotomized at medians for crosstabulatlions from
which Somer's d was computed.
* correlation coefficient significant at p<=.05

TABLE 4.8: EFFECTS OF CONTROLLING FOR STATUS ON THE RELATIONSHIP BETWEEN INSTITUTIONALIZATION AND CABLE POLICIES

VARIABLES:	CHANNEL CAPACITY	CHANNELS IN USE	LOCAL SERVICES	ACCESS CHANNEL(S)	TWO-WAY CAPABILITY
		Zero-order correlation coefficients			
LWV membership	.14* (414)	.10* (414)	.20* (415)	0.07 (415)	0.07 (415)
Out-of-State Ownership	-.38* (140)	-.22* (140)	-0.11 (140)	-.17* (140)	-.28 (140)
		Partial correlation coefficients controlling for:			
		Income Diversity			(N=)
LWV membership	0.06	0	0.09	0.03	0.06 (106)
Out-of-State Ownership	-.37*	-31*	-0.09	-.16*	-0.28 (106)
		Median Level of Education			
LWV membership	0.08	0.07	0.13	0.03	0.06 (106)
Out-of-State Ownership	-.37*	-.22*	-0.09	-0.16*	-.28 (106)
		Income Diversity and Median Education Level			
LWV membership	0.01	-0.03	0.02	0	-0.03 (105)
Out-of-State Ownership	-.36*	-.21*	-0.08	-.16*	-.28 (105)

* correlation coefficient significant at p<=.05

stratification model, controlling for league of Women Voters membership attenuates the relationships between status and policy indicators. If the level of community political organization were totally exogenous to the causal relationship between status and policy, the control for League membership would be expected to have no effect on the observed relationships between status and policy indicators. It appears, therefore, that community status and community political organizations are interdependent causes of variation in cable community interest policies. At the same time, the apparent null effect of controlling for the economic dimension of the institutionalization of community participation may indicate that this form of organized participation by the community in cable policy making is a relatively independent factor in determining community interest policies.

Examination of the results of the analyses relevant to the third critical hypothesis, presented in Table 4.9 (below), reveals even more about the apparent structure of a hybrid socio-political model. Specifically, the failure of controls for either political (LWV membership) or economic (out-of-state ownership) institutionalization, or both, to appreciably reduce the coefficients measuring the relationships between demographic factors and cable policy indicators indicates that demographic factors do not operate solely through their impact on community status and the institutionalization of community participation in cable policy-making. Rather, population size of a community, in particular, appears to exercise an influence on cable policy which is independent of any mediation by the institutionalization of participation of the community in policy making processes. A similar analysis (not presented in Tables) of the relationship between demographic indicators and indicators of organized community participation reveals that demographic factors influence institutionalization directly as well as through community status. Thus, population size appears to exert a strong pre-conditioning influence on both independent variables and on policies in a revised socio-political model of cable policy-making. A revised model of the socio-political determinants of cable policies is diagrammed in Figure 4.1 (p. 97).

The model depicted in Figure 4.1 reflects the finding that neither the pluralist nor the stratification model appears to be an accurate representation of reality by itself. Instead, a more complex set of causal relationships among social and political factors would appear to be at work in determining cable community interest policies. Our next step must be a comparison of the relative strength of the revised socio-political model described here and an economic model of cable policy determinants.

TABLE 4.9: THE EFFECTS OF CONTROLS FOR INSTITUTIONALIZATION ON THE RELATIONSHIP BETWEEN DEMOGRAPHICS AND POLICIES

Zero-order correlation coefficients

VARIABLES:	CHANNEL CAPACITY	CHANNELS IN USE	LOCAL SERVICES	ACCESS CHANNEL(S)	TWO-WAY CAPABILITY	(N=)
Total Population	.46	.42	.37	.24	.28	
	(409)	(409)	(410)	(410)	(410)	
Age Diversity	.12	.15	.09	.05	-.01	
	(414)	(414)	(414)	(415)	(415)	

Partial correlation coefficients, controlling for:

League of Women Voters membership

	CHANNEL CAPACITY	CHANNELS IN USE	LOCAL SERVICES	ACCESS CHANNEL(S)	TWO-WAY CAPABILITY	(N=)
Total Population	.45	.42	.32	.24	.27	(139)
Age Diversity	0.1	0.14	0.07	0.04	-0.02	(139)

Out-of-state ownership percentage

	CHANNEL CAPACITY	CHANNELS IN USE	LOCAL SERVICES	ACCESS CHANNEL(S)	TWO-WAY CAPABILITY	(N=)
Total Population	.43	.40	.36	.22	.23	(139)
Age Diversity	0.14	0.14	0.09	0.04	-0.03	(139)

LWV membership and Out-of-state ownership

	CHANNEL CAPACITY	CHANNELS IN USE	LOCAL SERVICES	ACCESS CHANNEL(S)	TWO-WAY CAPABILITY	(N=)
Total Population	.42	.40	.31	.22	.24	(138)
Age Diversity	0.09	0.13	0.06	0.03	-0.04	(138)

* correlation coefficient significant at $p <= .05$

Figure 4.1
A Socio-Political
Model

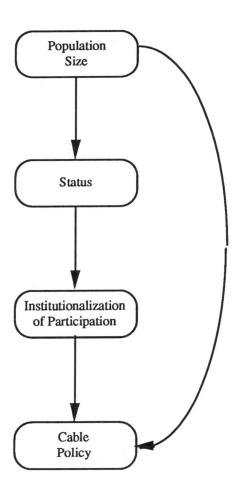

Comparison of Socio-Political and Economic Models

Unlike the pluralist and stratification models of cable policy determination, which invoke basically the same explanatory factors, the economic model employs a set of variables which is distinct from either of the socio-political explanations. We shall therefore examine the adequacy of the economic model by comparing it to the socio-political model suggested by the findings reported above. This comparison will be carried out by examining the results of multiple regression and discriminant analyses of data from a sample of 70 communities that had cable systems in operation in 1979 and for which all data on all relevant indicators are available.[8]   These analyses fitted regression (or discriminant) models based on the two models using each of the five cable policy indicators discussed above, thus, the results discussed below were drawn from analyses of ten separate models. These results are summarized in Tables 4.10 (below) and 4.11 (p. 100), which report descriptive and inferential statistics for each model, as a whole.

Looking first at the regression analysis results modelling the impact of each set of variables on the three continuous indicators of cable community interest policies (channel capacity, number of channels in use, and number of local services), we can see some indication that the adequacy of the socio-political and economic models as predictors of cable policy may depend upon the policy indicators used as criteria. Specifically, while the economic model is clearly superior for explaining variation in channel capacity (R^2=.71 compared to .30 for the socio-political model) and accuracy of prediction (Standard Error of the Estimate= 5.13 channels, compared to 7.78 channels), it is no better than the socio-political model in either explanatory power or predictive accuracy when the dependent variable is either actual channel usage or number of local services offered.

Despite the apparent superiority of the economic model for explaining channel capacity, closer examination of the regression coefficients associated with the variables in the two models is warranted. The economic model for predicting channel capacity suggests that community status, ownership by an multiple system operator(MSO), and profitability of the cable system will all be positively related to channel capacity, while stringency of federal regulation would have a negative impact on this indicator. Results of the regression analysis support the positive impact of community status (median income) and profitability (estimated income from basic subscriptions) but indicate that percentage ownership by MSOs has a negative impact and federal regulation has a positive impact. Regression coefficients suggest that one channel is added to a system's

TABLE 4.10
SUMMARY COMPARISON OF REGRESSION ANALYSES OF SOCIO-POLITICAL AND ECONOMIC MODELS OF CABLE POLICY DETERMINATION

DEPENDENT VARIABLE		SOCIO-POLITICAL MODEL	ECONOMIC MODEL
Channel	R^2	0.30	0.71
Capacity	adj R^2	0.27	0.68
	SEE	7.78	5.13
	MSE	60.56	26.35
	CV	37.8%	25.0%
	F	9.52	22.19
	p	0.000	0.000
Channels	R^2	0.41	0.41
in Use	adj R^2	0.38	0.34
	SEE	4.33	4.47
	MSE	18.79	19.96
	CV	30.4%	31.3%
	F	11.45	5.41
	p	0.000	0.000
Local	R^2	0.20	0.22
Services	adj R^2	0.15	0.12
	SEE	1.13	1.15
	MSE	1.28	1.33
	CV	55.7%	56.8%
	F	4.11	2.17
	p	0.005	0.040

total capacity for each increase of $1000 in median income and that 4 channels tend to be added for each $100,000 of monthly revenue from basic subscriptions. Systems which began operation after 1972, when the Federal Communications Commission first began strict regulation of cable systems tended to have over 9 more channels than those which started before 1968 (when the F.C.C. exercised no jurisdiction over cable systems).

While this last finding does not support the economic model, care should be taken before rejecting the model on this basis since systems franchised since 1972 have been required by F.C.C. regulations to implement minimum channel capacities which were much higher than earlier systems tended to have. While these data might be interpreted as evidence for the effectiveness of F.C.C. channel capacity requirements, they do not address directly the question of how many potential systems were discouraged by the stringency of the requirements imposed by the commission. Furthermore, improvements in cable technology may explain the higher capacities since 1972. Although examination of regression models including indicators of system age showed no effect of this variable on channel capacity, the discontinuous quality of improvements in cable technology may not have been fully captured in the continuous aging of the systems. An effective maximum capacity of twelve channels was increased to twenty in the late 'sixties and this almost certainly contributed to both the increased capacity of later systems as well as to the F.C.C.'s decision to require greater capacity after 1972.

The negative regression coefficient associated with percentage of system ownership by MSOs suggest that, contrary to the expectations of the economic model, systems wholly owned by MSOs tended to have five fewer channels of capacity than those which were operated as single systems. In other words, an increase of twenty percentage points in the proportion of the system owned by MSOs was associated with a reduction in capacity of 1 channel. This finding contradicts the expectation that the pooling of resources which could be accomplished by MSOs would induce higher channel capacities in systems which were part of such organizations. Nevertheless, the effect, while statistically significant the the $p <= .05$ level, is relatively small and examination of the standardized regression coefficient indicate that the apparent negative relationship between MSO ownership and channel capacity is attenuated when other variables in the economic model are held constant.

At the same time, only population and median income appeared to be significantly (and positively) related to channel capacities in the socio-economic model. Both of these variables could easily be subsumed by the economic model as aspects of the market in which cable systems operate. On the whole, then, the economic model still seems to be a better predictor of channel capacity than is the socio-political model.

Turning to channel usage and number of local services, summary statistics no longer appear to indicate the superiority of the economic model. In the case of both dependent variables, regression analyses of the the competing models yield practically identical results with regard to both explanatory power and predictive accuracy. Both models yield coefficients of determination (R^2) which indicate that they explain considerably less than one-half of the variation in channel usage and less than one-sixth of the variation in number of local services.

Likewise, regression coefficients associated with component variables fail to point to either the socio-political or economic model as dominant. With regard to channel usage, only channel capacity shows up as a statistically significant (at p=.05) predictor in either model. Channel capacity alone accounts for 38% of the variation observed in usage and the addition of other variables adds only 3% improvement in either model. Channel capacity also appears to be an important determinant of the number of local services offered with just over fourteen channels of capacity required in either model for an increase of one in the number of locally produced services offered. While the institutionalization of community political participation (as indicated by League of Women Voters membership) is significantly (and positively) related to local services, as would be predicted in the socio-political model, the stringency of federal regulation appears also to be significantly (and negatively) related to local services[9], as the economic model suggests.

The ambiguity regarding the relative superiority of either the socio-political or economic model remains in the interpretation of results of discriminant analyses conducted to examine the models as predictors of access channels and two-way capability.[10] Table 4.11 (below) presents summaries of the results of these analyses. None of the discriminant functions to which the summary statistics in the table does a very good job of differentiating cable systems with access or two-way capabilities from those without these services.

In the case of models predicting access channels, residual variation (R) exceeds ninety percent in both models (i.e., over 90% of the variation in the dichotomous access channel variable is *not* explained by the variables included in either discriminant function). Canonical correlations and eigenvalues are low and neither of the functions is statistically significant beyond the 70% level of confidence (p=.300). Although the economic model correctly classified almost 84% of the cases included in the classification phase of the analysis, this success

TABLE 4.11
SUMMARY COMPARISON OF DISCRIMINANT ANALYSES
OF SOCIO-POLITICAL AND ECONOMIC MODELS OF
CABLE POLICY DETERMINATION

		Socio-Political Model	Economic Model
Access	R	0.92	0.90
Channel(s)	Can.Corr	0.27	0.32
	Eigen.	0.08	0.11
	Wilks	0.93	0.90
	F	1.25	0.98
	p	0.300	0.456
	%correct	77.02%	83.97%
	Cpro	74.61%	76.64%
	Impr.	2.41%	7.33%
	N	248	237
Two-Way	R	0.58	0.52
Capability	Can.Corr	0.65	0.70
	Eigen.	0.72	0.94
	Wilks	0.58	0.51
	F	11.76	8.36
	p	0.000	0.000
	%correct	79.12%	84.25%
	C_{pro}	61.04%	67.11
	Impr.	18.08%	17.14%
	N	249	400

rate represents an improvement of less than 8% over chance (Impr.=7.33), given the *a priori* distribution of the cases classified into access and non-access systems. Although function coefficients in both models were unstable, both models suggest that channel capacity is the singly most important variable influencing the probability of a system having access channels.

While residual variation is reduced in the models predicting the existence of two-way capability, it is still over 50% in both models. The higher values of the canonical correlation coefficients and eigenvalues indicate that both of the functions discriminate between systems with two-way capabilities and those without fairly well. Although the economic model again allowed for an approximately 84% success rate in the classification phase, the nearly 80% success of the socio-political model represented a slightly larger improvement over chance. Thus it remains difficult to choose between the socio-political and economic models of cable policy determination for dimensions of policy which go beyond the potential diversity represented by channel capacity.

Summary

The examination of the bivariate hypotheses derived from each of the three pure-type explanations that have been offered for cable policies indicated that at least some of the factors suggested by each model may be related to community interest cable policies. Multivariate analyses indicated further that the stratification and pluralist models might be combined since both status and political variables appear to interact in their effects on community interest policies. By far the largest number of hypotheses supported by the data analyzed here were from the economic model. Furthermore, comparisons of the results of multiple regression and discriminant analyses based on the economic and socio-political models showed the economic model to be clearly superior in explaining channel capacities, but less effective when the dependent variables were uses of cable channels which represent typical community oriented interests in the medium. This suggests that reliance upon market forces may be justified only as long as the objective of implementing cable communications technologies is limited to maximizing the potential for genuine program diversity, but that the actual diversity is not likely to be induced by economic factors alone. In particular, the kinds of cable services that serve communities' interests seem less clearly influenced by economics though not necessarily more dependent upon social and political factors.

---

[1] This table and those following present five types of correlation coefficient. For relationships between interval level variables, both the unstandardized regression coefficient (b) and the Pearson's product-moment correlation coefficient (r) are presented. These coefficients were estimated from the sample of cabled communities ordinary least squares regression. Equations for which the F-ratio indicated a 95% confidence level or greater ($p \leq .05$) are highlighted with asterisks. Scattergrams of the cases included in the regression analyses were also examined for evidence of curvilinearity or heteroskedasticity. Instances where these problems arise are discussed in the text and and notes that follow. The third coefficient, Somer's d (d_{yx}), was calculated from crosstabulations of ordinal variables. For the relationships between the form of city government variable and the indicators of community interest cable policies either a phi coefficient (for 2 x 2 tables) or a contingency coefficient (for rectangular tables) are presented. Coefficients from tables whose Chi-squared value was statistically significant at the 95% confidence level are also highlighted by asterisks.

[2] Although, strictly speaking, television market rank is an ordinal variable, it was entered in the regression analyses as an interval level variable following the convention that scores representing more than 20 ranks may be treated as interval measures. In effect, the unit of measurement is a "market rank unit." The only adjustment which must be made is to remember that, since market rank scores increase as the size of the television market decreases, negative coefficients represent positive relationships between ordinary interval variables and market rank.

[3] The Pearson's product-moment correlation coefficient between television market and percentage of tv-market cabled bears this out (r=.77). This correlation would, no doubt, be even stronger were it not for broadcast reception problems in large television market cities like New York and Los Angeles.

[4] An examination of the scatter diagram of the relationship between television market rank and the number of communities served by each cable system suggests that there is a curvilinear relationship between these two variables with the mean number of communities served increasing as market rank increases (i.e., as size of the television market decreases) to about the 100th ranked market. Thereafter the relationship appears to be negative (i.e., fewer communities are served by systems in the second 100 television markets as the market rank increases). Furthermore, the distribution of the number of communities served is heteroskedastic with the largest variance occurring in the middle sized markets and less variance in the larger and smaller markets.

[5] Examination of the relationship between projected growth and both miles of system planned and age of system indicate that these two variables, at least, do contribute to system managers' growth estimates, miles planned positively, and system age negatively.

[6] 15.4% of the 104 systems with no MSO involvement and 20.6% of the 277 systems wholly owned by MSOs either had two-way channels of were planning such channels. 38.9% of the 36 systems with partial ownership by MSOs had or planned two-way capability. Although the differences between categories of MSO involvement are statistically significant (Chi-square = 8.99, p=.0112), the small number of systems with partial MSO ownership makes a conclusion that this relationship is curvilinear somewhat tentative. Visual inspection of scattergrams involving indicators of MSO participation in system ownership and interval level measures of diversity and localism did not reveal any clear curvilinearity in these relationships.

[7] Costner(1969); Sullivan(1971); Sullivan(1974); Van Valey(1971); Sullivan and Feldman(1979). A full description of the methods used to select the indicators used in the tests of multivariate models is contained in the Appendices.

[8] In order to be able to compare all of the models of cable policy-making suggested in the previous chapters, only those cases with valid values for all relevant variables in all models were included in the regression and discriminant analyses that follow. Although this subsample is biased toward larger communities, it seems reasonable to use it for purposes of comparing explanatory models. Nevertheless, the reader should be careful not to interpret the results derived from this subsample as descriptive of all cable systems in the U.S.

[9] Only during the period between 1972 and 1975, did the dummy variable for stringency of FCC regulation have a significant regression coefficient (at the 95% level of confidence).

[10] Discriminant analysis was applied because the dependent variables measuring the availability of access channels and two-way capability on the system are dichotomous.

Chapter 5

An Organizational Explanation for Cable Community Interest Policies

The explanatory models discussed in the previous chapters are not mutually exclusive. As noted, elements of each pure type of explanation are usually combined in analyses of cable policy. Although this suggests the potential utility of an explanation which combines elements of the pure types, no attempt has thus far been made to construct a coherent theory capable of accounting for the empirically successful elements of all three models within a single conceptual framework. In this chapter we shall consider such a theoretical model before going on to test the model against a "synthetic" multivariate model constructed from the factors which appeared to be most important to determining cable community interest policies in the results reviewed in chapter 4.

The model proposed here is based on an approach which has been variously identified with political economy, a theory of social organization, or a theory of the external control of organizations.[1] While these labels represent disparate concerns and methodologies, they all reflect a conscious effort to apply general propositions about social and economic behavior to the outputs of political institutions and the interaction of public and private organizations. This model is proposed with the belief that it can account for variation in the incidence of public interest uses of cable technologies at least as well as any of the pure models discussed earlier. Furthermore, as a conceptually integrated description of the operation of cable policy-making systems, the model should better explain which communities are likely to be well served by their cable systems than any simple synthesis of the existing types of explanations for cable public interest policies.

The model of cable franchising proposed here treats the franchise as a product of a "meta-organization" of actors in a given community. It employs a framework for the analysis of intra-organizational power as a base for examining the conditions under which cable regulatory policy is most likely to ensure the adaptability of cable systems to the needs and interests of the communities they serve. Like any theoretical model, the picture to be drawn here is an ideal-typical one which may not, and probably does not, conform to any particular cablesystem in all respects. However, the model is useful as a starting point from which to derive some general hypotheses relating characteristics of cable systems and the communities they serve to the extent of commitments to providing public interest cable services.

Structurally, the model involves three generalized actors involved in the pre-franchise bargaining process. From the descriptive model I extract a number of factors which may be related to the institutionalization, centrality, and non-substitutability of community representatives to the entrepreneurial and governmental decision-makers responsible for negotiating the provisions of a cable franchise. Finally, hypotheses relating these factors to the dimensions of community service policy identified in chapter 2 are presented.

A Model of Cable System Organization

Constructing a formal organization to operate a cable system is the objective of the process of drafting the system's franchise--a document which formalizes the relationships and interactions which will determine the system's operating policies. This does not imply, however, that the process of drafting a franchise is a simple one. As Kalba[2] has pointed out, this process is mainly one of bargaining and mutual accommodation between cable entrepreneurs and representatives of the communities in which they propose to operate a cable system.

The model of cable system organization to which we shall refer includes three types of actors who become involved in franchise negotiations:

1. The operator of the cable system, usually a business firm operated for a profit;

2. The franchising agency, ordinarily a local government, which may attempt to introduce public interest considerations into the cable decision-making process; and,

3. The community, whose interests the local government may attempt to represent and/or which may be more or less formally represented in franchise negotiations by nongovernmental community-interest groups.

These actors engage in negotiations over the provisions of a cable franchise within the general constraints imposed by technological and legal structures described in Chapter 1. The terms of the franchise are the result of the interaction among the three actors in a bargaining relationship. The outcome of this interaction is, in turn, largely determined by the specific aims of each of these actors and the degree of interdependence among them. This conceptualization of the structure within which cable policy is formulated highlights the political aspects of cable decision- making. Both the obvious involvement of the community's political machinery through the role of the local government as a franchising agent and the interdependence of community, government and commercial actors suggest the importance of the relative power of each actor in determining the specific cable policies to be implemented in a given community. The extent to which an actor is able to realize its goals for the structure and operations of the cable system depends upon the power it is able to exercise in the negotiation process. The pattern of interdependence upon which the power any single actor can exercise depends may be seen in the conflict and coincidence of the goals of all three actors.

Operator Goals

The primary goal of any cable system operator is ultimately the profitability of the cable system as a business enterprise. Specifically, profitability in the cable industry depends upon the cash flow generated by the system's operations. Cash flow is the difference between operating revenues and operating expenses before taxes, debts, and depreciation are deducted.[2] Since cash flow is the primary attraction of cable systems for investors, balance sheets and steady earnings are largely irrelevant to cable operators who focus their attention on the short-term availability of cash generated by their subscriber fees.

There are a number of strategies open to an operator seeking to maximize cash flow. First, the operator may attempt to maximize gross revenue. This may be done by either maximizing the number of subscribers to system services or by maximizing the rates charged for those services. Two concepts related to the level of subscription should be distinguished at this point: 1. Saturation, the proportion of households in a franchise area which are passed by the cable network and have potential access to cable services; and , 2. Penetration, the proportion of households with potential access to the system that actually subscribe to cable services. Although these terms have been used almost interchangeably, the distinction between them is important because the two concepts enter into an operator's strategic calculations very differently. Specifically, the operator of a cable system may choose (if the terms of the franchise allow) to maximize saturation, offering service universally to the households in the community and satisficing with regard to penetration. Alternatively, the operator may seek to extend lines only to areas with favorable demographics and offer a variety of services in an attempt to maximize penetration of these more profitable areas. Either of these strategies emphasize maximization of revenues.

An alternative strategy for maximizing cash flow is to minimize operating expenses. For a cable system operating expenses include:

1. Cost of maintaining the system and subscriber equipment;

2. Cost of producing, or otherwise acquiring, programs or services;

3. Labor costs (salaries and wages of employees); and,

4. Fixed costs such as fees paid to local government or utility pole rents.[3] The operating costs over which a system operator has the most control are those related to subscriber equipment and programming/services. Thus, operators may be expected to favor limited local origination and access programming (which are relatively expensive program sources), the limited use of subscriber equipment outside of converters necessary to allow television receivers to handle more channels, and limited use of other equipment necessary for non-broadcast or non-television cable services (e.g., utility meter reading, burglar/fire/health alarms, etc.).

Although either maximizing revenues or minimizing costs may be followed as a relatively pure strategy, it is most likely that the operator will seek an optimal level of subscription which can be attracted with a given package of services and try to set rates in order to attain a particular revenue goal.

Community Goals

The identification of the goals of any community is always problematic. Even in so-called intentional communities, explicitly stated goals are usually complemented by a set of unstated goals that form the hidden agenda of community members. However, it may be possible to infer some ideal-typical goals of communities in the cable franchising process by examining the types of demands which have historically arisen in franchise negotiations. Although community demands regarding cable system operations are to some extent unique to each community, there are three general issues which appear to have mobilized community participation in many cable franchising processes. In case studies of cable franchising, at least one of the following three issues has arisen whenever communities have organized for direct participation in the process:

1. "Good government" issues related to the conduct of the franchising process and the non-discriminatory provision of cable services to members of the community;

2. Consumer issues related to the rates charged for cable services, the quality of service, and the protection of subscribers' legal and civil rights; and,

3. "Community development" issues involving the availability of interactive services and access for members of the community or for public institutions to the use of cable channels on the system.

Good government issues have been raised partly because of the opportunities which exist in the franchising process for the corruption of public officials charged with overseeing public interests in the development and operation of a cable system. Similarly, the opportunities for trafficking in franchises (buying and selling cable franchises), bait and switch tactics (i.e., offering extensive services in order to secure the franchise and seeking relief from those promises once the franchise is granted), and other abuses have been publicized in a number of cities considering cable and have raised public concern over the propriety of the franchising process.

Related to good government issues has been a movement to consider municipal or subscriber ownership of cable systems as alternatives to commercial ownership and operation. Although the large capital outlays required to construct a cable system limit the realistic possibilities for local ownership of cable systems, community ownership has been actively pursued, especially by minority groups within several communities. Aside from full ownership, many communities have obtained a degree of control over cable system operations through joint ownership with commercial firms. Exactly how successful this strategy can be is unclear, particularly in cases where controlling interests remain outside the community. Nevertheless, many proponents of this type of public involvement argue that community interests in the management of its cable system's operations are best served by maximizing the percentage of the cable enterprise owned by members of the community or by the local government.

Another set of goals in which good government and consumer interests overlap involves the configuration of the cable system and the universal availability of services to residents of the community. In general, it appears that it is in any community's interest to seek maximum saturation as quickly as possible. This tends to insure the non-discriminatory availability of cable services throughout the community. As pointed out above, some operators may perceive an incentive to to limit coverage (saturation) to areas which hold the greatest promise of generating revenues, or at least begin operating in those areas long before extending coverage universally. Thus this goal of communities may bring them into direct conflict with system operators. Nor are issues arising from the question of geographic coverage necessarily resolved simply by maximizing saturation during the construction of the system. In many cases the geographic boundaries of a single community are ill-defined or a number of distinct communities may be involved in the development of a single franchise. In such cases, the base against which saturation may be measured is ambiguous and, therefore, subject to negotiation. Furthermore, economies of scale which apply in capital intensive enterprises like cable system development might support a reasonable argument for construction of the largest system possible regardless of community boundaries. Likewise, a regional system may offer advantages which would not be obtainable with separate systems in each community in the region. These advantages must be weighed against the potential loss of a degree of local control of the system and may make the community's optimal strategy in franchise negotiations unclear.

Unlike coverage goals, direct economic goals dictated by consumer interests are easy to specify. Interests of consumers in the community include, most obviously, the question of subscriber rates. Assuming that individual subscribers are rational, the goal of individual community members would be to minimize their contributions to the operation of the cable system. Thus they may be expected to seek to minimize the rates charged for cable services. There are three possible strategies which may be employed to this end:

1. The community may favor imposing uniformly low rates to all subscribers. This strategy is most likely to generate conflict which system operators attempting to maximize revenues.

2. The community may seek lower rates to at least some individual subscribers whose services would be subsidized by higher rates charged to institutional and organizational users of the cable system.

3. The community may seek rates set according to the cost of extending and maintaining services to particular users. In this case, rates could depend upon the length of the lines required to reach subscribers, the density of households (and actual subscribers) along cable lines, and the type of construction (e.g., above or below ground) in various areas covered by the franchise.

In general, communities have chosen the first of these strategies. Increasingly, until the Supreme Court's decision in *CCI v. Boulder* and the subsequent deregulation by the Cable Act of 1984, cities not only bargained for minimal rates but also established formal structures for rate regulation and required the provision of free channels for public, governmental, and/or educational uses.

Another economic goal of communities is a demand for the employment of local resources in building and operating the system. A cable system may be seen as a potential boon to the community as an employer, especially during the construction phase. Although this goal may be realistically pursued only larger communities, this type of demand has usually been associated with local union involvement in cable issues.

The set of community goals in which we are most interested includes demands regarding the number and quality of services provided by the cable system. A primary advantage of the cable medium is that it is not subject to the scarcity constraints faced by over-the-air broadcasting systems. Recognizing this, community groups have consistently sought to maximize the channel capacities of systems to be franchised. Although some systems built in the 1950s and 1960s are limited to carrying less than twelve channels of programming (usually 5), the modal number of channels carried in 1979 was twelve and in 1985 was thirty. Twelve channels is, in effect, the practical minimum based on the VHF channels which can be carried by an unmodified television tuner. The importance of maximizing the system's capacity to carry signals is related to the goal of increasing the diversity of messages available to users. The argument made in the case of cable has been carried over from broadcasting policy and ultimately derives from the notion of a free marketplace in which the competition among ideas may be depended upon for informing citizens in a democratic political system. A more pragmatic consideration behind the demand for maximum channel capacities is based on the notion that potential uses for cable channels may be expected to be discovered as persons become more aware of the possibilities of the technology. Unless some provision for this expansion is made when systems are first built, meeting the demand for future uses may require the equivalent of constructing a duplicate system where one already exists.

There are two basic ways channels can be filled, with broadcast (television and radio) signals or with non-broadcast services such as locally originated programs, pay-tv channels received from satellite transmissions, and non- broadcast interactive services like automatic utility meter reading and alarm services. Community goals regarding the types of services to be provided on cable systems depend largely upon the community's needs, the awareness within the community of the potential for services available, and the willingness to pay for those services either through subscriber fees or public expenditures. Generally, community groups have called for the provision of non-broadcast services like access channels and interactive capabilities. These demands once again bring the community and operator into direct conflict since non-broadcast services increase the cost of system operation more than broadcast services do.

Local Government Goals

Local governments enter the cable policy-making process either through their authority to oversee the use of public rights-of-way or through the authority to regulate monopolies. Franchising is most often required because a cable system operates as a local monopoly which depends upon the use of publicly owned infrastructures (utility poles, ducts, easements, etc.) Richard Posner identified two approaches to cable franchising that local governments can take. They may take a "concession" approach and grant the franchise to the highest bidder. Bids may involve lump-sum payments or periodic fees paid by the bidder chosen to receive the franchise. Alternatively, a bargaining approach may be used in which the government seeks the best mix of rates, fees and services from the firms bidding and, ultimately, chosen to receive the franchise. These two strategies are mutually exclusive, but either may be combined with post-franchise oversight or rate regulation by an administrative agency.

The precise goals of the local government in the franchising process depend to a great extent on the demands articulated by members of the community and upon the responsiveness of local officials to their constituencies. Since both of these factors vary widely among communities, it is difficult to specify the goals of local governments as generalized actors. Nevertheless, several observations can be made about the general directions which we might expect local government goals to take.

First, under the doctrine of *laissez faire*, governments (at least in capitalist systems) may be expected to demonstrate a preference for allowing market forces to operate by remaining outside of the decision-making processes of business enterprises. Thus, we would expect a general reluctance on the part of local governments in the U.S. to intervene in cable policy-making to any great extent. However, where public intervention may be justified as a means of compensating for deficiencies in market operations (as in the case of a natural monopoly), governments may attempt to assume the sole responsibility for managing public involvement. Consequently, where community groups demand effective involvement in cable decision-making, local governments will attempt to institutionalize that involvement under their authority rather than encouraging independent forms of citizen participation. Practically, this means a preference for indirect mechanisms (e.g., advisory boards) over more direct forms of participation (e.g., community ownership) which establish formal bargaining status for citizens or non-governmental community groups. A second point to keep in mind regarding the goals of local governments in the franchising process is the importance of the election-seeking of individual office-holders. If we may assume that governments view policies as means of inducing voters to support them in upcoming elections, policies with regard to franchising would depend on the perception of office-seekers of the likely response of their constituents to cable issues. Two implications may be derived from this proposition. First, the government will be unlikely to take a stand on cable issues unless constituents actively press particular demands relating to those issues. Furthermore, organized groups are more likely to be able to deliver (or withhold) the electoral support of blocs of voters large enough to affect election results. Second, since the most immediately obvious effects of any policy are its economic effects, officials seeking electoral support are likely to emphasize economic issues in cable policy over other issues. In particular, governments may favor rate regulation and local employment provisions over programming or other service requirements as conditions for awarding a franchise.

A third aspect of government interest in cable policies involves the franchise fees assessed against the system operator. Three types of franchise fees can be distinguished: fixed fees, where a lump sum payment is made at the time of obtaining the franchise, fees based on the number of subscribers served by the system, and fees assessed as a percentage of cable system revenues. The type of franchise fee may serve as a basis for inferring the goals of franchisors. If a fixed fee is specified, we may infer that, at the time of granting the franchise, the government was willing to remain aloof from the decision-making processes of the cable system franchise holder. This form of fee is relatively rare and is limited mainly to systems operating under franchises granted in the 'fifties and 'sixties.[4] If the fee assessed on the franchise is some form of head tax on the subscriber base, the government has a presumptive interest in maximizing penetration since its revenue from the cable system's operations will depend upon the size of that base. Although, per subscriber fees have been more common than flat fees, they are still relatively rare.[5] Most communities charge a franchise fee which is based on some percentage of the revenue collected by the system. If this type of fee is assessed on net revenue (profits) we may assume that the franchisor has an interest in maximizing the profitability of the system. Government revenue from franchise fees tends to be greatest when the fee is assessed as a percentage of gross revenues to the system. This last form is the preponderant type of fee applied. Aside from maximizing income to the franchising agent, basing franchise fees on gross revenues has a political advantage in that it de-emphasizes the government's interest in the profits of the system while maintaining the incentive to bargain for maximum saturation.

Finally, insofar as cable systems offer governments another medium of communication, local governments may also seek to obtain the use of government access channels or channels dedicated to other public institutions.[6] Cable channels may be used to facilitate interagency communications within the local government, carry a variety of outreach services (e.g., announcements of public meetings or the availability of public programs), and as a medium for campaign messages. However, the enthusiasm for government access channels may be dampened by two factors: 1. the difficulty in adapting established agency procedures to new media[7]; and, 2. the occasional reluctance of local politicians to expose their deliberations to publicity.

Community Power and Cable Policy

Using the goals specified in the preceding discussion, it is possible to develop indicators of the relative power of each of the actors in the model of cable policy determination from the degree of success each actor has had in translating its goals into policies established in the franchise and implemented in the cable system. Treating the actors in the franchising process as subunits of a relatively informal organization whose purpose is the negotiation of a cable franchise, we see them as parties in a three-way bargaining process.

Insight into the general determinants of power within organizations is provided by a "strategic contingencies" theory of intra-organizational power developed by Hickson, *et al.*[8] Although the theory was originally developed to explain power in formal organizations, it may be applied to the more informal type of organization represented in the franchise bargaining model introduced above. The theory builds upon a conception of organizations as systems which cope with uncertainties. The structure of the explanatory model involved is diagrammed in Figure 5.1 (below).

Beginning with the notion that power is a property of the relationship between actors in an organization rather than a property of the individual actors, Hickson, *et al.*, proposed a model which describes the power exercised by a subunit of an organization as a function of its control over the strategic contingencies affecting the activities of the other subunits. This control is determined by three variables: the ability of the subunit to cope with the uncertainties it faces in carrying out the mission of the organization as a whole, the centrality of its work flows to the overall activity of the organization, and, the substitutability of the subunit, i.e., its susceptibility to replacement by other actors or to routinization of its activities.

Defining uncertainty as the lack of information about the future states of the environment of the focal organization, we may begin to describe the relative control of the strategic contingencies affecting the organization of a cable system in terms of the uncertainties facing each of the actors in the model described above. Dependent upon meeting profit goals, cable system operators are mainly affected by uncertainties about the level of subscription which may be attained in a given community with a given package of services and rates. Also of concern are uncertainties about the specific requirements or conditions which will be imposed by franchisors and other regulatory agencies. As a result, Orton points out that,

> For the applicant, the franchise process involves an elaborate and highly competitive market research, public relations, and political lobbying effort, with many parallels to a political campaign... Unlike much other city business, however, the cable franchising process involves consumer preference projections as a key basis for the structure of the proposal.[9]

For their part, franchisors are also affected by the pervasive risk involved in designing a cable system franchise. However, the uncertainty facing local governments stems from the expectations of various constituencies regarding the goals of the community. Despite an apparently growing recognition of the importance of independent assessments of community communication needs[10], many local governments still depend upon market data presented by franchise bidders. Orton continues,

> ...Unfortunately, the data is gathered from a public that is largely ignorant of cable services, and thus of highly suspect reliability and validity. Moreover, the need to assemble an economically and politically attractive service package can also strongly tempt competing applicants to manipulate the data as necessary.[11]

Compounding the uncertainty of local franchising agents are questions about the willingness or ability of applicants for the franchise to meet its ultimate conditions. The case of Houston, Texas, illustrates

**Figure 5.1
The Organizational
Model**

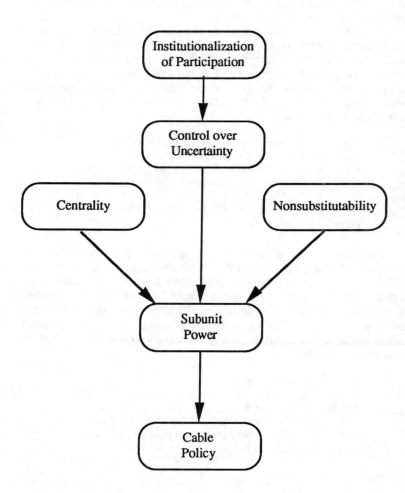

the implications of this uncertainty. The Houston city council divided the city into five areas and granted franchises to five separate operators without competitive bidding and without an adequate assessment of the franchisees' financial capabilities to provide services called for in the franchises. Soon after the award of the franchises, three of the five were sold off by the successful applicants because they could not meet the requirements of their contracts. As a result, eighteen months after the original franchises were granted, only about twenty subscribers in Houston were receiving cable services.[12]

Finally, at least until 1985, local franchisors have been uncertain about the exact division of responsibilities in the three-tiered system of cable regulation. The welter of overlapping jurisdictions, seemingly conflicting judicial decisions affecting cable regulation, and inconsistencies in state and federal cable policies have made attempts by local governments to represent constituents' interests in the franchising process extremely difficult.

The communities represented by local agencies are also faced with uncertainties which affect their role in the franchising process. First, individual members of a community that is contemplating a cable franchise usually have little knowledge about cable's potential uses. Ordinarily, cable is perceived as a means for retransmitting broadcast signals or receiving movies, sporting events, and news programming. As a result, individual households often find it difficult to reasonably evaluate the utility of cable service packages now possible. The decision on whether to subscribe is therefore based on limited information about the full range of technically feasible services.

Groups within the community may be able to overcome some of the information problems which affect individual households by focusing on uses of cable which are especially relevant to their members' common interests, but, in most cases, they remain somewhat uncertain about the responsiveness of cable operators and franchisors to group demands. In addition, groups face some of the same problems affecting operators and franchisors regarding the service needs of individual households.

Hickson, *et al.*, suggest that coping with uncertainties will increase a given subunit's power *vis-a-vis* other subunits of an organization only when the subunit is institutionalized as a distinct decision-making center within the system.[13]   Here, as in pluralistic theories, the institutionalization of an actor refers to the subunit's level of internal organization or structure. Institutionalization gives a subunit of an organization greater discretion over its responses to uncertainties and, hence, more control over the contingencies affecting the operation of the rest of the organization. Thus, the pluralistic argument that the institutionalization of community involvement in the franchising process is a key variable in explaining community interest policies may be interpreted within the context of this theoretical framework. Furthermore, the framework permits an interpretation of some of the negative findings in empirical tests of the institutionalization hypothesis since it places emphasis on two other properties of organizational subunits, their centrality and substitutability in the process of cable system organization. Pennings and Goodman point out that institutionalization may reinforce the effects of these two variables, but by itself may not be sufficient to determine a subunit's power in the organization.[14]

The centrality of a subunit to the activities of the organization of which it is a part may be understood as that subunit's importance to the successful achievement of the parent organization's purposes. Hickson, *et al.*, break this concept into two component dimensions, the pervasiveness and immediacy of the subunit's contribution to the attainment of organizational goals. If we take the goal of the meta-organization described in our model of the cable franchising process as the authorization and construction of a system to mediate between program suppliers and subscribers, the contribution of the operator to this goal is the offer to manage the operation of the system. The local government plays a highly central role since it is responsible for drafting and enforcing provisions of the franchise which establishes the parameters of the systems operation. Meanwhile, the community which is to be served by the cable system must articulate demands and preferences of its members regarding the franchise and cable system policies.

The pervasiveness of each of these roles to the construction and operation of a cable system refers to the extent to which decisions made in one subunit affects the working of the other subunits of the organization. This subdimension of a subunit's centrality is related mainly to the domain and scope of the subunit's power or influence over the activity of the organization as a whole.[15] It would seem that, in general, the most pervasive decisions in the franchising process originate within the local government while the community would have the least pervasive impact on the outcome of franchise negotiations. Although this general ordering of the relative pervasiveness of actors' decisions probably holds across cable systems, it also appears reasonable to expect that the pervasiveness of any single community's decisions will differ significantly from that of other communities based on the number, types, and intensity of demands expressed by the members of different communities during their franchising processes. Furthermore, the pervasiveness of community decisions may be augmented by the responsiveness of the franchising agent to publicly expressed preferences regarding the provisions of the franchise.

The immediacy of a subunit's work flows refers to the directness with which decisions made within the subunit are felt by other subunits. This subdimension of centrality would correspond to the weight of an actor's power or influence.[16] The immediacy of the community's impact on the outcome of franchise negotiations should therefore be related to the directness of community member involvement in the decisions affecting the ultimate franchise document. Furthermore, the community's immediacy to cable system decision-making should vary positively with the extent of local ownership of the firm which is awarded the franchise.

The substitutability of a subunit may also be broken down into two subdimensions, the interchangeability of individual actors within the subunit and the replaceability of the subunit as a whole. Again, focusing on the community actor in our model, the substitutability of individual subscribers (households or institutional cable users) would vary inversely with the total number of potential subscribers in the cable system's service area. The substitutability of the community as a whole would depend upon the size of the firm bidding on or designated to operate the cable system either in terms of the number of separate communities served or in terms of the relative proportion of total subscribers served by the firm within the specific community. *Ceteris paribus*, the larger the number of communities in which the operator is active (either as a bidder or as franchise holder), the more substitutable any individual community will be to that operator. Similarly, the greater the total number of subscribers served by a particular firm, the more substitutable (therefore less powerful) individual subscribers become. Finally, the smaller the proportion of the total subscriber base served by a firm represented by the subscribers in a given community, the easier it will be to replace that community with another.

Franchisors are, of course, much more constrained with regard to their ability to replace large blocs of constituents than are cable system operators but may still exercise some latitude in choosing the individuals to whom officials will look for political support and policy guidance. To a certain extent, operators may exercise a similar latitude when involved in simultaneous negotiations with a number of potential franchisors representing neighboring communities. In these situations they may choose to accede to the franchise terms which best suit their goals and reasonably argue that stricter terms in neighboring communities would be incompatible with the most efficient level of service.

In summary, the power of individual actors in our model of the cable franchising process is determined by each actor's level of institutionalization in the bargaining process, its centrality to the operation of the cable system, and the capability of the other two actors to replace its contribution to the system. We shall focus primarily on the power of the community actor since this should be reflected in the extent to which a cable system's service package includes a diverse selection of programming, including locally originated programs and interactive services. We may hypothesize that the extent to which community interests are addressed in cable policies will depend upon the level of institutionalization of community participation in cable system policy-making both during the franchise negotiations and in post-franchise operations. The greater the centrality of the community to cable system franchising and operations the more likely the system will accommodate community interests. Finally, the more difficult it is for the cable system operator to substitute one community for another or one individual for another within any community, the greater the extent to which a given community will see its interests in diversity, local programming, and interactive capability operationalized in cable services.

---

[1] The roots of the approach to explaining community power outlined in this chapter begin with Thompson's (1965) work on organization theory and Hirschman's (1970) treatment of the political economy of organizational control. The conceptual model on which the analysis here rests has been presented by Hickson, *et. al.* (1971) and elaborated by Hinings, *et. al.* (1974), and Pennings and Goodman (1977). Discussions of the concepts of centrality and substitutability of organizational subunits may be found in Pfeffer and Salancik (1978) and Hirschman (1970), respectively.

[2] Sloan (1979).

[3] Baer (1974).

[4] Less than 2% of the systems in operation in either 1979 or 1985. In the sample of cable systems collected for this study, 60% of the systems paying a fee other than one based on a percentage of gross receipts began operating in 1966 of earlier. Seiden (1968) has pointed out that even during the early period of cable system franchising in the United States, franchisors appeared to exhibit a steep learning curve with regard to the value of the percentage of gross revenue fee.

[5] about 3.5%

[6] Knight, *et. al.* (1982); Cable Television Information Center (1974).

[7] Yin (1974).

[8] Hickson, *et. al.* (1971).

[9] Orton (1981), p.2.

[10] Ayubi (1981); Wolfsohn and Kay (1980).

[11] Orton (1981), p.2.

[12] *Broadcasting* (1980); Enstad (1980).

[13] Hickson, *et. al.* (1971).

[14] Pennings and Goodman (1977).

[15] Kaplan (1964).

[16] *Ibid.*

Chapter 6

Examining the Organizational Model of Cable Policy Determination

As we have already seen, the most prominent explanations for cable policies are all somewhat deficient once we begin to consider their applicability to dimensions of community interests which go beyond the simple potential for diversity represented by channel capacity. The model which was outlined in the previous chapter has been offered as an alternative to the existing explanations as well as an alternative to a synthetic model that simply combines the elements of those pure-type explanations. In this chapter we shall examine the empirical support for the organizational model, first, as it exists for the bivariate hypotheses derivable from the model, and then in a comparison of the organizational model with a reasonable synthetic alternative.

Organizational Model
Bivariate Hypotheses

According to the organizational model outlined in Chapter 5, the ability of communities to obtain cable programming policies which reflect their interests, as communities, depends upon the power they can exercise in the franchising process. This power, in turn, is defined by the communities' control over strategic contingencies which affect the operations of their cable systems. Variables with determine a community's control over the strategic contingencies affecting cable system operations include the level of institutionalization of community participation in franchising and system operation, the centrality of community to cable decision-makers, and the substitutabilityof the community or individuals within it to the cable system's operations.

The role of variables related to the institutionalization of community participation has been discussed in connection with both socio-political and economic explanations for cable policy.[1] These findings need not be rehearsed here except to point out that the strongest support for the pluralist model, the negative relationship between out-of-state ownership and channel capacity, access and two-way capability may also be interpreted as support for the organizational model. Indeed, the relationship between local ownership and community interest policies may be better explained within the organizational framework since local ownership represents not only a form of institutionalization of community participation but also the centrality of the community to cable decision-makers. As such, the proportion of out-of-state ownership is reproduced in Table 6.1 (below), which displays the relationships between indicators of centrality and cable community interest policies.

The independent variables in Table 6.1 (below) may be divided into two dimensions of centrality: 1.) the pervasiveness of the impact of community decisions to the overall operation of the organization that runs the cable system, which is represented by the proportion of total MSO subscribers that are subscribers to a given system, the fraction of all systems in an MSO represented by a given system,[2] and, the percentage of ownership of a system held by individuals or firms with investments outside of the cable industry. 2.) the immediacy with which community actions are likely to be felt by the organization that operates the system, which is reflected in the percentage of a system owned by a multiple system organization, the proportion owned by out-of-state interests, the number of separate communities served by a system, and an indicator of whether the system has recently experienced a change of ownership. Four of these indicators were discussed above as they were relevant to other models of cable policy-making. Of the four, all but the number of communities served by a single system were significantly related to at least one of the dimensions of community interest cable policy. Of the three indicators in Table 6.1 which have not previously been examined, only the dichotomous indicator of a recent sale fails to attain significant relationships with any of the policy indicators. However, contrary to expectations based on the organizational model, the two indicators of the pervasiveness of community influence display consistently negative relationships with policy indicators. In both cases, the negative relationships might be explained in terms of the economic advantages of larger firms but, for the most part, the estimated coefficients are not significantly different from zero, so their interpretation as support for either model being considered here remains ambiguous.

Table 6.1: Relationship between the Centrality of the Community to Cable Decision Makers and Cable Community Interest Policies

	Channel Capacity	Channels in Use	Local Services	Access Channel	Two-Way Capability	(N=)
% of MSO subscribers	b=-.25 r=.02	b=-.70 r=.07	b=-.32 r=.15	d=-.09*	d=.05	(412)
% of MSO systems	b=-1.5 r=.08	b=-2.0 r=.17	b=-.68 r=.26	d=-.08*	d=.00	(417)
% own w/ other int's	b=.02 r=.11	b=.02 r=.16	b=.006 r=.29*	d=-.08*	d=.04	(415)
% owned by MSOs	b=-.11 r=.22	b=-.73 r=.21	b=-.005 r=.07	d=-.20*	d=-.18*	(313)
% outstate ownership	b=-.27 r=-.38*	b=-.11 r=.22	b=-.11 r=.11	d=-.35*	d=-.31*	(142)
# of Comm's served	b=.19 r=.09	b=.30 r=.20	b=.05 r=.14	d=.05	d=.06	(416)
Recently Sold?	d=.16	d=.17	d=.02	d=.15	d=.09	(417)

Independent Variables dichotomized at Median for crosstabulations with Access and Two-way variables

* correlation coefficient significant at $p \leq .05$

None of the indicators of centrality exhibit the kind of consistent relationships to all of the policy indicators found in the cases of population size, community wealth, federal regulation, League of Women Voters organization, television market rank, and system size discussed in Chapter 4. This may be an indication that centrality is not as useful a predictor of community interest policies as these other variables. However, at least according to one interpretation of the strategic contingencies framework on which our organizational model is based, an interaction of centrality and substitutability may be necessary for any effect of either to be observable. More conclusive evidence regarding the utility of the concept of centrality awaits multivariate analysis.

Variables arrayed in Table 6.2 (below) are indicators of the substitutability of either whole communities or of their individual residents to cable decision- makers. Again, five of the indicators in the table here appeared in previous tables and each of these is significantly related (in the expected direction) to at least one of the indicators of community interest policy; The projected growth of the system is related only to interactive capability. The negative relationships between penetration (subscribers per households in the system's service area) and cable policy indicators support the notion that subscribers become more substitutable as the potential demand for cable services increases. Similarly, the negative relationships between television market rank, cable penetration of the television market and community interest policies suggest that communities are more easily replaceable and consequently exercise less power in determining the extent of community interest programming in smaller markets than in larger markets. Only the indicator of subscriber density (subscribers per mile of plant in the system) does not conform to the expectation in the organizational model with regard to any dimension of community interest. This probably indicates a validity problem with this indicator of substitutability rather than bringing into question the validity of the model as a whole. The more subscribers attracted per mile of plant, the less each individual subscriber means to the system operator. This would be likely to offset the importance of subscriber density as a factor in determining the centrality of the community as a whole to the system's operator.

Indicators of substitutability in Table 6.2 which were not previously presented include system penetration (the proportion of subscribers in the service area of the system who have subscribed), system saturation of its service area (the proportion of households in the service area that are passed by the system), pay saturation (the proportion of households to which pay services are available that have subscribed to these premium services), and the existence of another

Table 6.2: Relationship between Substitutability of Community Actors and Cable Community Interest Policies

	Channel Capacity	Channels in Use	Local Services	Access Channel	Two-Way Capability	(N=)
Projected Growth	b=0.72 r=.24	b=.39 r=.20	b=.05 r=.12	d=.06	d=.11*	(310)
Subs/ HH In area	b=-10.9 r=-.42*	b=-6.7 r=-.40*	b=-1.1 r=-.31*	d=-.11	d=-.16	(217)
Subs/ HH Passed	b=-13.4 r=-.43*	b=-7.2 r=-.34*	b=-1.4 r=-.31*	d=-.13*	d=-.18*	(369)
Subs/ Miles	b=.03 r=.23	b=.02 r=.34*	b=.003 r=.20	d=.10*	d=.14*	(393)
HH in area/ HH passed	b=2.4 r=.15	b=1.8 r=.17	b=.62 r=.28	d=.11*	d=.10*	(417)
Pay Service Saturation	b=-1.1 r=-.17	b=-.38 r=-.08	b=-.09 r=-.09	d=.10	d=.13*	(91)
Twin System?	d=.17	d=.15	d=-.18	d=-.05	d=.13	(417)
Television Market	b=-.05 r=-.38*	b=-.03 r=-.35*	b=-.00 r=-.17*	d=-.12*	d=-.17*	(207)
TV market Saturation	b=.12 r=-.28	b=-.08 r=-.29*	b=-.007 r=-.12	d=.16*	d=-.18*	(205)

Independent Variables dichotomized at Median for crosstabulations with Access and Two-way variables

* correlation coefficient significant at $p <= .05$

cable system in the same community ("twin system?"). Except for the weak positive relationship between pay saturation and availability of interactive channels (which may be due to the small number of cases in which this situation occurs), all of the statistically significant relationships between these indicators of substitutability and community interest policies conform to organizational model expectations.

On the whole, Tables 6.1 and 6.2, appear to provide some support for the hypotheses derived from the organizational model, with the exception of the indicators of pervasiveness of community influence. This support, like that found for the bivariate relationships predicted by the models discussed earlier, is partial and equivocal until we can examine multivariate analysis results.

A Synthetic Model

As a benchmark for assessing the validity of the organizational model of cable policy making, we will use a synthetic alternative. Instead of reconceptualizing the process of cable policy-making, this alternative attempts to improve on the explanatory power of the pure-type models by combining their empirically successful elements in a single multivariate model. In effect, such a strategy for constructing a more generally applicable model would allow for an examination of the effects on the parameter estimates derived from one model of the controls for important variables derived from the other explanations. The use of such a model as a benchmark seems reasonable, since, as was pointed out in Chapter 3, the pure-type models identified there tend to be offered in pre-theoretical arguments which combine various elements of each. The construction of a synthetic model here recapitulates the process of identifying factors influencing cable policy in case studies. The major difference between this model and the stories derived from cases is that the elements of the model are included on the basis of a more general set of tests of the validity of the pure-type explanations.

Despite the seductive simplicity of this approach to constructing a general model of cable policy-making, the synthetic model lacks a necessary conceptual; underpinning. Perhaps the strategy of synthesizing elements of pure-type explanations would be an appropriate application of empirical theory-building if the explanations to be synthesized had equally strong empirical support for all of their attendant hypotheses. In this case, however, it is clear that none of the types of explanations we have examined is free from puzzling empirical findings and anomalies. This indicates that there is a need to attain a higher level of conceptual clarity before undertaking any effort at synthesis of empirical findings. Thus the synthetic model to be explicated here will be used only as a standard against which to judge the utility of the organizational model described in Chapter 5.

Based on findings from the sample of cable systems reported thus far, several principle must be taken into account in the construction of their synthesis. First, it is clear that maximizing channel capacity is a primary community interest in cable policy. As pointed out in Chapter 2, channel capacity is a value to be sought as a precondition of a cable system's adaptability to more specific needs of the community it serves. Given the importance of channel capacity as an indicator of community interest in potential diversity, it would appear from the findings reported in Chapter 4 that an economic explanation of cable system channel capacities must be at the core of any synthetic model of community interest policy determinants. Emphasis must be placed on market characteristics, regulatory environment, characteristics of the firms owning cable systems, and the viability of the systems as activities of these firms in explaining cable systems' policies.

It is also clear from the findings reviewed above that, once we go beyond the potential for diverse cable services, economic factors become less important *per se* and variables suggested by the socio-political model (specifically: demographic factors, socio-economic status, and community organization and involvement in policy-making) become relatively more important to determining a system's community oriented policies. In constructing a reasonable causal sequence, however, the socio-political factors cannot simply be added to the model after the effects of economic factors on specific policy indicators have been "removed" by prior entry in a regression model. Rather, a model more like that suggested by Richard Hofferbert[3] and applied with some success by Mazmanian and Sabatier to assessing determinants of California Coastal Commission policies[4] seems more appropriate. In such a model, pre-potent influences on policy include the physical, cultural, and socio-economic environment in which policy issues arise and decisions must be made. Although this study has put little direct emphasis on physical or cultural factors affecting cable policy, it seems reasonable to begin the synthetic explanation with demographic and socio-economic factors. Specifically, we enter community population size and status (after channel capacity in equations predicting localness and interactive capability) first in regression analyses. Next, it seems most reasonable to assume that the characteristics of firms which own cable systems would be related to the nature of the markets in which their systems operate. That is, larger firms with greater access to capital will be more likely to operate in larger communities than smaller firms. Firm characteristics would, in

Figure 6.1
A Synthetic Model

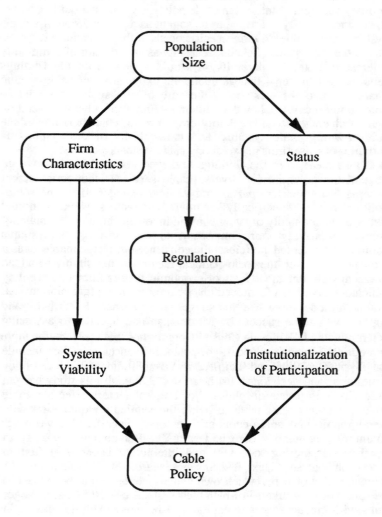

turn, influence the viability of cable operations while status and regulatory environment would affect the institutionalization of community involvement in cable policy- making. Higher status makes participation more likely while regulatory mechanisms offer an institutional channel for that participation. The overall model is diagrammed in Figure 6.1 (above).

Comparison of Synthetic and Organizational Models

Results of weighted least squares (WLS) regression analyses of the synthetic and organizational models are summarized in Table 6.3 (below). These results are based on regression analyses of data from a sample of 107 communities with populations of 10,000 or more that had cable systems in operation in 1979 using as dependent variables community interest policy indicators in both 1979 and 1985. The first three cable policy indicators (CHCAP: Channel Capacity, USED3: Channels in Use, and LOCAL: Local Services) were entered in ordinary least squares regressions; the remaining indicators (ACCESS: Access Channels, TWOWAY2: Two-way Capability, and TWOWAY3: Two-way Services) which are dichotomous were entered in weighted least squares analyses to derive estimates of linear probability models.[5] Independent variables entered in each regression analysis included current information on the system from the *Television Factbook* and information about the community in which the system operated from either the Factbook or the nearest preceding census of population and housing. The impact of each independent variable was examined in a three-step process. First, two indicators of each factor suggested by the synthetic or organizational explanation were entered and regression coefficients and t-ratios were examined to determine the more important predictor in each pair. These variables were then entered into another regression analysis and reexamined for both absolute and relative impact on each dependent variable (as indicated by the unstandardized and standardized regression coefficients). Based on the t-ratios associated with the regression coefficients, a final regression model was estimated which included only those predictors which had attained a probability level less than or equal to .05. Table 6.3 reports only the adjusted coefficients of determination for models which contained one indicator of each factor suggested by either the synthetic or organizational explanations as described above. In effect, then, the table summarizes and compares the explanatory power of the synthetic and organizational models of cable policy determination.

The results displayed in Table 6.3 confirm some expectations discussed in previous chapters. First, the two models appear fairly

TABLE 6.3
COMPARISONS OF SYNTHETIC
AND ORGANIZATIONAL MODELS

Dependent Variable	MODEL	R-SQUARED F-ratio 1979	1985
Channel Capacity	Synthetic	0.62 $F(9,97)=17.44$	0.45 $F(8,98)=9.92$
	Organizational	0.47 $F(8,98)=12.72$	0.15 $F(5,101)=4.81$
Channels in Use	Synthetic	0.39 $F(10,96)=7.70$	0.07 $F(10,96)=1.83$
	Organizational	0.42 $F(6,100)=13.69$	0.03 $F(9,97)=1.41$
Local Services	Synthetic	0.25 $F(10,96)=4.61$	0.11 $F(10,96)=2.25$
	Organizational	0.29 $F(6,100)=8.14$	0.13 $F(9,97)=2.68$
Access Channel(s)	Synthetic	$F(11,96)=10.36$	$F(8,98)=2.59$
	Organizational	$F(9,98)=12.92$	$F(10,97)=10.78$
TwoWay Capability	Synthetic	$F(11,96)=15.59$	$F(10,97)=13.58$
	Organizational	$F(9,98)=19.43$	$F(11,96)=14.80$
TwoWay Service	Synthetic	$F(11,96)=4.06$	$F(10,97)=15.45$
	Organizational	$F(9,98)=8.36$	$F(10,97)=9.47$

All values of coefficients of determination are adjusted for the degrees of freedom in respective models. Only F statistics are reported for the last three dependent variables since coefficients of determination computed in WLS models are not directly comparable to OLS coefficients.

close in terms of the respective proportions of variation in the dependent variables each of them explains. The widest distance between them is the .30 difference in proportion of variation explained between the 1985 models predicting channel capacity. Given that the synthetic model was constructed from components of simpler models which had already proved empirically successful as determinants of cable policy, this closeness in explanatory power is less important for judging the relative power of the synthetic and organizational models than it is as an indication of the validity of using the synthetic model as a benchmark.

Second, as suggested in Chapter 2,[6] The relative ability of the two models to explain different aspects of community interests in cable service policies varies. The synthetic model was clearly superior to the organizational model as a predictor of channel capacity (the potential diversity of cable services offered by a system) in both 1979 and 1985, and, perhaps, as a predictor of channel usage, availability of access channels, and two-way services in 1985. In all other cases, the organizational model appears to have at least a slight advantage. The superiority of the synthetic model in the case of 1979 channel capacity is probably somewhat misleading since a separate regression analysis involving the simpler economic model was apparently even better than our benchmark with an adjusted R^2 value of .60.[7]

Finally, coefficients of determination and F-ratios were lower in 1985 than in models estimated for 1979. A *post hoc* interpretation of this result suggests that it should have been expected since the systems in 1985 were, on the whole, more distant in time from their original franchising dates. It was at the time of the original franchise that the impact of dependent variables in either of the models compared in Table 6.3 should have been greatest since the major decisions about cable services would be made at that time based on the perceptions and expectations of those involved in the franchise process. After the original franchise period, changes in system policies would be likely to be incremental or non-existent. Thus, when the component variables of these models were observed, one should have expected to find some attenuation of the explanatory ability (and goodness of fit) of either model from the time of the negotiation of the original franchise. This, of course, suggests that the best test of the models would involve indicators observed as close as possible to the original franchise date. Ideally, we would like to know the information available to the parties involved in the negotiations at the precise time that bargaining was being conducted. Such observations were, unfortunately, impossible given the resources available for this study. Furthermore, reports of such information would be prone to considerable unreliability since they would depend upon self-reports of the perceptions of principals to the negotiations. Consequently, we must content ourselves with less than ideal data.

Taking all of this into account, the results displayed in Table 6.3 provide preliminary evidence for two conclusions. First, with regard to channel capacity, economic factors seem most important to maximizing potential diversity of cable services. The widening of the gap between the two models may indicate that the relative importance of economic over organizational considerations increased over the period between 1979 and 1985. Thus, the perception that the cable industry had attained a state of development by the late 1970s that was mature enough to allow market forces to operate without regulatory interference appears to have been an accurate reading of this particular standard of public interest. We have already reviewed some evidence to the same effect in data on the expansion of channel capacities reported in Chapter 2. The information provided by these analyses points to the validity of the economic explanation for this trend. Second, beyond the simple potential for diversity, the organizational power of communities in the franchising process appears to replace purely economic factors as the determinant of maximum commitment by cable systems to community interests. In the 1979 models (in which we can have somewhat more confidence if the reasoning outlined above is valid), all of the other indicators of community interest policies appear to be better explained in the organizational than in the synthetic model. This suggests that the assessment of the cable industry as mature on the basis of its maximization of channel capacities alone is incomplete.

The findings in Table 6.3 are suggestive of these conclusions at the broadest level. The relative explanatory power of the models is not enough *per se* to support the choice of either model as the better explanation of cable policies. For the dichotomous variables, in particular, R^2 values cannot be interpreted as simple proportions of variation explained and are therefore not even presented. Examination of the regression coefficients associated with each of the indicators entered as predictors must also show that the hypotheses suggested by each model holds up under controls for other significant variables in each model. The results of such an examination for the 1979 and 1985 data are summarized in Tables 6.4 and 6.5, respectively (below). These are the results of regression analyses which only the predictors which were statistically significant at or beyond the 95% confidence level in the full models are entered. Values for the coefficients of determination (R^2) in these two tables are lower than those in Table 6.3 due to the deletion from the regression analyses variables which were

TABLE 6.4: MOST IMPORTANT PREDICTORS
OF COMMUNITY INTEREST POLICIES, 1979

Dependent Variables	Most Important Indicators (First set of indicators from synthetic, second from organizational model. Signs in parentheses indicate signs of regression coefficients)	R-Squared F-ratio
Channel Capacity, 1979	SCHYR80(+), FCC1-3(+), TINC79(+)	0.52 $F_{(5,101)}=23.90$
	MARKT(-), FCC1-3(+)	0.44 $F_{(5,101)}=17.54$
Channels in Use, 1979	CHCAP79(+)	0.40 $F_{(1,105)}=72.88$
	CHCAP79(+)	0.40 $F_{(1,105)}=72.88$
Local Services 1979	USED379(+), OTH79PC(+)	0.15 $F_{(2,104)}=10.56$
	CHCAP79(+), LPERV279(-), PEN279(-) , SRVD79(+), LWVMEM(+)	0.29 $F_{(5,101)}=9.60$
Access Channel(s) 1979	USED379(+), LWVMEM(+) $F_{(43104)}=41.01$	
	USED379(+), LPERV279(-)	$F_{(3,104)}=40.77$
TwoWay Service, 1979	CHCAP79(+), FCC1-3(+)	$F_{(6,101)}=26.94$
	CHCAP79(+), SUBST279(-), MARKT(+)	$F_{(4,103)}=41.31$
TwoWay Planned, 1979	CHCAP79(+), FCC1-3(-), MSO79PC(+)	$F_{(7,100)}=7.19$
	CHCAP79(+), FCC1-3(++-)	$F_{(5,102)}=7.33$

All coefficients of determination are adjusted for degrees of freedom.

TABLE 6.5: MOST IMPORTANT PREDICTORS OF
COMMUNITY INTEREST POLICIES, 1985

Dependent Variables	Most Important indicators (First set from synthetic model, second from organizational model. Signs in parentheses indicate signs of regression coefficients.)	R-Squared & F-ratio
Channel Capacity 1985	TOTPOP80(+), MDNINC80(+), SYSAGE85(-), TINC85(+)	0.42 $F(4,102)=18.46$
	MSO85PC(-), MARKT(-)	0.15 $F(2,104)=9.99$
Channels in Use 1985	CHCAP85(+)	0.40 $F(1,105)= 5.47$
	CHCAP85(+)	0.40 $F(1,105)= 5.47$
Local Service 1985	TINC85(+)	0.09 $F(1,105)=11.87$
	SRVD85(+)	0.09 $F(1,105)=11.58$
Access Channel(s) 1985	CHCAP85(+)	$F(2,105)=54.69$
	CHCAP85(+), LPERV285(-)	$F(3,104)=43.05$
TwoWay Service 1985	FCC1-3(+)	$F(4,103)=27.56$
	FCC1-3(+), SRVD85(+)	$F(5,102)=24.85$
TwoWay Planned 1985	FCC1-3(+), PINC85(+)	$F(5,102)=15.43$
	FCC1-3(+), MARKT(-)	$F(5,102)=16.67$

All coefficients of determination are adjusted for degrees of freedom.

not significant at the 95% level of confidence. Models will be compared with regard to each of the six dependent variables and years displayed in the tables in turn.

Findings for both 1979 and 1985 suggest that community status and system viability were clearly the most important factors in the synthetic model determining cable system channel capacities. Community status is represented by median 1970 level of education (SCHYR70) in 1979 and median 1980 income (MDNINC80) in 1985. System viability is indicated by estimated system income in 1979 and 1985 (TINC79 and TINC85) and, in part, by community population (TOTPOP80) and age of the system (SYSAGE85) in 1985. These indicators were related in the direction that the synthetic model would predict (i.e., all positively, except system age which was negatively related to channel capacities). Although the positive relationship between the stringency of federal regulations (FCC1-3) in the 1979 model seemingly contradicts the synthetic model's predictions, this finding may be discounted since the data included only information on communities which had cable systems in operation by 1979. Arguments about the impact of regulation on cable system development ordinarily make the claim that regulatory stringency discourages not so much the provision of cable services by systems as the development of cable systems at all. This variant of the hypothesis cannot be tested using data only from communities in which this hurdle has already been passed. The positive impact of federal regulations on channel capacity should, therefore, be interpreted only as an indication that systems beginning operation tended to comply with the FCC rules regarding capacity in effect at the time.

In the organizational model, substitutability of the community, as indicated by television market rank (MARKT) is negatively related to channel capacity in both 1979 and 1985. While stringency of federal regulation (FCC1-3) again appears with a positive relationship in the 1979 test, it was replaced by multiple system ownership percentage (MSO85PC) in 1985. Both indicators can be interpreted as partial measures of the centrality of the community to the firm that owns the cable system as well as reflections of the institutionalization of community participation in decision-making for cable systems. However, the indicators entered in the organizational models consistently explain less of the variation in channel capacities for systems in the sample than do those in the synthetic models in both years. Thus the superiority of the synthetic benchmark over the organizational model observed in the examination of coefficients of determination in Table 6.5, appears to reaffirm support for the primacy of economic variables in maximizing channel capacities.

The instrumental value of channel capacities in determining the extent to which the more specific and ultimate dimensions of community interest are served is demonstrated in the analyses of factors influencing channel usage. In both years and in both models examined, only channel capacity remained to explain 40 percent of the variation in channels used when other indicators that did not demonstrate statistically significant relationships to the number of channels used were eliminated from the analyses. On the one hand, this could be taken as further evidence for the overall superiority of the synthetic (and especially the economic) model of cable policy determination since economic factors affecting channel capacity would indirectly determine usage. On the other hand, it seems reasonable to interpret the ambiguity of support for either model in this finding as an indication that something other than economic factors may determine exactly how channels available on cable systems will be filled. There is support for the latter interpretation in the results of analyses taking the number of local services offered by cable systems in 1979 as the dependent variable. In that year, only channels in use (USED379) and percentage of the system held by owners with financial interests outside the cable industry (OTH79PC) remained in the fully reduced synthetic model regression analyses. Together these variables accounted for only about 15 percent of the total variation in number of local services in the sample. At the same time, indicators of centrality (LPERV279), substitutability (PEN279, SRVD79) and institutionalization of community participation (LWVMEM) all remained in the fully reduced organizational model regression, along with channel capacity (CHCAP79). These variables accounted for about twice the total proportion of variation in local services (29 percent) as was explained in the synthetic model. All indicators in both models behaved as expected with the exception of the indicator of pervasiveness (LPERV279) the number of communities served by a cable system (SRVD79). The positive relationship between this indicator of the substitutability of a single community and number of local services, however, cannot be interpreted as conclusive evidence against the organizational model since the number of communities served by a single system often exceeds one in cases where adjoining communities cooperate in negotiating a franchise to increase their bargaining power as well as avail themselves of any economies of scale which might accrue to a larger cable system. The effect of joining such a cooperative franchising venture on the substitutability of each community involved would, in such cases, be offset by the increased centrality of the larger franchise area that could be offered to the ultimate franchisee. The negative impact of the proportion of all systems owned by an MSO represented by a single system

(LPERV279) is more problematic since it directly contradicts the expectation derived from the organizational model. On the whole the finding in this multivariate model would lead us to reject at least the pervasiveness dimension of centrality as an explanatory factor in the model. The only other alternative would be to question the validity of the indicator as a measure of pervasiveness of community influence. This problem aside, the rest of the evidence from this analysis of 1979 data appears to support the organizational model.

The success of the organizational model in explaining local services in 1979 is not carried over into the analyses in 1985. As we have already noted, the explanatory power of both synthetic and organizational models was attenuated over the 6 year period covered by these data.[8] In the synthetic model only estimated income (TINC85) remained in the organizational model. Each variable alone accounted for less than 10 percent of the variation in local services. This basis of the results of regression analyses including indicators of all relevant attenuation may be the result of the distance in time from the original negotiation of the franchises in systems in 1985.[9] Nevertheless, on the variables in both models, the organizational model appears, on the whole to be superior for explaining commitment to local services.

Analyses of the final three dependent variables in Tables 6.4 and 6.5 are based on results of weighted least squares estimates of linear probability models predicting the presence of at least one access channel (ACCESS), interactive capability (TWOWAY2), and actual interactive services (TWOWAY3). For these variables, the interpretation of coefficients of determination is complicated by the fact that dependent variables are weighted before entry into analyses. Because of this R^2 values calculated for these models are not comparable to those reported above for the interval-level policy indicators and are not reported. However, the results of t-tests for the significance of regression coefficients associated with each independent variable can be used to test the hypothesis that no relationship actually exists between each independent variable and the dependent variable, holding all other independent variables constant while the F-ratios tell us about the goodness of fit of each model as a whole. Thus the results summarized in Tables 6.4 and 6.5 are indications of the relative success of the conceptual models examined in this chapter as explanations of the probability of having these three kinds of cable policies.

In 1979, both models include channel usage (USED379) as a significant predictor of the availability of an access channel. This relationship is not necessarily of any substantive importance since we would expect the addition of an access channel to increase the number of channels used in any system. In the synthetic model the indicators remaining in the model after all non-significant independent variables were eliminated included estimated system income (TINC79) and League of Women Voters membership (LWVMEM). These represent the system's viability and the institutionalization of community participation in cable policy making, respectively. Examination of the unstandardized WLS regression coefficients revealed that LWV membership had a greater impact on the probability of having an access channel than did estimated income.[10] Thus the relative importance of the economic viability of the system appears less than the institutionalization of community participation in this realm of decision-making. Beyond this reversal of the importance of factors suggested by the synthetic model, support for the organizational model is lacking. Again, the logged proportion of all systems owned by an MSO that is represented by any single system (LPERV279 and LPERV285), presumed indicators of the pervasiveness of a community's influence on the firm that owns the system, were negatively related to the probability of having access service(s). The organizational model suggests that the probability of having an access channel would be positively related the increases in the magnitude of this quantity, i.e., negatively related to the number of systems included in the MSO.   Contrary to the model's prediction, it appears that the probability of having an access channel is positively affected by the number of systems owned by the firm which operates any given system.   This would appear to support the synthetic model's predictions rather than those of the organizational model.

Findings relevant to interactive capabilities and services are similarly ambiguous. In general, the results of both 1979 and 1985 analyses support the organizational model, however, there are perplexing anomalies.

First, in 1979, factors suggested in the organizational model were somewhat more successful in predicting the probability of two-way communication capabilities than were those derived from the synthetic alternative. In that year, only channel capacity and stringency of federal regulation had significant effects in the synthetic model. The effect of regulation, however, was positive, contrary to the economically based expectations of the model. In the same year, channel capacity was joined by indicators of substitutability of both subscribers and the community in the organizational model. Here, an unexpected positive relationship between market size and two-way capability detracts from support for the organizational model and suggests a relationship which might have been predicted in the synthetic model under the guise of market characteristics. To further confuse matters, the probability of two-way capabilities in 1985, was once again positively related to the stringency of federal regulations and to the number of communities served. The ambiguity of these factors with regard to inferences about the validity of either of the models examined here has been discussed above. The overall effect of the analyses is to weaken confidence in the organizational model without strengthening confidence in our empirically synthesized benchmark.

In 1979 the synthetic model appears to be superior to the organizational model. Channel capacity, federal regulation, and percentage ownership by an MSO all affect the probability of two-way service as the synthetic model would predict. Interestingly, in that year, the analysis of the organizational model suggests that the role of federal regulation was specified by MSO ownership in a way that makes this conclusion more convincing. That is, in the organizational model (which was identical to the synthetic except for the absence of MSO ownership percentage) the impact of federal regulations were positive for both of the earlier periods of FCC regulation but negative for the deregulatory period since 1975. When the control for MSO ownership is introduced, all three periods of federal regulation seem to have had a negative impact on the probability of offering interactive services that the synthetic model would have predicted.

In 1985 the apparent superiority of the synthetic model evaporates slightly. The positive impact of MSO ownership percentage drops out but is replaced by estimated income from pay services. However, the impact of federal regulation is once again positive. As discussed above, this does not necessarily contradict the expectations derived from the economic contribution to the synthetic model, but it does bring into question the meaning of the 1979 finding of a negative federal effect. The organizational model includes this positive impact of federal regulation and a negative impact of market size, both of which the model would predict.

Summary

An overall summary of the findings reported in the previous section would necessarily be somewhat misleading. On the whole the safest conclusion to draw out of these analyses is that there is no single model which can predict the extent to which all dimensions of community interests will be served by cable systems. While channel capacities and the probability of two-way service(s) appear to be more responsive to the primarily economic factors in the synthetic model, the availability of local services, probability of access channel(s) and of two-way capability seem to be more dependent on the power of communities as treated in the organizational model. This pluralism of explanations for community interest cable policies does however have some clear implications for regulatory policy and we will turn to these in the next chapter.

---

[1] See Table 9, in Chapter 4, at p. 85.

[2] The natural logarithm of this fraction was used to correct for the possible distribution of fractional scores in which the numerator is always 1.

[3] Hofferbert(1969).

[4] Mazmanian and Sabatier(1980).

[5] Although WLS analyses are inferior means of estimating parameters of probability models to logit and probit analyses, they were chosen for these data because linear probability models estimated with WLS analysis retain more comparability with the OLS regression analyses than do nonlinear models. There is no theoretical reason to believe that the impact of the independent variables included in these analyses on the probabilities of access channels or two-way capabilities is nonlinear. Although the R^2 value produced by a WLS estimate may not be interpreted as the proportion of variation explained by the model (and is therefore not reported in Tables 6.1-6.3), F-ratios may be used to estimate goodness of fit of whole models, and t-ratios can be used to test the effect of each independent variable on the probability of the value for the dependent variable being 1 (instead of 0). See, Aldrich and Nelson, 1986, for a discussion of various strategies for analysis of dichotomous variables.

[6] *Supra*, p. 73.

[7] Economic models predicting channel capacity and other dependent variables in 1985 were also examined but had R^2 values less than those attained in the synthetic model regressions.

[8] R^2 values in Table 6.1 were .11 for the synthetic and .13 for the organizational model.

[9] cf., *supra*, pp. 139-140.

[10] b=.002 for LWVMEM, b=.0000007 for TINC79. Thus an increase of 1 in the membership of the LWV would appear to improve the probability of having an access channel by two-tenths of a percent while an increase of $1,000 in system income would improve this probability by less than one-tenth of a percentage point.

Chapter 7

Regulating Cable Communications To Promote Community Interests

In this chapter I will draw out the implications of the determinants of community interest policies for the appropriate functions of regulatory policy in the field of cable communications. In particular, the focus shall be on the question of what the findings of the research reported in the preceding chapters suggest regarding the capabilities of cable firms to serve community interests and the congruence of corporate and community goals in cable policy-making during the 1980s and into the next century. In addition, analyses of data relevant to the impact of regulatory policies will be presented to supplement this discussion and serve as a base for an the impact of the *Cable Communications Policy Act of 1984* as well as the potential effects of the more recent *Cable Consumer Protection and Competition Act of 1992*.

The discussion of appropriate regulatory functions builds on Scholz's four-fold schema.[1] Scholz proposes that the appropriate function of public regulatory activity depends upon two general factors, the capability of regulated firms and the congruence of firms' incentives with the public goals to which their activities are relevant. When both firms' capabilities and the congruence of firms' incentives with public goals are high, regulation should be directed at preserving the efficiency of the market in which the firms operate. When capabilities are limited but incentives for the firm are congruent with public goals, regulation should be directed at ensuring the reliability of firms by supplementing their mechanisms for detecting and correcting social errors. On the other hand, when capabilities are high but incentives are not congruent with public goals, regulatory policy should address firms' motivations with either positive or negative incentives.

Finally, when both capabilities of firms and the congruence of their incentives with public goals are low, regulation should attempt to ensure the adaptability of firms to public goals by addressing both the reliability of their operations and their motivation.

These functions are related to the avoidance of social errors, or, at least, the reduction of such errors to within margins acceptable to the society at a given point in time. These errors may be classified as marginal, when they fall within the limits of public tolerance, or they may be more serious. Serious errors may involve articulation errors, when firms produce either too little or too much of a good to meet the demand for that good, or control errors, when the firms ability to manipulate their environment allows them to impose costs on customers or third parties.[2] Insofar as diversity, localism, and interactive capabilities of cable systems are significant public goals, failures to provide appropriate levels of these goods in any community must be considered social errors committed in the process of franchising and operating cable systems. The purpose of cable policy, then, involves avoiding, or correcting, the errors of minimizing the diversity, localness, and interactive capability of cable systems. Scholz suggests that, in general, this form of error correcting regulation is best accomplished by creating redundant channels for detecting and correcting the errors which are most likely to occur in an industry given the structure of capabilities and incentives of firms in that industry.

With its multiple tiered regulatory structure, the cable industry in the 1970s provided an excellent study in the possibilities and problems of redundancy in error correcting mechanisms. However, before examining the structure and functioning of cable regulation in greater detail we must first examine the unique structure of capabilities and incentives within which cable firms (and their regulators) operate.

Despite some difficulties, firm capabilities are relatively simple to conceptualize. In formal economic terms, the capability of any firm may be defined as the firm's ability to produce a net increment to the welfare of consumers while avoiding (or compensating) welfare losses to third parties. The extent of any firm's ability to do this, in turn, depends on three factors: 1. the firm's access to technologies capable of producing goods or services which increase consumers perceived welfare; and, 2. the firm's access to information on the willingness to pay for its products; and, 3. the firm's access to information on the external effects its operations impose on others. A purely economic analysis of firm capabilities would maintain a focus on the ability of firms to use their access to these factors to produce changes in individual welfare. However, this exclusive emphasis on individual welfare and preferences may cause us to lose sight of the significant social values which may be furthered (particularly at the level of the community) by applying cable technologies. Although it may be possible, in principle, to formally represent the interests of communities in the cable franchising process as the sums of individual preference satisfactions, the pervasive uncertainty regarding the actual advantages of implementing community service policies over the dimensions we have been discussing would this sort of reduction ill advised. The argument of proponents of limited operator responsibility for community interest services has typically taken the form of an appeal to the failure of market demand to justify implementing services which cable systems are technologically capable of providing. Thus despite the technical capacity of cable communication systems to provide a wide variety of information and entertainment services that would clearly benefit the communities they serve, the claim is made that these benefits are not sufficient to offset the net costs absorbed by the firm which offers these expensive services in highly uncertain markets. Yet, unless services are offered within a community, the uncertainty of subscribers about their potential uses (and consequently, benefits) remains high and the unprofitability of providing such services becomes a self-fulfilling prophecy. It makes sense, therefore, to treat the dimensions of community interest cable policy as relatively indivisible (i.e., public) goods, at least until the benefits individuals can derive from these goods are more widely recognized.

Technologically, cable firms appear eminently capable of serving community interests. The ability of cable systems to carry a variety of communications services can be taken for granted. Channel capacities are now practically unlimited, programming sources are proliferating and the technologies for local production of video programming are diffusing rapidly. It was this capability with regard to the potential diversity of cable programming which has contributed to the perception of the industry as "mature" and, thus, ready for deregulation. The Cable Consumer Protection and Competition Act of 1992 represents a reconsideration with regard to the ability of firms to exercise self-restraint in setting subscription rates (as well as a concession to broadcasters who may have lost revenues due to the availability of cable). However, little attention has been paid to the information problems which limit cable firms capabilities and motivations in the areas of actual diversity, especially diversity of local programming and interactive services. As we shall see, cable firms capabilities vary significantly over the dimensions of community interest in cable system policies.

The congruence of firms' incentives with the goals of the public is more difficult to assess. It depends upon the firm's willingness to structure its activities in a way which maximizes the net gain in social, as opposed to individual, welfare. Determining the congruence of firm and community goals requires, first, that we ascertain the goals of the firm. When the organization in which we are interested is a commercial enterprise like a cable firm, the goals of the firm may be assumed to always include at least a desire to cover operating costs, at least in the long run, while appropriating any surplus value created as profits. Beyond the profit motive, the goals of any particular firm may vary over industries, over firms within an industry, and over time. While variation over these dimensions may complicate any analysis of the congruence of firm goals and the goals of the public, the ubiquity of the profit motive helps to establish a "baseline" from which analysis may proceed. In particular, the profitability of cable operations is judged by the cash flow which a system can generate. This implies a strong incentive to either attract and maintain a subscriber base or maximize subscription rates, either of which will maximize the monthly income of a system, even at the expense of net losses in the short term.

The greater difficulty in assessing the congruence of firm and public goals is presented by the necessity of determining the goals of the public for any activity potentially subject to regulatory intervention. Public goals shift in response to the public's perception of the capabilities of the firms in any industry and the extent to which the government is held responsible for maximizing social welfare. The historical development of cable policy as it has been outlined in chapter 1, above, points to the importance of changing public perceptions of industrial capabilities in influencing policy at all levels of government. When the potential uses of cable technologies were not well understood and cable systems were seen as substitutes, and potential competitors, of broadcasting, regulations at the federal level were primarily protective of over-the-air television stations. These were perceived as the primary electronic mass communication media at the time. When the possible uses of cable were publicized and more widely recognized, federal regulations were imposed to maximize the commitment of cable operations to these services. Perhaps more than coincidentally, the rules formalized in the F.C.C.'s 1972 Report and Order also tended to favor existing broadcasting operations at the expense of cable system operators. At any rate, after 1975 public perceptions of cable system capabilities as a threat to broadcasting began to shift. Competition between broadcasting and other video media, including cable, came to be seen as healthy. Sentiments favoring deregulation of cable as well as broadcasting operations, which marked much of the 1980s, testified to the importance of the change of public expectations for regulatory policy. On one hand, communications media, including cable, were seen as capable of efficient competition, on the other, the feeling that government should not be responsible for interventions in potentially efficient markets was widespread. The point of the discussion in this chapter is an informed assessment of the validity of the increasingly popular conception of the cable industry as a "mature" industry in which governmental intervention of any type is unnecessary due to the development of adequate incentives and capabilities of cable firms and the consequent reduction of the importance of government action to assure the provision of an optimal level of cable service. To help in this assessment, a review of former policies affecting the cable industry will be useful.

The Structure and Functions of Cable Regulation

As mentioned above, the system of cable regulation which existed prior to the passage of the National Cable Communications Act of 1984 appeared to provide an excellent opportunity to examine the role of redundancy of information channels in the regulation of corporate behavior in the cable communications industry. For the nearly twenty years between the mid-1960s and 1984, cable systems around the United States operated under a variety of local, state and federal regulatory mechanisms. Although regulation at different levels of government usually involved explicit provisions regarding jurisdictional responsibilities, there was often a considerable overlapping of authority, most often with higher levels setting minimum standards which could be superseded by more stringent provisions in either the franchise ordinance or in state statutes. Furthermore, the stringency of regulations affecting cable system operations varied considerably not only from one cable franchise to the next but also across states and even at the federal level across communities of varying size and distance from television broadcasting stations. While this patchwork of regulations undoubtedly contributed to confusion both within the cable industry and among the various regulatory authorities,[3] it also afforded a rare opportunity to observe a variety of regulatory mechanisms affecting cable activities. Although rough, the indicators of state, local and federal level regulation of cable systems included in the study appear to indicate that regulatory policies have had at least some effect on the attainment of community interests. Zero order correlations between regulatory policy indicators and both diversity and interactive capability of cable system offerings are positive. However, the picture presented by bivariate correlation coefficients is substantially altered when we examine these relationships under controls for other variables entered in multiple regression and discriminant analyses. Table 7.1 (below) presents the results of regression analyses of regulatory policy effects on the potential and actual diversity and the number of types of local

**TABLE 7.1: IMPACT OF REGULATORY POLICIES
ON COMMUNITY INTEREST POLICIES
(controlling forsignificant non-policy predictors)**

| | Dependent Variable | | | | | | | | |
| | Channel Capacity | | | Channel Usage | | | Local Types | | |
	r	b	ß	r	b	ß	r	b	ß
FCC1	-.02	-.20	-.01	.49	.26	.45	-.20	-.78	-.34
FCC2	.29	11.52*	.41	.44	4.04*	.25	-.08	-1.11	-.28
FCC3	.43	7.88	.43	.10	-1.43	-.13	.07	-.57	-.22
STATE1	-.26	-7.83*	-.54	-.01	2.94	.35	.07	.93	.46
STATE2	-.04	-3.91	-.21	-.12	2.95	.28	.01	.89	.35
STATE3	.01	-4.47	-.20	.42	1.33	.10	.01	.47	.15
STATE4	.26	-4.38*	-.42	-.09	2.85*	.48	.01	.51	.35
RTREG	.06	.07	.00	.36	2.40	.20	-.21	-.57	-.20
MDINC	.32	.0006	.16						
BASE$	.16	.00003*	.35						
AGE	-.57	-.20	-.18						
MSO%	-.16	-.04	-.11						
SCHOL	.13	2.14	.23						
PENET	-.30	.61	.04						
TVMKT	-.43	-.02	-.16						
CHCAP				.49	.26*	.45	.19	.05	.39
PERV2							.02	.13	.11
CONST	-4.83			4.91			1.25		
R^2		.65			.55			.23	
adj. R^2		.45			.42			0	
S.E.E.		5.42			3.22			1.03	
F		.25			4.31			.95	
p		.004			.001			.51	

*indicates that regression coefficient (b) is significant at the .05 level.

programming services offered by cable systems in the sample collected for this study. We shall discuss the impact on community interests of regulatory policy at each level of government in turn. Starting at the federal level, the deregulation of the cable industry which commenced in the mid-1970s, appears to have promoted an increase in the potential diversity of cable services, as measured by systems' channel capacities, as well as the actual diversity of cable programming, as indicated by the number of channels actually in use. Positive regression coefficients associated with the deregulatory period of federal policy and negative coefficients relating the period of strictest federal regulation and channel usage support this conclusion. However, the impact of federal deregulation on the number of types of local services offered by cable systems in the sample appears to have been negative. The strongest negative effects are associated with the period of deregulation at this level. Furthermore, two facts make the interpretation of the positive impact of deregulation on potential and actual diversity somewhat less than straightforward. First, while the period of deregulation has the unstandardized regression coefficient (b) with the largest magnitude, the effect of the strictest period of federal regulation (between 1972 and 1975) was also positive. Standardized coefficients (ßs) for both these periods are about equal, indicating similar relative effects for both periods, taking all other variables entered in the analysis into account. Second, the increase of potential and actual diversity in cable system services since the early 1970s may be attributed to the rapid development of cable technology (e.g., coaxial cable capable of carrying more channels without deterioration of signal quality) and the almost simultaneous increase in the availability of more program sources (e.g., satellite pay-tv operations and the development of cable programming networks) during the twenty years between the 1970s and 1990s. Since the indicator of federal regulatory activity is based on the time period during which cable systems began operating, the secular effects of these two trends cannot be ruled out using these data.

Discriminant analyses of factors influencing the availability of access channels and interactive channels reported in Table 7.2 (below), suggest that federal regulation may have had a positive impact of access channels and a negative impact on two-way capabilities. This inconsistency of effects is somewhat troubling since both access and interactive channels were mandated for systems with over 3500 subscribers in the FCC's 1972 *Report and Order*.

Overall, the deregulation of the cable industry at the federal level appears to be having its intended effects, especially on the number of channels being made available, but also on the implementation of interactive capabilities. Whether the increasing diversity and

TABLE 7.2
IMPACT OF REGULATORY POLICY VARIABLES
ON THE AVAILABILITY OF
ACCESS AND INTERACTIVE CHANNELS
(results of discriminant analyses controlling for
significant non-policy predictors)

| | Dependent Variable | | | |
| | Access Channel | | Two-Way Channel | |
	unst	stan.	unst.	stan.
FCCREG	.37	.38	-.28	-.27
STATREG	.32	.38	.07	.08
RATREG	.60	.00	-.69	-.30
CHCAP	.07	.48	.21	1.16
PERV1	-.75	-.46		
PERV2			-.02	-.01
MSO%	.00	.11		
OOS%			.01	.29
CONSTANT	-2.05		-3.12	

R	.76	.07
CAN. COR.	.44	.69
EIGENVALUE	.24	.93
WILK'S λ	.80	.52
χ^2	14.79	36.93
p	.02	.0000
CORRECTLY		
CLASSIFIED	88.56%	93.44%
C_{pro}	75.45%	85.25%
IMPROVEMENT	13.11%	8.19%
N	73	73

interactive capability associated with the latest period of federal policy can be attributed to that policy or to technological changes which have effectively promoted a more competitive national market for communication services, further deregulation would seem to be warranted as a means of avoiding inefficiencies which were imposed by at least some of the federal government's interventions in the market. Despite the general support for federal deregulation provided by these finding, it is also fairly clear that one specific federal requirement-- the mandatory provision of local access channels--was effective in promoting the interests of communities in this area. Whether this effect could be obtained more efficiently by alternative policy actions is an open question at this time.

The importance of unfettered competition to maximizing channel capacities in the national market is borne out by the evidence of uniformly negative effects of state intervention on this dimension of community interest All types of state level regulations affecting cable, from those most protective of cable industry interests to those most restrictive of cable operations are negatively related to total channel capacities. However the direction of this relationship reverses when we examine the impact of state laws on actual diversity, localness, access and interactive capabilities. State laws which are either the most comprehensive or the most protective of cable industry interests seem to have the strongest effect on actual diversity and localness. This may indicate that states with comprehensive regulatory agencies dedicated to cable policy are "captives" of industry interests. Nevertheless, regardless of the type of state laws involved, state action appears to have promoted all of the dimensions of community interest in cable policy except that of potential diversity. In addition, the strictness of state regulation appears to be positively related to the availability of both access and interactive channels (although the relationship to the latter is negligible).

Once we move beyond the dimension of potential diversity to questions of how channels available on cable systems are actually used, it is clear from the data presented here that regulation by the states, i.e., closer to the local level, is effective in promoting community interests. This may be interpreted as a suggestion that the effectiveness of regulation as a promoter of community interests increases as the level at which controls are imposed approaches the level of the community itself. It may be that state agencies and legislatures are more likely to possess information relevant to the actual level of demand for community interest services. This information may reduce uncertainties enough to affect the capabilities of cable firms to provide these services. As we shall see, however, this must remain for the time being, no more than a plausible hypothesis.

Moving to the weakest indicator of cable policy, whether or not subscription rates are regulated at the local level, we can observe mixed effects. Local rate regulation appears to have had no appreciable impact on either potential diversity (channel capacity) or the availability of access channels. The existence of rate regulation has apparently had a negative impact on the number of types of local service offered by systems and the availability of interactive channels. At the same time there was a weak positive effect indicated for this variable on actual diversity. The assumption made when the rate regulation variable was selected for these analyses was that communities which went as far as regulating rates could be inferred to have a commitment to stricter regulation of other decisions and activities of cable operators as well. The instability in measured impacts of this variable may indicate that the strictness of local regulations do not have a cumulative structure. Rather, there may be dimensions of strictness of regulatory policy at the local level which vary independently of one another. Thus one community may emphasize rate regulation as an issue of consumer protection while the next imposes strict franchise provisions regarding some community interest service without any formal post-franchise regulations.

Whether or not we accept the assumption upon which the use of the rate regulation variable in this study was predicated, the pattern of effects indicated in Tables 7.1 and 7.2 could be explained by a purely economic model of cable policy-making. The negative impacts of rate controls on localness and interactive capability could be direct results of a reluctance of cable system operators to offer such expensive services under a constraint which would lower potential system income. Similarly, an operator faced with administratively determined rates might fill more of the channels available to him/her in order to possibly attract more subscribers and thus maximize income under such a constraint. This explanation is plausible since a variety of satellite, network and syndicated cable services are available for carriage at essentially no cost to systems. Finally, the lack of any impact of local regulation on channel capacities may be taken as evidence of the primacy of technological factors over policy which we have already discussed with regard to the determinants of the potential diversity of cable services.

As we shall see, the lack of more elaborate and accurate indicators of local regulatory policy is undoubtedly the greatest deficiency of this research. Clearly a micro-level analysis of the effects of local policy decisions on the provision community interest services is needed to answer the many questions this study leaves unaddressed.

Diversity as a goal of regulatory policy

The results of analyses discussed above and in the preceding two chapters make two points regarding the goal of diversity very clear: 1. We must distinguish between potential diversity as it is represented in the channel capacity of cable systems and the actual diversity of cable services as indicated by the use of cable system channels; and, 2. It is relatively safe to assume that market forces are adequate to induce a relatively strong commitment by cable firms to maximum channel capacities but much less safe to trust to the market the actual diversity of cable offerings.

The success of economic indicators in predicting channel capacities of the systems in our sample suggest that social errors in providing a maximum level of potential diversity in cable services are likely to be marginal. When they occur, it appears likely that these errors would be corrected by cable firms responding to the exercise by communities and individuals of their "exit" option.[4] The technology required to provide relatively unlimited channel capacities is widespread and inexpensive. For their part, cable system operators are induced to offer a large number of channels in order to effectively compete with broadcast and other alternative sources of video programming (e.g., satellite, videotape, disk, or over- the-air subscription television). Furthermore, channel capacity is almost universally recognized by franchisors as an important attribute of any cable system and they are likely to avoid franchise proposals which include limited capacities and favor those which promise more extensive potential services. Finally, the public widely recognizes increased channel capacity as a feature of cable service which differentiates it from over-the-air broadcasting. The awareness of the potential for expanded channel capacities by the public and its representatives means that the demand for cable services is fairly inelastic with regard to differences in channel capacities. Increases in potential diversity of cable services attract subscribers, but any attempt by operators to provide fewer channels than the number widely perceived as feasible will reduce appreciably the rate at which households subscribe. Thus, both the capability and motivation of cable firms to avoid the social error of suboptimal channel capacity are high, and economic factors related to competitiveness of most cable franchises are sufficient to ensure that cable operators will try to serve community interests along this instrumental dimension. Since cable system operators can provide extensive channel capacities and since this can be done relatively cheaply with a certain return for the investment in technology, they are likely to respond sensitively to market forces. The function of public policy seeking to increase channel capacities in such a situation is the ensure that market-mediated messages are not distorted by concentrations of economic power or other imperfections in the market.

When we turn to the measures of actual diversity, however, a different picture emerges. In general, the number (and percentage) of available channels actually in use appears less responsive to purely economic factors. Rather, the implementation of actual diversity seems much more dependent upon the ability of communities to exercise an effective "voice" option regarding cable policies. Despite the availability of diverse sources of programming, system operators are faced with a high degree of uncertainty about the actual level of demand in any given community for many of the services which could be provided. This uncertainty increases the likelihood of articulation errors as cable firms incorrectly guess at which services and what levels of service to provide. Furthermore, beyond inexpensive syndicated and network programming, the cost of providing many of the services for which cable is uniquely suited limits the motivation of operators to offer those services. When this lack of motivation is coupled with limited understanding of the uses to which cable could be put (as is often the case), the possibility of control errors also arises. In such a situation, the institutionalization of community involvement in cable policy-making, particularly when coupled with a high level of centrality of the community to the operator, amplifies the efficacy of the voice option making the provision of actual diversity more likely.[5]

With regard to actual diversity, then, the function of regulatory interventions should involve an attempt to assure that franchisees will reliably meet the specific demands for programming which exist in any given community. As long as this demand includes only the less expensive syndicated and network programming which is available for carriage by any cable system, there is little reason to be concerned about the motivation of operators. They can be depended upon to recognize the income maximizing effects of offering services which meet subscribers' (or, potential subscribers') preferences, once these preferences are known to them.

Regulatory bodies can do two things to help ensure a reliable response to this demand. First, they can promote the expression of community interests which will reveal the specific dimensions of this demand. This may be accomplished by a variety of means similar to those employed under the FCC's ascertainment policy for broadcasting licensees. Second, regulators can communicate the demands of each community to franchisees. These actions, to some extent, imply that the locus of regulatory authority most appropriate for promoting the

actual diversity of cable programming would be closer to the level of
the community to be served than to the national cable market. At any
level, some institutionalized channel for conveying more information
about the preferences of communities for cable services would probably
be adequate to remedy the information deficiency which has reduced
the capability of cable operators to provide as many of the
programming services as they might.

Localness and Interactive Capability

As we turn our attention to more specific indicators of community
interests in cable policy, the importance of non-market factors becomes
even clearer. In particular, the localism of cable services seems much
more dependent upon the effective exercise of the community's voice
than on the exit option. Here, the relative explanatory ability of the
organizational model[6] indicates that communities which can clearly
express their demands for services molded to their unique needs are
much more likely to see those demands met by their cable franchisees
than are communities without the mechanisms for this expression. A
part of the reason for this may be that the number and types of local
services required by any given community are more dependent on local
conditions than on general factors reflected in market demand. The
institutionalization of community involvement in cable decision-
making can decrease the uncertainty faced by both cable operators and
franchisors and thereby reduce the probabilities that articulation errors
will occur in the provision of cable services. However, because of the
additional expense involved in providing useful local or interactive
cable services, it seems that the functions of regulation must also
include an attempt to ensure that operators have the proper level of
motivation to undertake this expense.

Uncertainty on the part of potential subscribers means that the
elasticity of demand for cable services is high with regard to the
provision of local and interactive services. That is, subscriptions in any
community are not likely to be affected much by relatively small
changes in the types or levels of local or interactive services offered.
Most subscribers think of cable as the extension of broadcasting it was
originally introduced to be. They are therefore unlikely to exercise
their exit option by not subscribing (or discontinuing their
subscriptions) when less than optimal levels of non-broadcast service
are provided by their cable system. Likewise, a sort of inverse
elasticity of demand may obtain for those few who, recognizing the
community interest in cable, refuse to subscribe until more local and

interactive services are provided. In such a situation of highly elastic demand, the probability of articulation errors is very high because the normal channel of market communication is restricted. More importantly, the probability of control errors is also high since operators of cable systems may depend upon the elastic demand for their ordinary services to protect their subscriber bases while they avoid the provision of expensive local and interactive services.

The case of local and interactive service policies also provides a classic example of the dilemma of exit and voice identified by Hirschmann.[7] Those in any community who are most sensitive to the level of community interests represented in cable services are the least likely to subscribe in the first place. This reduces their centrality to cable system operators and limits the effectiveness of their voice in communicating the demand for community oriented services. At the same time, as long as there are enough subscribers who will continue to pay for more ordinary cable services, these subscribers may be easily substituted for those demanding expensive community oriented services. The refusal of the few demanders of community interest services to subscribe is, therefore, not likely to register with operators keeping their eyes on the all important cash flow of their systems.

According to Scholz's argument about the functions of regulatory policy, the problems of obtaining local and interactive cable services include the high probability of both articulation and control errors and thus call for regulations which attempt to ensure a maximum adaptability of cable system operators to the demands of the communities they serve. This seems to imply that , by their very nature, local and interactive services will have to be guaranteed at the local level. The demand for these services can only be determined at this level and the demands of different communities will certainly vary widely with local circumstances. In addition the requirements of any given community for local and interactive cable services are likely to vary over time. Perhaps the only thing constant in this particular situation, at least until technology changes to reduce the costs of these services, is that operators of cable systems will prefer not to offer local or interactive services if they can get by without them.

The Cable Communications Policy Act and Community Interests

To a large extent, the purpose of the *Cable Communications Policy Act of 1984* was to simplify the baroque structure of cable regulations which had grown by accretion since the late 1960s. The main provision of the Act pre-empts all regulatory authority of state and local governments in this area of policy and places it in the hands of the federal government. As the analyses reported above indicate, this might be a prescription for disaster regarding community interest cable services were it not for the fact that the FCC is officially committed in the Act to completing the deregulation of the cable industry it began in the mid-1970s. The states are effectively cut out of the cable regulation business, which may be a problem considering the success they have apparently had in encouraging community interest services. However, it is likely that the elimination of the overlapping jurisdictions which pre-dated the 1984 Act will have as many salutary effects (due to the simplification of the regulatory structure) as it has disadvantages.

The most important aspects of the Act, and the provisions which bear closest scrutiny in the coming years are those affecting the local franchising process. Before the passage of the Cable Communications Policy Act, local regulation aimed at promoting community oriented dimension of cable service could be accomplished in two ways, either in the provisions of the franchise itself, or, in post franchise regulation of cable system operations. With pre-emption of local regulatory authority, the importance of the franchise as a regulatory instrument in this area will most certainly increase. The Act specifies procedures for granting and renewing franchises, but these are not mandatory. They may be ignored if both franchisor and potential franchisee agree to other procedures. While local franchising agents are allowed to require public, educational and governmental access channels as a condition for granting the franchise, they may not specify particular programs, or even general types of programming for the system. The law also requires the deregulation of basic subscription rates. In return for accepting these reductions in their bargaining authority, local franchisors are given permission to extract up to five percent of a system's gross annual revenues as a franchise fee. The Act has been endorsed by both the cable industry and representatives of city government officials who were involved in the negotiations over its final form. The question we must consider in closing this chapter is what the effects of the Act are likely to be, given the findings reported here about the determinants of community interest policy.

First, and foremost in the minds of cable industry lobbyists and conservative legislators involved the getting the act passed, it seems that the Cable Communications Policy Act of 1984 has appropriately chosen to sanction the deregulation of the cable industry at the national level. Although the Act may allow for some concentration of ownership in its provisions allowing newspaper ownership of cable systems within their local markets, it continues the ban on telephone or broadcasting company ownership within their service areas. This will hopefully provide adequate protection of competition in communications markets to assure efficiency. Federal regulation beyond this market preserving function has already shown itself to be inefficient.

As suggested above, the exclusion of the states from regulatory authority over cable operations, is probably also a good idea. Although state regulations do appear to have been positively related to the extent of cable system commitments to community interest policies, it is likely that this effect could be better obtained by controls imposed at the local level. The states may have served their purpose in the theory of federalism as laboratories for public policy and the functions they performed could be devolved to local governments responsible for franchising cable systems.

Consequently, it is the impact of the Cable Communications Policy Act on local authority which is likely to be most regrettable. Although the final version of the bill , which was originally introduced by former Senator Goldwater of Arizona, does preserve considerable prerogatives that might have been lost in the Goldwater version, it still leaves much to be desired regarding the bargaining power of franchising agents. By completely removing the local authority to regulate cable operations after the franchise has been granted, the Act reduces the flexibility of local governments attempting to promote the adaptation of cable service policies to unique, and possibly changing, local needs and demands. In effect, it has restricted the degrees of freedom available to franchisors in bargaining with cable operators over the terms of their franchises. When post-franchise regulation was a possibility, less care needed to be exercised in hammering out the franchise provisions since unforeseen contingencies could be addressed by changes in regulatory policies after the franchise was in effect. The removal of the authority to engage in continual oversight of cable decisions will undoubtedly reduce the centrality of any community to its operator, especially if the. operator is a multiple system owner. To the extent that the centrality of communities has contributed to their obtaining community interest services, this provision is likely to reduce the provision of these services. Nevertheless, the observable impact of this aspect of the Act may be minimized since relatively few communities chose to establish ongoing regulatory bodies to oversee cable operations.

A similar conclusion may be reached regarding the specific type of post-franchise regulation examined in this study, i.e., the regulation of basic rates. Few communities exercised their option to engage in this form of intervention when it was open to them. Furthermore, the deregulation of rates may provide some of the extra incentive required for firms to try newer and more expensive services. This might have the effect of increasing the likelihood of these services, including local programming and interactive channels, being offered as successful attempts in this direction diffuse throughout the industry. Even if this happens, however, those who are the unfortunate pioneers may find themselves paying considerably higher rates than may be necessary, given the demand once others become aware of the utility of these services.

Another aspect of the Cable Act which is questionable is the non-mandatory nature of the franchising and renewal procedures. As written, the procedures carefully balance the concerns of franchisors seeking to represent community interests with the rights of franchisees to due process. It is possible that franchisors and operators can mutually agree on better(i.e., fairer, more efficient, or more effective) procedures for franchise renewals, but to assume that local officials beset with the problems of administration of a variety of programs will be consistently able to match the bargaining prowess of experienced representatives of cable firms stretches the normal bounds of credibility. For this very reason we can expect that cable operators will be more likely to suggest variances from the federally mandated procedures than will their local official counterparts in the franchise renewal process. It would, of course, be more than mildly surprising if these changes in the standard procedure resulted in benefits to communities greater than(or even equal to) those reaped by cable firms.

Finally, the prohibition of specific programming requirements by franchisors, while reasonable if we consider the potential for censorship that these kinds of controls would raise, may be a mixed blessing. As pointed out above, an important function of public regulation of cable operations in the promotion of community interests is the information channel which could be provided by a local franchising agency armed with knowledge of the specific needs and demands of the community. Although many of these needs may be served through an elastic interpretation of the access channel privileges granted to franchisors under the Act, the removal of more specific controls from the repertoire of regulatory mechanisms available to them is certain to reduce the specificity with which community interests can be identified. This would tend to limit the information-providing role that could be played by local governments as well as reducing their capacity to manipulate the incentives facing cable firms. Thus, at least with regard to the dimensions of cable communications policy which have been the central concern of this research, the Cable Communications Act of 1984, while better than it might have been, is not as good as it could be.

---

[1] Scholz(1981).

² The typology of social errors presented here is based on that developed by Benveniste(1981). Although Benveniste includes another type, which he calls "commons errors", I felt that the abuse of common property resources could be subsumed under the more general category of control errors since it represents an exercise of an organization's control over its environment albeit to the detriment of shareholders in the resource.

³*Los Angeles Times*, January 19, 1982.

⁴ See, Hirschmann(1970).

⁵ See, D.J. Hickson, C.R. Hinings, C.A. Lee, R.E. Schneck, and J.M. Pennings(1971) on the roles of centrality, nonsubstitutability, and institutionalization in determining bargaining power in organizations. See, also, C.R. Hinings, D.J. Hickson, J.M. Pennings, and R.E. Schneck, (1974), and, J.M. Pennings and P.S. Goodman(1977).

⁶ See, Godek(1983), chapter 7.

⁷ Hirschmann, *op. cit.*

Chapter 8

Conclusions and Recommendations for Cable Communication Policies

A theory of the determinants of community interest cable policies is needed to act as a practical guide to public action capable of minimizing the social errors of cable organizations and maximizing the adaptability of cable firms to the specific interests of the communities in which they operate. We have examined a number of candidates for such a theory available in the literature on cable policy and found them wanting. We have also examined an organizational power explanation for cable commitments to public interests and compared this to a synthetic model of the process of organizing and maintaining a cable system based on the empirically successful elements of the pure-type explanations. Although an economic model has considerable appeal as an explanation for the variation in the potential diversity of services offered by cable systems, the empirical support for this model's explanation of one dimension of community interest does not rule out the organizational alternative. Indeed it appears that an organizational interpretation of the findings based on the economic model allows us to clear up some problems caused by possible inconsistencies in the economic model.

Furthermore, we have found that purely economic factors seem to decline in usefulness as we shift our focus from an explanation of potential diversity, a general and instrumental interest of communities, to more specific community interests in the localism and interactive capabilities of cable services. These dimensions appear to depend less upon the economic constraints under which cable systems operate and more upon social and political factors unique to each community and the success of the community in organizing to represent its interests to a cable system operator.

Finally, in contrast to prevailing opinion in contemporary policy-making institutions, we have seen that government, at all levels, but especially local government, can and has been able to apply regulatory authority on behalf of the realization of community interests in cable policies.

In this chapter I shall review the practical implications of the findings reported in the previous chapters. This discussion will be organized first by the dimensions of community interest identified in this study and second, within each dimension, by the levels at which official public intervention in cable operations may take place, i.e., at the levels of federal, state, and local governments. The aim of this discussion is to establish strategies appropriate at each level of government to foster conditions which will ensure the greatest adaptability of cable firms to the needs and desires of communities.

As I present the recommendations suggested by the findings of this study I shall assess the current status and future possibilities for regulatory policy affecting cable communications. Policy is not made in a vacuum and the course set by policies implemented at the present time will affect future decisions. It is, therefore, wise to assess the feasibility of the policies suggested by the findings of this study in terms of policies already in effect. Some notion of where we are headed will help in determining what we need to know before taking our next steps. I will conclude with suggestions for further study.

Policies to Encourage Diversity in Cable Services

Diversity is a primary value of cable communications. The ability of cable systems to meet the needs of the communities in which they operate depends first of all on their capacity to offer an expanded selection of channels for the transmission of information and entertainment programming. This fact was not lost on the cable industry which has sold itself almost exclusively as an instrument for increasing the variety of programs available for consumption by individual households. Beyond this, however, the evidence I have presented here indicates that the capability of cable systems to offer a wide variety of communications services is fundamental to the fulfillment of their community interest potential.

The first problem of designing public policies to encourage cable system policies that serve community interests is one of balancing the potential diversity offered by an expanded number of communication channels with the ultimate goals of localism and interactive capability that represent a genuine fulfillment of cable's potential for serving community interests. This problem is made particularly acute since local and interactive cable services depend upon the availability of extra channels. However, the seemingly obvious solution of maximizing channel capacities by protecting the economic viability of cable systmes will not, by itself, ensure that the extra channels will be devoted to local and interactive services. Unless communities can organize themselves to present clear sets of demands for services that will further their collective interests, the same market forces which are likely to promote potential diversity will also fill available channels with a superficially diverse but actually relatively standardized menu of movies, sports, and syndicated television productions. Furthermore, even well-organized communities may be frustrated in their attempts to obtain cable service packages tailored to their specific needs unless they can muster the resources to make themselves central to cable decision makers' deliberations and non-substitutable in the operation of cable enterprises. The full flavor of this problem becomes apparent when we recognize that the effective presentation of demands for community interest policies of cable systems is certain to increase the cost of operating cable systems thus potentially reducing their profitability. In this situation some tradeoffs may have to be made among the total capacity of the system, its commitments to community interest services, and subscribers' rates.

Compounding the problem caused by the paradox of diversity is a problem of equality in the availability of cable services to potential subscribers. This problem has two important aspects. First, since the resources which make communities more or less central and non-substitutable to cable operators are not equally distributed among communities, some may be able to use their superior bargaining positions to obtain excellent packages of community oriented cable services without significantly affecting the overall capacities of their cable systems or the rates charged for the services made available. Operators in these communities may recoup their losses in other communities which are less able to exercise a great deal of bargaining power in franchise negotiations either by providing sub-optimal (from the community's point of view) service packages or by charging higher rates for any given level of service. This sort of inter-community inequality is not exactly the same kind of problem as that which is the motive for many stratification theories of cable policy, but its overall impact is similar. It is an articulation error in which some communities are under-served while others may even be over-served by cable systems.

The second aspect of the problem of equality is the individual level economic discrimination which may make those households most likely to benefit from community services the least likely to subscribe. If subscription rates must increase in order to support community interest services without cutting back on the potential capacity systems may need to respond to future needs and demands, cable services may price themselves out of the reach of the poorer members of any community. In either aspect, the problem of equality raises the possibility that some observers' fears of an ever-widening "information gap" between rich and poor will come true.

It seems clear that the federal government must take a leading part in setting up the paramenters of cable regualtion. The Congress appears to have recognized this as the appropriate role for the federal government in the *National Cable Communnications Policy Act*[1] which assigned exclusive jurisdiction over cable regulation to the federal government and established a set of minimum requirements for services provided by systems with over twenty channels. However, as we shall see later in this chapter, simply recognizing the leading role of the federal government in regulating the cable industry is not likely to effectively address the problems entailed in the attempt to guarantee diversity. Minimum channel capacity requirements similar to those imposed by the F.C.C. in its 1972 *Report and Order*[2] but taking into account current technological capabilities are necessary to ensure that all communities will be able to begin franchise negotiations from a uniform baseline of total channel capacity. In addition, the federal government should continue to maintain technical standards affecting signal quality and system construction. Within these broad constraints, market forces may operate to promote maximum channel capacities, as our findings about the impact of FCC deregulation of channel capacities attest. However, market forces cannot be relied upon to solve the problem of equality in either of its above-mentioned aspects. Nor are markets alone likely to produce optimal levels of community interest cable services. Unfortunately, experience in other areas of policy-making where the states and/or local governments have exercised primary jurisdiction suggests that these governments are not likely to be effective guarantors of equality. Thus, it seems that a more extensive federal administration of cable markets than that which is mandated in the *National Cable Communications Act of 1984* and its successors will be necessary.

In general, the federal government should attempt to structure cable markets to compensate for the effects of the kinds of community characteristics which have been found in this study to reduce communities' bargaining power in the franchising process.[3] Minimal federal standards for franchises in specific types of communities could be used to guarantee a rough equality among communities and between local franshiching agencies and cable system operators. These standards may be established so as to apply only as much authoritative intervention as is necessary to create conditions in which market forces could operate without aggravating inter-community differences in franchise bargaining power. Although the exact structure of cable markets which will provide the most equitable results is not perfectly clear in the abstract, the findings of this study suggest several broad guidelines.

First, since the power of any given community is apparently related to its size and to the availability of alternatives to cable, federal regulations should constrain market forces to an extent which is roughly inverse to the size of the community. Thus market forces may be given a freer reign in large metropolitan areas than in smaller communities outside of the major broadcast markets. In particular, federal rules regarding the ownership of cable systems in smaller communities should emphasize incentives for smaller MSO's while firms of all sizes should be encouraged to compete for larger communities' franchises.

Also, with regard to the question of cross-ownership, the restrictiveness of federal regulations should probably be inversely related to the size of the communities and/or the nature of the communications markets within which they operate. Although the data examined in this study clearly indicate that ownership by diversified firms has a positive impact on public interest cable policies, the issue of cross-ownership of different media within a single community raises a number of questions unrelated to the narrow dimension of cable diversity treated here. In particular the value of maximazing the diversity of sources of all types of communications may override the value of a cable system with a large channel capacity. Nevertheless, it seems reasonable to assume that source diversity will be directly related to community or market size and that rules prohibiting cross-ownership could safely be more relaxed in these communities than in smaller ones.

The roles of the states in encouraging cable diversity is less clear than that of either the federal or local governments. Although state cable policies do not appear to have had a significant effect on channel capacities of cable systems, it appears that states with comprehensive cable regulation (either by independent cable commissions or through existing agencies for the regulation of utilities) were successful in encouraging the actual use of available channels. Where state agencies can put the weight of their authority behind the demands of communities, these agencies can serve a useful function as intermediaries between the broad dictates of the federal government and the specific needs of communities under their jurisdictions. However, their role should be limited to generating incentives to use cable system capacities to meet community needs for localism and interactive cable services. State licensing and taxation of cable systems or firms should not be allowed to interfere with the operations of federally structured markets for cable services since these would tend to increase the costs of operating cable systems in an unequal fashion. This could ultimately lead to the kinds of inequalities in the extension of cable service that federal regulations should be designed to constrain. On the other hand, state-level service requirements would probably be unable to reflect local needs as accurately as provisions of locally negotiated franchises. Consequently the most appropriate role for the states in this policy area would be in supporting the ascertainment of local needs and the subsidization of local services.

In terms of promoting the overall potential for diversity in cable programming the role of local governments can also be relatively limited. The major responsibilities of local franchising agencies should lie in the areas of determining local needs for cable services and negotiating with potential operators for franchise provisions which meet those needs. The data we have examined in this study indicate that cable systems which are economically viable are capable of providing the basic potential, in terms of channel capacities, upon which genuinely local cable services can be built. Furthermore, the incentives to maximize channel capacities seem to be relatively strong. As pointed out in Chapter 1, this kind of situation suggests that the appropriate role of regulatory policy should be the preservation of markets with only the minimal intervention of authority to guarantee a type of "equality of opportunity" for communities to seek the particular cable services which will best meet their needs.

Localism and Interactive Capabilities

Policies to promote the localism and interactive capabilities of cable sevices must operate in a somewhat different situation that those aimed at maximizing channel capacities. The capability and willingness of cable operators to provide cable service packages tailored to local needs are limited by a variety of factors, not the least of which are the expense of producing non-standardized programming and the limited profitability of local live originations and recorded programs produced for very specific local audiences. Perhaps an even greater problem is the uncertainty faced by cable operators and others involved in franchising regarding the nature and extent of local services with will efficiently and effectively meet local communications needs. This uncertainty has an irreducible component since the innovation of new services and technologies will undoubtedly promote the perception of new needs and generate new demands. Thus cable operators who are principally responsible for the operation of cable systems not only have little incentive to promote localism but are also practically incapable of doing so in an effective way.

This kind of regulatory situation calls for policies which will ensure the adaptability of cable firms to the specific goals of the communities they seek to enter. Here, the problem is almost exactly the reverse of the problem of equality in the potential diversity of cable services. Rather than promoting equality, this dimension of community interest calls for the differentiation of services and specialized application of cable and related technologies to the potentially unique situation of each community. This reversal of the nature of the regulatory policy problem suggests a similar reversal of the relative importance of the roles of the three levels of government. While the federal government may effectively establish uniform national standards for cable diversity it is particularly unsuited for the the role of determining in each community the package of services which will serve that community's unique needs and interests. Despite some problems which may be caused by the differential responsiveness of local governments to various interests in any community, it appears that the local level is the most appropriate for government action to promote the adaptation of cable services to community needs.

Local responsibility for franchising has been, and should continue to be the cornerstone of policies promoting localism. Although assistance in ascertaining community needs may be provided by higher levels of government, the ultimate responsibility for negotiating a franchise must rest with local government. Furthermore, procedures which ensure the involvement of local citizens groups and the organization of significant community interests appear to be essential at this level.

The specific provisions of franchises are, of course, the responsibility of each franchising agency. Nevertheless, the general features of local policies to ensure the adaptability of cable firms to local needs may be outlined:

1. *Universal Service.* Franchisors should take care to ensure that the effective service area of the cable system (i.e., households passed) will be entirely wired and all services operational in as short a time as possible. Beyond acting as a guarantor of intra-community equality in the availability of cable services, such a provision can prevent cable operators from targeting specific areas where demands for community interest programming are minimal and then claiming that this minimal demand in specific areas justifies cutting community interest services for the entire community. Aside from coverage of the service area, the requirement for universal service should involve a provision stipulating that all community interest channels (i.e., local origination and access channels) be provided as a part of the basic service package along with the standard retransmission of broadcast signals.

2. *Regulation.* Provision should be made for continuous, or at least periodic, review of the system's performance. This may be accomplished by requiring relatively frequent renewal and renegotiation of the franchise or by continuous monitoring of system performance as a condition for automatic renewal "on good behavior."

Some flexibility regarding the regulation of rates is necessary, with rate regulation policies determined by local conditions. Regardless of local conditions, the regulation of rates charged for "extra" pay services (e.g., movie channels) is less essential than the regulation of rates for basic services (including community interest services). Also, rate regulation, even for basic services, is less justifiable in communications markets where a variety of alternatives to cable are available than in areas where cable systems approach a monopolistic position in the provision of voice and video communications.

Whether or not rates are directly regulated, the franchise should spell out acceptable justifications for any change in the system's rate structure and require operators to notify the public of proposed changes in rates and the justification for those changes in rates in time to hold public hearings before new rates go into effect. Tying changes in rates to franchise renewal periods could be another way to assure community input on rate policies.

3. *Ownership.* Within the guidelines for system ownership provided by the federal structuring of cable markets discussed above, franchisors should attempt to maximize local participation in system ownership. All cynicism about the cable industry proctice of "rent-a-citizen" aside, the data examined here seem to indicate that community service is positvely related to the extent of local (at least as opposed to out of state) ownership of systems.

In addition, in reviewing applicants for a franchise, local governments should favor smaller MSO's (in terms of numbers of subscribers served) over larger ones. An exception to this general rule may be made if the community granting the franchise is very large relative to others served by the franchise applicant.

4. *Community Involvement.* The franchise should contain provisions for the explicit involvement of community groups and encouragement of citizen participation in the cable policy-making process. The institutionalization of community involvement should begin as soon as possible in the franchising process and should carry over th the management of local channels and any local regulatory functions.

5. *Operator Support.* The franchise should cast the cable system operator in the role of local programming facilitator similar to that mandated for the Canadian cable industry. This means that the system operator should be responsible for providing necessary studio and

equipment facilities for locally produced programming. In addition, a staff to assist (or carry out) production of programming and maintenance of studio(s) and equipment should be provided. Finally, the operator should be assigned responsibility, perhaps with the cooperation of a community advisory board, for the scheduling and promotion of local programming.

6. *Ascertainment.* The franchising agent, with the cooperation of other representatives of the community, should assume the responsibility for the initial ascertainment of community needs. Once the franchise has been granted and the system is operating, provision should be made for continuous or periodic assessement of the community's changing communications needs. This assessment may involve the system operator in his/her role as local programming facilitator but must include official and unofficial representatives of community interests. This kind of institutionalized community involvement in policy-making can go a long way toward reducing the uncertainty concerning the appropriate role for the cable system within the community and increasing the adaptability of cable firms to community goals.

Although the roles of state and federal governments are necessarily limited by the nature of the problem of assuring localism, there are some general functions which may be performed at these levels in support of communities' efforts to maximize the adaptability of cable firms to their needs. On the whole, the guiding principle of state involvement in cable matters should be the protection and encouragement of a basically local franchising process which maximizes the opportunities for community involvement in decision-making and the importance of communities to the organization which operate systems within the state's boundaries.

Although federal involvement in cable policy is primarily restricted to creating the structural conditions in which markets can operate to maximize the number of channels available to any community there are some important policy decisions affecting local cable services which must be made at the federal level. First among these is the protection of the cable user's right to privacy. Policy protecting cable subscribers' privacy will become more important as the implementation of interactive services becomes more widespread and especially as cable systems become more important elements of networks for computerized data transmission and videotext. Similarly, problems may arise over copyrights to locally produced cable programming which will require federal attention. Aside from providing for the equal protection of the rights of cable service users, the role of the federal government in encouraging local and interactive cable services should be limited to the preservation of markets within which cable operators and communities may negotiate over the provision on cable services which will be most beneficial to the communities involved.

Suggestions for Future Research

While the statistical models examined in chapters 6 and 7 were fairly successful in accounting for variation in cable system channel capacities in the subsample to which they were applied, other dimensions of community interest cable policy are more difficult to predict (or explain) on the basis of these models. They have been used in this study solely to compare the relative adquacy of a number of possible general explanations for cable policies. I have attempted to derive from these comparisons some guidance as to the appropriate functions of regulatory policies which assume that maximizing the community interest potential of cable systems is a goal worth pursuing.

It is possible that a more complete specification of the general factors affecting cable decisions can yield statistical models which "explain" more variation in the dimensions of localism and interactive capability than the analyses presented here. The specification and testing of such a model is one promising avenue for future research. However, one conclusion which may be drawn from the analyses conducted for this study is that general models of cable policy determinants are not likely to reduce the statistically unexplainable proportion of variation in indicators of cable policy beyond a certain point, even with perfectly valid indicators of general policy determinants. This is because of the inherent uniqueness of each community which faces the myriads fo decisions that must be made when cable comes to town. While guidance relevant to the regulatory framework within which these dicisions are to be made may be taken from studies of general determinants like this one. The most important questions about cable policy, and the most important directions for future research in this policy area, will be asked at the level of each community granting (or renewing) a cable franchise.

One set of such questions centers on the understanding of the impact any given set of cable services is likely to have in a community. That is, what are the community's precise interests in the use of the cable system? Questions like this can only be answered by inventing and exploring the ways in which this set of communication technologies can be applied to provide collective, as well as private, benefits for the members of any community.

Another area in which this kind of community-specific research must be applied is in active experimentation with a variety of organizational forms for the development and use of cable's potential for local and interactive services. The key to this kind of research will be the cooperation of cable operators, local officials and citizens in finding ways to use cable for their mutual benefit. The policy recommendations presented in this chapter are aimed at pointing out ways that general factors affecting decisions about cable policies can be used to ensure that these policies can be made in such an atmosphere.

Finally, continuous research on the uses of both cable and other media of communication will be necessary to maintain some grasp of what genuine community interests in these media may be. While new communication technologies will always have inherent advantages for particular purposes and uses, the interaction of available media must also be considered. As individuals and communities discover new uses for older media as the use of newer ones diffuses, the nature of community interests in the organization of both old and new media must necessarily change. Also improvements in the carrying capacity or efficiency of existing media can qualitatively change the uses to which these media can be put. Thus the availability of fiber optics, for example, is likely to bring cable systems and telephone service providers into either direct competition or cooperation as phone lines and cable lines converge in their ability to carry voice and video communication

In a dynamically developing situation like that which curently affects communications in contemporary societies, the best uses of media are likely to be difficult to envision *a priori*. Because of the uncertainty engendered by continuous development, the role of industries, governments and communities in organizing and reorganizing their media of communications is likely to change. Perhaps the most valuable lesson to be gleaned from the history of cable communication policies is that societies must stand ready to adapt to these changes. If they do they are likely to thrive, if they aren't, they will suffer.

---

[1] *Cable Communications Policy Act of 1984*, Public Law 98-549, 98 STAT. 2779, 47 U.S.C. 609 note, October 30, 1984.

[2] 36, *F.C.C. 2d*, 143, 240-241(1972).

[3] See Roof, Trauth, and Huffman(1995) on the distinction between structural and content regulation.

APPENDIX
Variable Names, Definitions, and Sources

Variable Name	Definition and Source
FCCREG	Period of FCC Regulatory Activity (least strict to most strict), coded as follows: 0: pre-1968 1: 1968-1972 2: post 1975 3: 1972-1975 *Source:* Computed from *TV Factbook* information on date system began operating
FCC1- FCC3	Dummy variables corresponding to the three periods of FCC regulatory policy
STATREG	Types of state legislation relevant to cable operations (least strict to most strict), coded as follows: 0: No state laws 1: Protective legislation 2: Balanced legislation 3: Restrictive legislation 4: Comprehensive regulation *Source:* Briley, Sharon A., "State Regulation of Cable TV: Prospects and Problems," The Cable-Broadband Communications Book, (M.L. Hollowell, ed.), Communications Press:Wash., D.C., 1977.
STATE1- STATE4	Dummy variables corresponding to the four types of state laws affecting cable operations

Variable Name	Definition and Source
RTREG	Regulation of system's rates, coded as follows: 0: no rate regulation 1: rates regulated *Source:* N.C.T.A. survey of cable systems, 1979.
MDINC	Community median income *Source:* U.S. Census of Population, 1980.
BASE$	Estimated Monthly income from basic subscribers *Source:* Calculated from information in T.V. Factbook.
AGE	Age of cable system *Source:* Calculated from information in T.V. Factbook.
MSO%	Percentage of system owned by multiple system operators *Source:* Calculated from ownership information in T.V. Factbook.
SCHOL	Median years of schooling in community *Source:* U.S. Census of Population, 1980.
PENET	Penetration rate of system *Source:* Calculated as ratio of subscribers to number of households passed from information in T.V. Factbook.
TVMKT	Television market rank *Source:* T.V. Factbook
OOS%	Percentage of system owned by out-of-state interests *Source:* Calculated from ownership information in T.V. Factbook.
PERV1	Proportion of all subscribers served by an MSO (if applicable) which is represented in a given system *Source:* Calculated from subscriber information in T.V. Factbook.
PERV2	Proportion of total number of systems served by an MSO (if applicable) represented by any single system *Source:* Calculated from information in T.V. Factbook.

Bibliography

Agostino, Donald Edward, (1974) "A Comparison of Television Channel Use Between Cable Subscribers and Broadcast Viewers in Selected Markets," dissertation, Ohio University, 1974.

Aldrich, John H., and Forrest D. Nelson, (1986) "Logit and Probit Analysis for Multivariate Analysis with Qualitative Dependent Variables," *New Tools for Social Scientists*, (Berry & Lewis-Beck, eds.), Sage:Beverly Hills, California, 1986.

Anderson, Chuck, (1975) *Video Power: Grass Roots Television*, Praeger:New York, New York, 1975.

Ash, Stephen B., and John A. Quelch, (1983) *Videotex Technology and Its Marketing Impact*, Lexington Books, D.C. Heath & Co.:Lexington, MA, 1983.

Asher, Caroline D., (1977) "Purging Madison Avenue from Canadian Television II," *Law and Policy in International Business*, V. 9, No. 3, 1977.

Aufderheide, Pat, (1992) "150 Channels and Nothin' On," *The Progressive*, Vol. 56, No. 9, September, 1992.

Ayubi, Yolanda, (1981) "Cable Television and City of Milwaukee Residents: Results of a Needs Ascertainment Study," Interim report prepared for the Milwaukee Citizens Cable Advisory Committee and Officials of the City of Milwaukee, Wisconsin, August, 1981.

Babe, Robert E., (1975) *Cable Television and Telecommunications in Canada: An Economic Analysis*, Michigan State University Press:East Lansing, Michigan, 1975.

Bablitch, Mary Beth, and Stuart Langton, (1983) *Cable, Public Television and the Interactive Viewer: Three Parties to a New Television Experience*, Lincoln Filene Center for Citizenship and Public Affairs, Tufts University:Medford, Massachusetts, 1983.

Bablitch, Mary Beth, Stuart Langton, and Ken Thomson, (1983) *The Cable Connection: A Model for Citizen Participation in Community Cable Television*, Lincoln Filene Center for

Citizenship and Public Affairs, Tufts University:Medford, Massachusetts, 1983.

Bablitch, Mary Beth, and Ken Thomson, (1982) "The Cable Connection: A Model of Citizen Participation in Community Cable Television," *Citizen Participation*, V. 3, No. 6, July-August, 1982.

Bachrach, Peter, and Morton Baratz, (1970) *Power and Poverty: Theory and Practice*, Oxford University Press:London, U.K., 1970.

Baer, Walter S., (1985) "Telephone and Cable Companies: Rivals or Partners in Video Distribution," *Video Media Competition* (E.M. Noam, ed.), Columbia University Press:New York, 1985.

Baer, Walter S., (1974) *Cable Television: A Handbook for Decisionmaking*, Crane, Russak & Co.:New York, New York, 1974.

Baer, W. S., M. Botein, L. L. Johnson, C. Pilnick, and R. K. Yin, (1974) *Cable Television: Franchising Considerations*, Drane, Russak and Co.: New York, 1974.

Baldwin, T. F., et.al., (1978a) "Michigan State University-Rockford Two-Way Cable Project. Issues: Final Report." Michigan State University, East Lansing, Michigan, June, 1978.

Baldwin, T. F., M. D. Wirth, Jayne Zenaty, (1978b) "The Economics of Per program Pay Cable Television," *Journal of Broadcasting*, Volume 28, Number 2, Spring, 1978.

Barnet, Stephen R., (1970) "Cable Television and Media Concentration, Part I: Control of Cable Systems by Local Broadcasters," *Stanford Law Review*, Volume 22, January, 1970.

Baukus, Robert A., (1976) "Making Cable Work" Project, Summary Statements, Sept. 27, 1975-January 29, 1976. Connecticutt University, Storrs Institute of Public Service, 1976.

Becker, Lee B., and Shelzaf Rafaeli, (1981) "Cable's Impact on Media Use: A Preliminary Report from Columbus," Paper presented at the annual convention of the Association for Education in Journalism, East Lansing, MI, August, 1981.

Bednarczyk, Susan, and Jean Rice, (1977) "Five Years Later: Looking at Cable Access Experiments," *The Cable-Broadband Communications Handbook, 1977-1978*, (M. L. Hollowell, ed.), Communications Press:Washington, D.C., 1977.

Bell, Donald L., Esq., (1993) "Price Discrimination: Territorial Pricing for Cable Television Services and the Meeting Competition Defense under the Cable Television Consumer Protection and Competition Act of 1992," *Journal of Legislation*, v. 19, no. 1, 1993, pp. 63-77.

Benveniste, Guy, (1981) *Regulation and Planning: The case of Environmental Politics.* Boyd & Fraser:San Francisco, California, 1981.

Bernstein, Peter W., (1979) "Television's Expanding World," *Fortune,* Volume 99, Number 13, July 2, 1979.

Berryman, S. E., (1978) "Cable, Two-Way Video, and Educational Programming: The Case of Day Care," Rand Corporation:Santa Monica, California, Report Number R-2270-NSF, October, 1978.

Bertrand, Claude-Jean, (1985) "Cable Television in France," *Cable Television and the Future of Broadcasting* (R.M. Negrine, ed.), St. Martin's Press:New York, 1985.

Besen, S. M., B. M. Mitchell, R. G. Noll, B. M. Owen, R. E. Park, and J. N. Rosse, (1977) "Economic Policy Research on Cable Television: Assessing the Costs and Benefits of Cable Deregulation," *Deregulation of Cable Television,* (P. W. MacAvoy, ed.), American Enterprise Institute:Washington, D.C., 1977.

Beutel, Phillip, (1990) "City objectives in monopoly franchising: the case of cable television," *Applied Economics,* v. 22, no. 9, September , 1990, pp. 1237-1247.

Blalock, Hubert M., (1969) *Theory Construction: From Verbal to Mathematical Formulations,* Prentice-Hall:Enclewood Cliffs, New Jersey, 1969.

Blazar, William A., M. E. Spector & J. Grathwol, (1985) "The Sky Above, the Teleport Below," *Planning,* v. 50, no. 12, December, 1985.

BM/E Magazine, editors, (1973) *CATV Operator's Handbook: Second Edition,* Tab Books:Blue Ridge Summit, Pennsylvania, 1973.

Bolick, Clint (1984) "Cable Television: An Unnatural Monopoly," Cato Inst. Policy Analysis No. 34, Cato Institute, Washington, D.C., March 13, 1984.

Borko, Stephen B., (1974) "Local Government Experience with Cable Television," *Municipal Yearbook, 1974,* International City Managers Association:Washington, D.C., 1974.

Botein, Michael, (1985) "The FCC's Regulation of the New Video Technologies: Backing and Filling on the Level Playing Field," *Video Media Competition* (E.M. Noam, ed.), Columbia University Press:New York, 1985.

Box, G. E. P., and J. M. Watz, (1973) "Criterion for Judging the Adequacy of Estimation by an Approximating Response Polynomial," Technical Report Number 9, Department of Statistics, University of Wisconsin:Madison, WI, 1973.

Bradburn, Norman M., (1970) "Survey Research in Public Opinion Polling with the Information Utility--Promises and Problems," *The*

Information Utility and Social Choice, (Sackman & Nie, eds.), AFIPS Press:Montvale, NJ, 1970.

Branscomb, Anne W., (1975) "The Cable Fable: Will It Come True?" *Journal of Communications*, Volume 25, Number 1, Winter, 1975.

Brants, Kees, and Nick Jankowski, (1985) "Cable Television in the Low Countries," *Cable Television and the Future of Broadcasting* (R.M. Negrine, ed.), St. Martin's Press:New York, 1985.

Bretz, Rudy, (1975) "Public Access Cable TV: Audiences," *Journal of Communications*, Volume 25, Number 3, Summer,1975.

Briley, Sharon A., (1977) "State Regulation of Cable TV--Progress and Problems," *The Cable-Broadband Communications Book*, (M. L. Hollowell, ed.), Communications Press:Washington, D.C., 1977.

Broadcasting, editors, (1980) "Special Report: Prospecting for Cable Franchises: The Gold Rush of 1980," *Broadcasting*, March 31, 1980.

Brownstein, Charles N., (1978) "Interactive Cable TV and Social Services," *Journal of Communications*,, Volume 28, Number 2, Spring, 1978.

Bunce, Richard, (1976) *Television and the Corporate Interest*, Praeger:NY, NY, 1976.

Burns, Red, and Lynn Elton, (1978) "Reading, PA: Programming for the Future," *Journal of Communications*, Volume 28, Number 2, Spring, 1978.

Burns, Red, (1975) "Local Origination and Public Access: Community Information Systems," *Cable Handbook, 1975-76: A Guide to Cable and New Communications Technologies*, (M. L. Hollowell, ed.), Publicable, Inc.:Washington, D.C., 1975.

Burt, Ronald S., (1977) "Power in a Social Topology," *Power, Paradigms and Community Research*, (Liegert & Imershein, eds.), Sage:Beverly Hills, CA, 1977.

Buchanan, James, and Gordon Tullock, (1974) *The Calculus of Consent: Logical Foundations of Constitutional Democracy*, Ann Arbor Press:Ann Arbor, MI, 1974.

Buske, Sue Miller, (1980) "Improving Local Community Access Programming," *Public Management*, June, 1980.

Cable Television Information Center, (1974) "Local Government Uses of Cable Television," Cable Television Information Center:Washington, D.C., 1974.

Cable Television Information Center, (1972) "Cable Television Options for Jacksonville," The Urban Institute:Washington, D.C., 1972.

Cable Television Information Center, (n.d.) "Discussion Outline: Public Policy Issues Pertaining to Cable Television," Cable Television Invormation Center:Arlington, Virginia, (not dated).

Caldwell, Geoffrey, (1985) "Cable Television in Australia: A Study of Repose," *Cable Television and the Future of Broadcasting* (R.M. Negrine, ed.), St. Martin's Press:New York, 1985.

California Public Broadcasting Commission, (1982) *The Impact of AB699: Community Service and Cable Rate Deregulation*, California Public Broadcasting Commission:Sacramento, CA, April 15, 1982.

Campbell, D. T., and D. W. Fiske, (1959) "Convergent and Discriminant Validation by the Multitrait-Multi-method Matrix," *Psychological Bulletin*, Vol. 56, 1959.

Campbell, Vincent N., (1974) "The Televote System for Civic Communication: First Demonstration and Evaluation," American Institute for Research in the Behavioral Sciences:Palo Alto, CA, September, 1974.

Cantor, Muriel and Joel M. Cantor (1986) "Regulation and deregulation: Telecommunications politics in the United States," *New Communications Technology and the Public Interest*, Ferguson(ed) Sage:Beverly Hills, California, 1986.

Carmines, Edward G., and R. A. Zeller, (1979) *Reliability and Validity Assessment*, Sage:Beverly Hill, CA, 1979.

Caron, André, and James R. Taylor, (1985) "Cable at the Crossroads: An Analysis of the Canadian Cable Industry," *Cable Television and the Future of Broadcasting* (R.M. Negrine, ed.), St. Martin's Press:New York, 1985.

Carpenter-Huffman, Polly, R. C. Kletter, and R. K. Yin, (1974) *Cable Television: Developing Community Services*, Crane, Russak & Co.:NY, NY, 1974.

Cass, Ronald A.(1981) *Revolution in the Wasteland: Value and Diversity in Television*, University Press of Virginia: Charlottesville, Virginia, 1981

Charles River Associates, (1973) "Analysis of the Demand for Cable Television," CRA Report Number 178-2, Charles River Associates:Canbridge, MA, April, 1973.

Checkoway, Barry, and Jon VanTil, (1978) "What Do We Know About Citizen Participation? A Selective Review of Research," *Citizen Participation in America* (S. Langton, ed.), Lexington Books:Laxington, MA, 1978.

Chisman, Forrest P., (1977) "Public Participation and FCC Policy Making," *Journal of Communications*, Vol. 27, No. 1, Winter, 1977.

Clark, Terry Nichols, (1976) "Community Structure, Decision-Making, Budget Expenditures, and Urban Renewal in 51 Cities," *Community Politics: A Behavioral Approach*, (Bonjean, Clark & Lineberry, eds.), Free Press:NY, NY, 1971.

Clark, Terry Nichols, (1968) *Community Structure and Decision-Making: Comparative Analyses*, Chandler:San Francisco, CA, 1968.

Clarke, Peter, F. Gerald Kline, Hazen Schumacher, and Susan Evans, (1978) "Rockford, Illinois: In-Service Training for Teachers," *Journal of Communications*, Vol. 28, No. 2, Spring, 1978.

Cleland, Margaret, (1976) *Cable in Connecticutt: A Citizen's Handbook*, Connecticutt University, Storrs Institute for Public Service, Connecticutt Commission for Higher Education:Hartford, CN, June, 1976.

Cole, Jr., John P., (1981) "FCC Deregulation," *Current Developments in CATV 1981*, (G. Shapiro, ed.), Practicing Law Institute:Washington, D.C., 1981.

Coleman, James S., (1977) "Notes on the Study of Power," *Power, Paradigms and Community Research*, (Liebert & Imershein, eds.), Sage:Beverly Hills, CA, 1977.

Comanor, William S., and Bridger Mitchell, (1971a) "Cable Television and the Impact of Regulation," *Bell Journal of Economics and Management Science*, Vol. 2, No. 1, Spring, 1971.

Comanor, William S., and Bridger Mitchell, (1971b) "The Lost Generation: A Correction," *Bell Journal of Economics and Management Science*, Vol. 2, No. 2, Autumn, 1971.

Commission on Radio and Television Education, (1975) "Kabelvision Kiruna: CATV -- Experimental Application of a New Channel in a Neighborhood Society," Commission on Radio and Television Education:Stockholm, Sweden, May, 1975.

Committee for Economic Development, (1975) *Broadcasting and Cable Television: Policies for Diversity and Change*, Committee for Economic Development:New Yrok, April, 1975.

Connecticutt State Commission on Educational and Informational Uses of Cable TV, (1975) "Public Use of Public Channels: Opportunities in Cable Telecommunications. First Report to the General Assembly," Connecticutt State Commission on Educational and Informational Uses of Cable TV:Hartford, CN, February 15, 1975.

Connell, Eileen, (1978) "Reading, PA: Training Local People," *Journal of Communications*, Vol. 28, No. 2, Spring, 1978.

Costner, Herbert L., (1969) "Theory, Deduction, and Rules of Correspondence," *American Journal of Sociology*, Vol. 75, 1969.

Crandall, R. W., and L. L. Fray, (1974) "A Reexamination of the Prophecy of Doom for Cable Television," *Bell Journal of Economics and Management Science*, Vol. 5, Spring, 1974.

Cupps, P. Stephen, (1977)   "Emerging Problems of Citizen Participation," *Public Administration Review*, Vol. 37, No. 5, September/October, 1977.

Dahl, Robert A., (1961) *Who Governs? Democracy and Power in an American City*, Yale University Press:New Haven, CN, 1961.

Dawson, R. E., and J. A. Robinson, (1963) "Interparty Competition, Economic Variables and Welfare Policies in American States," *Journal of Politics*, Vol. 25, 1963.

Dent, Gary A., (1977) "Booby Traps of Cable TV Appraisal," *Banking*, Vol. 69, No. 3, March, 1977.

Dickson, Edward M., (1974) *The Video Telephone: A Preliminary Technology Assessment*, Sage:Beverly Hills, CA, 1974.

Dolan, Edward V., (1984) *TV or CATV?: A Struggle for Power*, Associated Faculty Press:Port Washington, New York, 1984.

Doty, Pamela, (1975) "Public Access Cable TV: Who Cares?" *Journal of Communications*, Vol. 25, No. 2, Winter, 1975.

Draper, Norman R., and Harry Smith, (1981) *Applied Regression Analysis* (2nd edition), John Wiley & Sons:NY, 1981.

Drexel Library Quarterly, editors, (1973) *Cable Television for Librarians*, (Special Issue), *Drexel Library Quarterly*, Vol. 9, No. 12, January and April, 1973

Dunlop, Robert A., (1970) "The Emerging Technology of Information Utilities," *Information Utilities and Social Choice*, (Sackman and Nie, eds.), AFIPS Press:Montvale, NJ, 1970.

Dunnett, P.J.S., (1990) *The World Television Industry*, Routledge, Chapman & Hall, Inc.:London, 1990.

Dyer, James A., and David B. Hill, (1981) "Cable Television and Diversion form Local Television News," Paper presented at the 7th Annual Conference of the Midwest Association for Public Opinion Research (MAPOR), Chicago, IL, October 23-24, 1981.

Efrein, Joel L., (1975) *Cablecasting Production Handbook*, Tab Books:Blue Ridge Summit, PA, 1975.

Enstad, Robert, (1980) "How a City Gets Hooked on a Cable TV Franchise," *Chicago Tribune*, August 31, 1980.

Etzioni, Amitai, et. al., (1975) "Participatory Technology: The MINERVACommunications Tree," *Journal of Communications*, Vol. 25, No. 2, Spring, 1975.

Eulau, Heinz, (1970) "Some Potential Effects of the Information Utility of Political Decision-Making and the Role of the Representative," *The Information Utilities and Social Choice*, (Sackman and Nie, eds.), AFIPS Press:Montvale, NJ, 1970.

Feldman, Nathan E., (1970) "Cable Television: Opportunities and Problems in Local Program Origination," Report Number R-570-FF, Rand Corp.:Santa Monica, CA, September, 1970

Ferguson, Marjorie (1986) *New Communication Technologies and the Public Interest*, Sage:Beverly Hills, California, 1986.

Flathman, Richard E., (1966) *"The Public Interest" An Essay Concerning the Normative Discourse of Politics*, John Wiley & Sons:NY, 1966.

Foote, J.S., (1990) *Television Access and Political Power*, Praeger:New York, NY, 1990.

Forbes, Dorothy, and S. Layng, (1978) *The New Communicators: A guide to Community Programming*, Communications Press:Washington, D.C., 1978.

Fuss, Helvyn, and Leonard Waverman, (1981) *The Regulation of Telecommunications in Canada*, Technical Report No. 7, Economic Council of Canada:Ottowa, Ontario, Canada, March, 1981.

Garay, Ronald, (1988) *Cable television : a reference guide to information.* Greenwood Press:New York, NY, 1988.

Garay, Ronald, (1978) "Access: Evolution of the Citizen Agreement," *Journal of Broadcasting*, Vol. 22, No. 1, Winter, 1978.

Geller, Henry, (1985) "The Role of Future Regulation: Licensing, Spectrum Allocation, Content, Access, Common Carrier, and Rates," *Video Media Competition* (E.M. Noam, ed.), Columbia University Press:New York, 1985.

Gillespie, Gilbert, (1975) *Public Access Television in the United States and Canada: With an Annotated Bibliography*, Praeger:NY, 1975.

Gittell, Marilyn, with B. Hoffacker, E. Rollins, S. Foster, and M. Hoffacker, (1980) *Limits to Citizen Participation: The Decline of Community Organizations*, Sage:Beverly Hills, CA, 1980.

Goldman, Ronald J., (1979) "Demand for Telecommunication Services in the Home," Paper presented at the annual meeting of the International Communications Association, Philidelphia, PA, May, 1979.

Gomery, Douglass, (1995) "The giants take over cable television," *American Journalism Review*, v. 17, no. 4, May, 1995, p.46.

Goodman, Robert(1982) "Government versus Cable TV," *Lincoln Review*, V. 3, pp. 23-46, June, 1982.

Gross, Peter A., (1980) "Cable and Pay Television," *Network Television and the Public Interest*, (M. Botein & D. M. Rice, eds.), Lexington Press:Lexington, MA, 1980.

Guelph University, Office of Continuing Education, (1973) *Proceedings: Cable Broadcasting in the Community*, Guelph University, Edmonton, Alberta, Canada, February, 1973.

Hamburg, Morton I., (1983) "Cable Television Franchising and Local Regulation," *Law and the Television of the 80's*, (New York School of Law), Oceana Publications Inc.:New York, New York, 1983.

Hanna, William, S. Niculescu, and S. Silver, (1977) "A Framework for the Study of Urban Politics and the Quality of Urban Life," *Power, Paradigms and Community Research*, (Liebert & Imershein, eds.), Sage:Beverly Hills, CA, 1977.

Harris, Marilyn, and Melodee Williams, (1978) "Television Comes to the Classroom in Irvine--Anyone Can Become a Star!" *Thrust for Educational Leadership*, V. 8, No. 1, October, 1978

Hazlett, Tom(1982) "The Viewer is the Loser!" *Reason*, v. 14, pp. 25-35, July, 1982.

Head, Barry, (1973) "Voices over the Cable: CAn the Public Be Heard?" *Harper's Magazine*, V. 246, No. 1474, March, 1973.

Heeter, Carrie, and Bradley S. Greenberg, editors(1988) *Cableviewing*, Ablex:Norwood, N.J., 1988.

Henry, Jane B., (1985) "The Economics of Pay-TV Media," *Video Media Competition* (E.M. Noam, ed.), Columbia University Press:New York, 1985.

Herbst, Adrian E., (1993) "Background and Development of the Cable Television Consumer Protection and Competition Act of 1992," *Current Municipal Problems*, v. 19, no. 4, 1993, p. 487-508.

Hickson, D. J., C. R. Hinings, C. A. Lee, R. E. Schneck, and J. M. Pennings, (1971) "A Strategic Contingencies Theory of Intra-Organizational Power," *Administrative Science Quarterly*, V. 16, No. 2, June, 1971.

Hill, David B., and James A. Dyer, (1981) "Extent of Diversion to Newscasts from Distant Stations by Cable Viewers," *Journalism Quarterly*, V. 58, pp. 552-555, Summer, 1981.

Hinings, C. R., D. J. Hickson, J. M. Pennings, and R. E. Schneck, (1974) "Structural Conditions of Intra-Organizational Power," *Administrative Science Quarterly*, V. 19, No. 22, 1974.

Hirschman, Albert O., (1970) *Exit, Voice and Loyalty: Responses to Decline in Firms, Organizations, and States*, Harvard University Press:Cambridge, MA, 1970.

Hollander, Richard S., (1985) *Video Democracy: The Vote-from-Home Revolution*, Lomond Publications:Mount Airy, Maryland, 1985.

Hollins, Timothy, (1984) *Beyond Broadcasting: Into the Cable Age*, BFI Books:London, U.K., 1984.

Hollowell, Mary Louise, ed., (1983) *The Cable/Broadband Communications Handbook: Volume 3, 1982-1983*, Communications Press, Inc.:Washington, D.C., 1983.

Hollowell, Mary Louise, (1980) *The Cable/Broadband Communications Book*, Communications Press:Washington, D.C., 1980.

Hollowell, Mary Louise, (1977) *The Cable/Broadband Communications Book*, Communications Press:Washington, D.C., 1977.

Hollowell, Mary Louise, (1975) *Cable Handbook, 1975-76: A Guide to Cable and New Communications Technologies*, Publicable, Inc.:Washington, D.C., 1975.

Horn, Harold E., (1981) "Local Government and Cable Television," *Telecommunication and Productivity*, (M. Moss, ed.), Addison-Wesley:Reading, MA, 1981.

Horwitz, Robert Britt. (1989) *The irony of regulatory reform : the deregulation of American telecommunications*, New York : Oxford University Press, 1989.

Howard, Herbert H., (1981) "Ownership Trends in Cable Television, 1972-1979," *Journalism Quarterly*, V. 58, 288-291, Summer, 1981.

Howard, Niles(1981) "Cable TV: The Race to Wire America," *Dun's Business Month*, V. 118, pp. 79-80,84-85, November, 1981.

Huffman, John Leonard, (1974) "Cable Television in Iowa: An Analysis of Local Ordinances in 1973," dissertation, University of Iowa, 1974.

Hunter, Floyd, (1953) *Community Power Structure*, University of North Carolina Press:Chapel Hill, NC, 1953.

Hurwitz, Sol, (1980) "Media: Next Phase," *Journal of the Institute for Socioeconomic Studies*, V. 5, pp. 50-64, Autumn, 1980.

International City Managers' Association, (1972) *Public Management*, (Special Issue), V. 54, No. 7, July, 1972.

International Institute of Communications, (1977) "The Financing of Community and Public Access Channels on Cable Television Networks in Member Countries of the Council of Europe," International Institute of Communications:London, U. K., 1977.

Irwin, Manley R., (1981) "Technolocy and Telecommunication: A Policy Perspective for the 80's," Working Paper Number 22, Economic Council of Canada:Ottowa, Ontario, Canada, March, 1981.

Jacobsen, Robert E., (1977) *Municipal Control of Cable Communications*, Praeger:New York, 1977

James, Lawrence R., S. A. Mulaik & J.M. Brett(1982) *Causal Analysis:Assumptions, Models, and Data*, Sage:Beverly Hills, CA, 1982.

Jeffres, Leo, (1978) "Cable TV and Viewer Selectivity," *Journal of Broadcasting*, V. 22, No. 2, Spring, 1978.

Jeffres, Leo, (1976) "Consequences of the Television of Abundance: Introduction of Cable Television into a Small Minnesota Community," Paper presented at the annual meeting of the

Association for Education in Journalism, College Park, Maryland, August, 1976.

Jeffries, Winslow Albert, (1975) "The History and Development of Cable Television in America and the Gary Communications Group, Inc.," Master's thesis, University of Illinois, Chicago, Illinois, 1975.

Jesuale, Nancy with Ralph Lee Smith, (1982) *CTIC Cablebooks: Volume 1: The Community Medium*, Cable Television Information Center:Arlington, Virginia, 1982.

Johnson, Leland L., (1975) "The Social Effects of Cable Television," Rand Corp.:Santa Monica, CA, March, 1975.

Johnson, Leland L., (1975) "Expanding the Use of Commercial and Non-Commercial Broadcast Programming on Cable Systems," Rand Report R-1677-MF, Rand Corp.:Santa Monica, CA, January, 1975.

Johnson, L. L., W. S. Baer, R. Bretz, D. Camph, N. E. Feldman, R. E. Park and R. K. Yin, (1972) "Cable Communications in Dayton Miami Valley: Basic Report," Rand Corp.:Santa Monica, CA, 1972.

Johnson, Nicholas, and G. G. Gerlach, (1972) "The Coming Fight for Cable Access," *Yale Review of Law and Social Action*, V. 2, No. 3, Spring, 1972.

Johnson, William H., (1980) "Structure and Ownership of the Cable TV Industry," *The Cable/Broadband Communications book, Volume 2, 1980-81*, (M. L. Hollowell, ed.), Knowledge Industry Publications:White Plains, NY, 1980.

Jouhy, Ernest, (1985) "New Media in the Third World," *Video Media Competition* (E.M. Noam, ed.), Columbia University Press:New York, 1985.

Kald, Lynda Lee, (1978) "Political Uses of Cable Television," *State Government*, V. 51, No. 4, Autumn, 1978.

Kalba, Konrad K., and J. M. Guite, with B. Ayvazian and M. Savage, (1980) *Service Innovation in the U.S. Cable Industry: The Role of Subscriber Scale and Other Factors*, Kalba Bowen Associates:Cambridge, MA, 1980.

Kalba, Konrad K., and Y. M. Braunstein, with L. S. Levine and M. Savage, (1978) *The Impact of Firm Size and Subscriber Scale on Cable Television Services*, Kalba Bowen Associates:Cambridge, MA, 1978.

Kalba, Konrad K., (1975) "City Meets the Cable: A Case Study in Technological Innovation and Community Decision-Making," dissertation, University of Pennsylvania, 1975.

Kalba, Kas, (1974) "Urban Telecommunications: A New Planning Context," *Socio-Economic Planning Science*, V. 8, 1974.

Kalba, Kas, (1973) "Communicable Medicine: Cable Television and Health Services," *Socio-Economic Planning Science*, V. 7, 1973.

Kamieniecki, Sheldon, (1980) *Public Participation in Environmental Policy-Making: The Cast of Water Quality Management*, Westview Press:Boulder, CO, 1980.

Kaplan, Abraham, (1964) "Power in Perspective," *Power and Conflict in Organizations*, (R. L. Kahn & E. Boulding, eds.), Tavistock:London, U. K., 1964.

Kaplan, Stuart J., (1978a) "Current Status of Cable Television in the Top 100 Markets," *Journalism Quarterly*, V. 55, Summer, 1978.

Kaplan, Stuart J., (1978b) "The Impact of Cable Television Services on the Use of Competing Media," *Journal of Broadcasting*, V.22, No. 2, Spring, 1978.

Kasperson, Roger E., and M. Breitbart, (1974) "Participation, Decentralization, and Advocacy Planning," Commission on College Geography Resources, Paper Number 25, Association of American Geographers:Washington, D.C., 1974.

Kay, Peg, (1978) "Policy Issues in Interactive Cable Television," *Journal of Communications*, V. 28, No. 2, Spring, 1978.

Kellner, Douglas, (1990) *Television and the Crisis of Democracy*, Westview Press: Boulder, CO, 1990.

Kellner, Douglas, (1987) "Public Access Television: Alternative Views," *American Media and Mass Culture: Left Perspectives*, D. Lazere (ed.), University of California Press: Berkeley, Ca., 1987.

Klaver, Fanca, (1976) "Media in the Netherlands," Council of Europe, Committee for Out-of-School Education and Cultural Development, Strasbourg, France, September, 1976.

Kleman, Daniel A. and W. Shartzer, (1972) "Cable TV and the Central City," *Public Management*, V. 54, No. 7, July, 1972.

Knight, F. S., H. E. Horn, and N. J. Jesuale, eds., (1982) *Telecommunications for Local Government*, International City Management Association:Washington, D.C., 1982.

Korte, David Owen, (n.d.) "The Franchise Procedure," Paper prepared for the Cable Television Information Center, Arlington, VA, not dated.

Krasnow, Erwin G., and L. D. Longley, (1978) *The Politics of Broadcast Regulation*, St. Martin's Press:NY, 1978.

Ksobiech, Kenneth J., (1975) "The Columbus Video Access Center: A Research Analysis of Public Reaction," Indiana University, Institute for Communications Research, Bloomington, IN, April, 1975.

Lane, Kenneth, (1979) "Which Way Cable?" *The Humanist*, V. 39, No. 45, September/October, 1979.

Langton, Stuart, (1978) *Citizen Participation in America*, Lexington Books:Lexington, MA, 1978.

Laudon, Kenneth C., (1977) *Communications Technology and Democratic Participation*, Praeger:NY, 1977.

Ledbetter, Jr., Theodore, and Gilbert Mendelson, (1972) *The Wired City: A Handbook on Cable Television for Local Officials*, Urban Communications Group, Inc.:Washington, D.C., 1972.

Le Duc, Don R., (1976) "Cable TV Control In Canada: A Comparative Policy Study," *Journal of Broadcasting*, V. 20, No. 4, Fall, 1976.

Leepson, Marc, (1982) "Cable TV's Future," *Congressional Quarterly, Editorial Research Reports*, V. 2, No. 12, 1982.

Lemelstrich, Noam, (1980) *Two-Way Communication: Political and Design Analysis of a Home Terminal*, Sage:Beverly Hills, CA, 1974.

Levin, Harvey, (1980) *Fact and Fancy in Television Regulation*, Russell Sage Foundation:NY, 1980.

Levin, Harvey J., (1973) "Television's Second Chance: A Retrospective Look at the Sloan Cable Commission," *Bell Journal of Economics and Management Science*, V. 4, No. 1, Spring, 1973.

Levy, Jonathan D., and Peter K. Pitsch, (1985) "Statistical Evidence of Substitutability Among Video Delivery Systems," *Video Media Competition* (E.M. Noam, ed.), Columbia University Press:New York, 1985.

Lewis, Peter M., 1978) *Community Television and Cable in Britain*, British Film Institute:London, U. K., 1978.

Lewis, Richard, (1986) "Cable TV: The Medium Carries the Message," *PCWorld*, December, 1986.

Liebert, Roland L., and A. W. Imershein, (1977) "Three Faces of Power: The Development of Paradigmatic Alternatives in Community Research," *Power, Paradigms and Community Reserach*, (Liebert & Imershein, eds.), Sage:Beverly Hills, CA, 1977.

Lindblom, Charles E., (1977) *Politics and Markets: The World's Political Economic Systems*, Basic Books:NY, 1977.

Lippke, James A., (1975) "The Profit and Loss in Local Programming: Cable Operator's Perspective," *Cable Handbook, 1975-76: A Guide to Cable and New Communication Technologies*, (M> L> Hollowell, ed.), Publicable, Inc.:Washington, D.C., 1975.

Lowl, Theodore, (1979) *The End of Liberalism: The Second Republic of the United States*, W. W. Norton and Co.:NY, 1979.

Lucas, William A., K. A. Heald, and J. Bazemore, (1979) "The Spartanburg Interactive Cable Experiments in Home Education,"

Rand Report No. R-2271-NSF, Rand Corp.:Santa Monica, CA, February, 1979.

Lucas, William A., (1975) "Two-Way Cable Communications and the Spartanburg Experiments," Rand Paper No. P-5484, Rand Corp.:Santa Monica, CA, August, 1975.

Lucas, William A., and Karen Posner, (1975) "Television News and Local Awareness: A Retrospective Look," Rand Report No. R-1858-MF, Rand Corp.:Santa Monica, CA, October, 1975.

Lucan, William A., and R. K. Yin, (1973) "Serving Local Needs with Telecommunications: Alternative Applications for Public Service," Rand Report No. R-1345-MF, Rand Corp.:Santa Monica, CA, November, 1973.

Lyall, R. Duncan, and C. F. DeKay, (1976) "Estimation of an Urban Cable Demand Model and Its Implications for Regulation for Major Markets," Center for Metropolitan Planning and Research, Johns Hopkins University:Baltimore, Maryland, 1973.

MacAvoy, Paul W., ed., (1977) *Deregulation of Cable Television: Ford Administration Papers on Regulatory Reform*, American Enterprise Institute:Washington, D.C., 1977.

MacAvoy, Paul W., (1976) "Memorandum on Regulatory Reform in Boradcasting," Domestic Council Review Group on Regulatory Reform:Washington, D.C., 1976.

MacKenna, David W., (1981) "The Cabling of America: What about Municipal Ownership," *National Civic Review*, V. 70, pp. 307-314, 330, June, 1981.

MacRae, Jr., Duncan, (1970) "Some Political Choices in the Development of Communications Technologies," *The Information Utilities and Social Choice*, (Sackman and Nie, eds.), AFIPS Press:Montvale, NJ, 1970.

Mandelbaum, Seymour J., (1972) *Community and Communications*, W. W. Norton & Co.:NY, 1972.

Marchese, Lamar V., (1972) "A Feasibility Study of Cable Television Utilization for Community Development in Central Appalachia," Master's thesis, University of Florida, 1972.

Marsden, Peter V., and E. O. Laumann, (1977) "Collective Action in a Community Elite: Exchange, Influence Resources and Issue Resolution," *Power, Paradigms and Community Research*, (Liebert & Imershein, eds.), Sage:Beverly Hills, CA, 1977.

Marvick, Dwaine, (1970) "Some Potential Effects of the Information Utilities on Citizen Participation," *The Information Utilities and Social Choice*, (Sackman and Nie, eds.), AFIPS Press:Montvale, NJ, 1970.

May, Judith V., (1971) *Citizen Participation: A Review of the Literature*, Institute of Government Affairs, University of California, Davis, CA, 1971.

Maynard, Jeff, (1985) *Cable Television*, Sheridan House:Dobbs Ferry, New York, 1985.

Mazmanian, Daniel A., and P. A. Sabatier, (1980) "A Multivariate Model of Public Policy-Making," *American Journal of Political Science*, V. 24, No. 3, August, 1980.

Mazmanian, Daniel A., and Jeanne Nienaber, (1979) *Can Organizations Change? Environmental Protection, Citizen Participation, and the Corps of Engineers*, Brookings Institution:Washington, D.C., 1979.

McCavitt, Wm. E., and P.K. Pringle, (1986) *Electronic Media Management*, Focal Press:Stoneham, Massachusetts, 1986.

McCombs, Maxwell E., (1972) "Mass Media in the Marketplace," *Journalism Monographs*, No. 24, Association for Education in Journalism:Lexington, KY, August, 1972.

McCombs, Maxwell E., and C. H. Eyal, (1980) "Spending on the Mass Media," *Journal of Communications*, V. 30, Winter, 1980.

McKenna, Joan, (1974) *Cable Television and the Future*, Quantum Communications, Inc.:Berkeley, CA, 1974.

Mengel, Lucia M., (1974) "Cable Television Franchising in Florida: An Analysis of Selected Franchises," Communications Research Center, Florida State University, Tallahassee, Fl, 1974.

Mergers and Acquisitions, editors, (1995) "Sell-Offs: Remapping Cable TV," *Mergers and Acquisitions*, v. 29, no. 5, March, 1995, p. 7.

Milbrath, Lester, and M. L. Goel, (1977) *Political Participation*, Rand, McNally:Chicago, IL, 1977.

Miller, Nicholas P., and Alan Beals, (1981) "Regulating Cable Television," *Washington University Law Review*, V. 57, No. 1, December, 1981.

Minnesota Cable Communications Board, (1979) "Minnesota Cable Communications and Local Self-Determination: A Practical Guide for Communities that Want to Announce Their Own Communications Needs and Plan Their Own Communications Services," Minnesota Cable Communications Board:St. Paul, MN, 1979.

Minnesota Cable Communications Board, (n. d.) *Cable TV Rates: Your Rights and Obligations*, Minnesota Cable Communications Board:St. Paul, MN, not dated.

Minnesota Cable Communications Board, (n. d.) "Cable and Minnesota Communities," Minnesota Cable Communications Board:St. Paul, MN, not dated.

Mitchell, B. M., and R. H. Smiley, (1974) "Cable, Cities and Copyrights," *Bell Journal of Economics and Management Science*, V. 5, No. 1, Spring, 1974.

Mitnick, Barry M., (1980) *The Political Economy of Regulation: Creating, Designing, and Removing Regulatory Forms*, Columbia University Press:NY, 1980.

MITRE Corp., and Office of Telecommunications Planning, (1974) "Cable Television Financial Performance Model Description and Detailed Flow Diagram," MITRE Corp.:Bedford, MA, 1974.

Montgomery, D.C., and E. A. Peck, (1982) *Introduction to Linear Regression Analysis*, John Wiley & Sons:NY, 1982.

Morrison, Donald G., (1969) "On the Interpretation of Discriminant Analysis," *Journal of Marketing Research*, V. 9, May, 1969.

Moss, Mitchell L., ed., (1978a) *Two-Way Cable Television: An Evaluation of Community Uses in Reading, Pennsylvania*, National Science Foundation:Washington, D.C., April, 1978.

Moss, Mitchell L., (1978b) "Reading, PA: Research on Community Uses," *Journal of Communications*, V. 28, No. 2, Spring, 1978.

Moss, Mitchell L., (1977) "Cable TV and Community Services: A Challenge for Local Government," *National Civic Review*, V. 66, No. 7, July, 1977.

Munger, Frank, (1969) "Opinions, Elections, Parties and Policies: A Cross-State Analysis," Paper presented at the American Political Science Association meeting, September, 1969.

Muth, Thomas A.(1979) *State Interest in Cable Communications*, Arno Press:New York, New York, 1979.

National Cable Television Association, (1980) *1979-1980 Cable Services Report: Local Programming*, National Cable Television Association: Washington, D.C., 1980.

National Cable Television Association, (1974a) *Over the Cable*, National Cable Television Association:Washington, D.C., 1974.

National Cable Television Association, (1974b) *Local Origination Directory*, National Cable Television Association:Washington, D.C., 1974.

National Cable Television Association, (1973) "Cable Television and Education: A Report from the Field," National Cable Television Association: Washington, D.C., 1973

National League of Cities, (1985) *Cable Franchising and Regulation: A Local Government Guide to the New Law*, National League of Cities and U.S.Conference of Mayors in Cooperation with Arnold & Porter:Wash., D.C., 1985.

National League of Cities, (1975) *Cable Television: Basic Questions and Answers for City Officials*, National League of Cities, Conference of Mayors, 1975.

Negrine, Ralph M., editor (1985) *Cable Television and The Future of Broadcasting*, St. Martin's:New York, NY, 1985.

Negrine, Ralph M., (1985) "Cable Television in Great Britain," *Cable Television and the Future of Broadcasting* (R.M. Negrine, ed.), St. Martin's Press:New York, 1985.

Neustadt, Richard M., (1982) *The Birth of Electronic Publishing: Legal and Economic Issues in Telephone, Cable, and Over-the-Air Teletext and Vedeotext*, Knowledge Industry Publications:White Plains, NY, 1982.

Newsweek, editors, (1981) "Cable TV: Coming of Age," *Newsweek*, August 24, 1981.

Nie, Norman, C. H. Hull, J. G. Jenkins, K. Stinbrenner, and D. H. Dent, (1975) *SPSS: Statistical Package for the Social Sciences*, (2nd Edition), McGraw-Hill:New York, NY, 1975.

Nie, Norman, (1970) "Future Developments in Mass Communications and Citizen Participation," *The Information Utilities and Social Choice*, (Sackman and Nie, eds.), AFIPS Press:Montvale, NJ, 1970.

Nimelman, Andrew A., (1982) "Of Common Carriage and Cable Access: Deregulation of Cable Television by the Supreme Court" *Federal Communications Law Journal*, V. 34, pp.167-192, Winter, 1982.

Noam, Eli M., (1985) *Video Media Competition: Regulation, Economics, and Technology*, Columbia University Press:New York, 1985.

Noam, Eli M., (1985) "Economies of Scale in Cable Television: A Multiproduct Analysis," *Video Media Competition* (E.M. Noam, ed.), Columbia University Press:New York, 1985.

Noam, Eli M., (1982) "Towards an Integrated Communications Market: Overcoming the Local Monopoly of Cable TV," *Federal Communications Law Journal*, V. 34, pp. 209-257, Spring, 1982.

Noll, Roger G., M. J. Peck, and J. J. McGowan, (1973) *Economic Aspects of Television Regulation*, Brookings Institution: Washington, D.C., 1973.

O'Brien, David J., (1975) *Neighborhood Organization and Interest-Group Processes*, Princeton University Press:Princeton, MJ, 1975.

O'Donnell, Thomas, and Jay Gissen, (1982) "A Vaster Wasteland?" *Forbes*, May 24, 1982.

Olson, Mancur, (1977) *The Logic of Collective Action: Public Goods and the Theory of Groups*, Harvard University Press:Cambridge, MA, 1977.

O'Neill, J. S., and S. Polk, (1972) "Service: The Immense Benefit of Cable," *Public Management*, V. 54, No. 7, July, 1972.

Ophuls, William, (1977) *Ecology and the Politics of Scarcity*, Freeman:San Francisco, CA, 1977.

Oppenhiem, Jerrold, (1974) "Television and the Poor," *Cable Report*, V. 3, No. 11, December, 1974.

Organization for Economic Cooperation and Development, (1979) *Technology on Trial: Public Participation in Decision-Making Related to Science and Technology*, Organization for Economic Cooperation and Development:Paris, France, 1979.

Orton, Barry, (1981) "Cable Television: Pre-Franchise Expectations and Subsequent Audience Behavior," Paper presented at the seventh annuyal conference of the Midwest Association for Public Opinion Research, Chicago, IL, October 23-24, 1981.,

Othmer, David, (1973) "The Wired Island: The First Two Years of Public Access Cable Television in Manhattan," Fund for the City of New York:New York, 1973.

Owen, Bruce M., (1981) "The Rise and Fall of Cable Regulation," *Case Studies in Regulation*, (L. W. Weiss & M. W. Klass, eds.), Little, Brown & Co.:Boston, MA, 1981.

Owen Bruce M. and R. Braeutigam, (1978) "Regulation of a New Technology: Cable Television," *The Regulation Game: Strategic Use of the Administrative Process*, Ballinger Publishing Co.:Cambridge, MA, 1978.

Owen, Bruce M., J. H. Beebe, W. G. Manning, (1974) *Television Economics*, Lexington Books:Lexington, MA, 1974.

Padden, Preston R., (1972) "The Emerging Role of Citizens' Groups in Broadcast Regulation," *Federal Communications Bar Journal*, V. 25, No. 2, 1972.

Page, Clint, (!978) "CATV: Two-Way Access to City Hall," *Nation's Cities*, V. 16, No. 5, May, 1978.

Park, Rolla Edward, ed., (1973) *The Role of Analysis in Regulatory Decision-Making: The Case of Cable Television*, Lexington, MA, 1973.

Park, Rolla Edward, (1972) "Prospects for Cable in the 100 Largest Television Markets," *Bell Journal of Economics and Management Science*, V. 3, No. 1, Spring, 1972.

Park, Rolla Edward, (1970) "The Potential Impact of Cable Growth on Television Broadcasting," Rand Report No. R-587-ff, Rand Corp.:Santa Monica, CA, 1970.

Parker, Edwin B., (1970) "Information Utilities and Mass Communication," *The Information Utilities and Social Choice*, (Sackman and Nie, eds.), AFIPS Press:Montvale, NJ, 1970.

Pennings, Johannes M., and P. S. Goodman, (1977) "Toward a Workable Framework," *New Perspectives in Organizational Effectiveness*, Jossey-Bass:San Francisco, CA, 1977.

Pergler, P., (1980) "The Automated Citizen: Social and Political Impact of Interactive Broadcasting," Occassional paper No. 14, The Institute for Research on Public Policy:Montreal, Quebec, Canada, August, 1980.

Phillips, Mary Alice Mayer, (1972) *CATV: A History of Community Antenna Television*, Northwestern University Press:Evanston, IL, 1972.

Pool, Ithiel De Sola, ed., (1973) *Talking Back: Citizen Feedback and Cable Technology*, MIT Press:Cambridge, MA, 1973.

Possner, Karen, (1977) "Options for Cable Television Regulation," *The Cable/Broadband Communications Book: 1977-78*, (M. L. Hollowell, ed.) Communications Press:Washington, D.C., 1977.

Posner, R. A., (1972) "The Appropriate Scope of Regulation in the Cable Television Industry," *Bell Journal of Economics and Management Science*, V. 3, No. 1, Spring, 1972.

Posner, R. A., (1970) "Cable Television: The Problem of Local Monopoly," Rand Memorandum RM-6309-ff, Rand Corp.:Santa Monica, CA, 1970.

Press, S. James, (1972) *Applied Multivariate Analysis*, Holt, Rinehart and Winston:NY, 1972.

Practicing Law Institute, (1985) *The New Era in CATV: The Cable Franchise Policy and Communications Act of 1984*, Practicing Law Institute:New York, N.Y., 1985.

Prewitt, Kenneth, (1970) "Information and Politics: Reflections on Reflections," *The Information Utilities and Social Choice*, (Sackman and Nie, eds.), AFIPS Press:Montvale, NJ, 1970.

QCTV, Limited, (1978) "QCTV: An Innovator in the West," QCTV Ltd.:Edmonton, Alberta, Canada, 1978.

Reinemer, Vic, (1981) "Cable TV and Public Power Belong Together," *Public Power*, V. 39, pp. 12-21, September-October, 1981.

Reuben, Gabriel H., (1970) "Using Cable Television to Involve Parents," *Educational Television*, V. 2, No. 1, January, 1970.

Rice, Jean, ed., (1983) *Cable TV Renewals and Refranchising*, Communications Press Inc.:Washington, D.C., 1983.

Rice, Jean, (1980) "Cable Access: Promise of the '80's," *The Cable Broadband Communications Book: Volume 2, 1980-81*, Knowledge Industry Press:White Plains, NY, 1980.

Rivkin, Steven R., (1978) *A New Guide to Federal Cable Television Regulations*, MIT Press:Cambridge, MA, 1978.

Rivkin, Steven R., (1974) *Cable Television: A Guide to Federal Regulations*, Crane, Russak Co.:NY, 1974.

Roman, James W., (1983) *Cablemania: The Cable Television Sourcebook*, Prentice-Hall:Englewood Cliffs, New Jersey, 1983.

Rood, Thomas R., (1977) "Cable Television: A Stutus Study of Services and Community Access in the State of Michigan," dissertation, Wayne State University:Detroit, MI, 1977.

Roof, E. Dana, Denise M. Trauth, and John L. Huffman, (1993) "Structural Regulation of Cable Television: A Formula for Diversity," *Communications and the Law*, v. 15, no. 2, June, 1993, pp. 43-70.

Rosenbaum, Nelson, (n. d.) *Citizen Participation: Models and Methods of Evaluation*, Center for Responsive Governance: Washington, D.C., not dated.

Rosenbaum, Walter A., (1976) "The Paradoxes of Public Participation," *Administration and Society*, V. 8, No. 3, November, 1976.

Rosener, Judy B., (1978) "Citizen Participation: Can We Measure Its Effectiveness?" *Public Administration Review*, V. 38, No. 5, September/October, 1978.

Ross, Darryl Allen, (1973) "A Survey of Municipal Officials' Attitudes Toward Cable Television," dissertation, Ohio University, 1973.

Ross, Leonard, (1974) *Economic and Legal Foundations of Cable Television*, Sage:Beverly Hills, CA, 1974.

Rothstein, Larry, (1978) *New Directions in Mass Communications Policy: Implications for Citizen Education and Participation*, Department of Health, Education, and Welfare publication number (oe)78-07003, U. S. Department of Health, Education and Welfare:Washington, D.C., 1978.

Rouse, Virginia, (1975) "Community Television: It's Working in Columbus, Indiana," *Educational and Industrial Television*, V. 7, No. 4, April, 1975.

Rutter, Laurence, (1980) *The Essential City: Local Government in the Year 2000*, International City Management Association:Washington, D.C., 1980.

Sabbah, Francoise, (1985) "The New Media," *High Technology, Space, and Society*, (Castells, ed.), Sage:Beverly Hills, California, 1985.

Sackman, Harold, and B. W. Boehm, (1972) *Planning Community Information Utilities*, AFIPS Press:Montvale, NJ, 1972.

Sackman, Harold, (1971) *Mass Information Utilities and Social Excellence*, Auerbach:Princeton, NJ, 1971.

Sackman, Harold, and N. Nie, eds., (1970) *The Information Utilities and Social Choice,*, AFIPS Press:Montvale, NJ, 1970.

Salmons, Henry, (1984) "Cable Operators take a Bruising," *New York Times*, Section 3, pp. 1,22, March 4, 1984.

Savage, R., (1980) *The Literature on Systematic Quantitative Comparison in American State Politics*, Report No. 11, Center for the Study of Federalism:Temple University:Philadelphia, PA, 1980.

Schacht, Michael, and Rolf-Rüdiger Hoffman, (1985) "Cable Television in West Germany," *Cable Television and the Future of Broadcasting* (R.M. Negrine, ed.), St. Martin's Press:New York, 1985.

Schäfer, Helmet, (1985) "A European View of Competition and Control in a Multimedia Society," *Video Media Competition* (E.M. Noam, ed.), Columbia University Press:New York, 1985.

Schattschneider, E. E., (!975) *The Semi-Sovereigh People: A Realist's View of Democracy in America*, Dryden Press:Hinsdale, IL, 1975.

Schiller, Don, Bill E. Brock, and Fred Rigby, (1979) *CATV Program Origination and Production*, Tab Books:Blue Ridge Summit, PA, 1979.

Schmid, A. Alan, (1976) *Property, Power, and Public Choice*, Praeger:NY, 1976.

Schoenberger, Carl F., (1979)   "Probable Two-Way Cable Applications in the Next Five Years," Fourth Annual Conference on Cable Reliability, Society of Cable Television Engineers and the Broadcast, Cable and Consumer Electronics Society:Denver, CO, February 27-28, 1979.

Scholz, John T., (1981) "Regulating Corporate Behavior: Bounded Rationality, Reliability, and Adaptability," Paper presented at the 6th annual Hendricks Symposium, University of Nebraska, Lincoln, NE, April 30-May 1, 1981.

Schubert, Glendon, (1960) *The Public Interest: A Critique of the Theory of a Political Concept*, The Free Press:Glencoe, IL, 1960.

Scott, James D., (1976) *Cable Television: Strategy for Penetrating Key Urban Markets*, University of Michigan:Ann Arbor, 1976.

Seiden, Martin H., (1972) *Cable Television U.S.A.: An Analysis of Government Policy*, Praeger:NY, 1972.

Seiden, Martin H., (1965a) *Report to the Federal Communications Commission: An Economic Analysis of Community Antenna Television Systems and the Television Industry*, Federal Communications Commission:Washington, D.C., February 12, 1965.

Seiden, Martin H., (1965b) *CATV Sourcebook: Including Exclusive Data Tables on TV and Microwave*, Tab Books: Thurmont, Maryland, 1965.

Shapiro, George H., ed., (1981) *Current Developments in CATV, 1981*, Practicing Law Institute:NY, 1981.

Shapiro, George H., (1980) "Up the Hill and Down: Perspectives on Federal Regulation" *The Cable/Broadband Communications Book,*

Volume 2, 1980-81, (M. L. Hollowell, ed.), Knowledge Industry Publications:White Plains, NY, 1980

Simon, Jules F., (1981) "The Collapse of Consensus: Effects of the Deregulation of Cable Television," *Columbia Law Review*, V. 81, pp. 612-638, April, 1981.

Sloan, Allan, (1979) "Bring Plenty of Money," *Forbes*, December 10, 1979.

Sloan Commission on Cable Television, (1971) *On the Cable: The Television of Abundance*, McGraw-Hill:New York, 1971.

Smith, Desmond, (1979) "Mining the Golden Spectrum," *The Nation*, V. 228, No. 20, May 26, 1979.

Smith, Ralph Lee, (1970) *The Wired Nation: Cable TV: The Electronic Communications Highway*, Harper, Colophon:NY, 1970.

Sparkes, Vernone M., (1985) "Cable Television in the United States: A Story of Continuing Growth and Change," *Cable Television and the Future of Broadcasting* (R.M. Negrine, ed.), St. Martin's Press:New York, 1985.

Sparkes, Vernone M., (1979) "The Users of Cable TV Access Channels: A Study of the Diffusion and Adaption of a Communications Innovation," Paper presented at the annual meeting of the Association for Education in Journalism, Houston, TX, August, 1979.

Sparkes, Vernone M., (1976) "Community Cablecasting in the U. S. and Canada: Different Approaches to a Common Objective," *Journal of Broadcasting*, V. 20, No. 4, Fall, 1976.

Sparkes, Vernone M., (1975) "Local Regulatory Agencies for Cable Television," *Journal of Broadcasting*, V. 19, No. 2, Spring, 1975.

Sparkes, Vernone M., (1974) "Municipal Agencies for the Regulation of Cable Television: Current Developments and Issues," dissertation, Indiana University, 1974.

Stein, Ira C., (1985) *Cable Television: Handbook and Forms*, Shepard's/McGraw-Hill:Colorado Springs, Colorado, 1985.

Steiner, Robert L., (1972) *Visions of Cablevision: The Prospects for Cable Television in the Greater Cincinnnati Area*, S. H. Wilder Foundation:Cincinnati, OH, 1972.

Stoller, D., (1982) "Growing Impact," *Cablevision*, p. 52, May 10, 1982.

Stone, Clarence, (1980) "Systemic Power in Community Decision-Making," *American Journal of Political Science*, V. 74, No. 4, December, 1980.

Stonecash, Jeff, and S. W. Hayes, (1981) "The Sources of Public Policy: Welfare Policy in the American States," *Policy Studies Journal*, V. 9, No. 5, Spring, 1981.

Stonecash, Jeff, (1979) "Assessing the Roles of Politics and Wealth for Public Policy," *Political Methodology*, V. 6, No. 4, 1`979.

Strasser, Judith, (n. d.) "Why Wire the Nation?" Unpublished paper, Stanford University, not dated.

Strouse, James C., (1975) "The Wired Nation: Social and Political Implications," *The Mass Media, Public Opinoin and Policy Analysis: Linkage Explorations*, Merrill:Columbus, OH 1975.

Sullivan, John L., and Stanley Feldman, (1979) *Multiple Indicators: An Introduction*, Sage:Beverly HIlls, CA, 1979.

Sullivan, John L., (1974) "Multiple Indicators: Some Criteria for Selection," *Measurement in the Social Sciences: Theories and Strategies*, (H. M. Blalock, ed.), Aldine:Chicago, IL, 1974.

Sullivan, John L., (1971) "Multiple Indicators and Complex Causal Models," *Causal Models in the Social Sciences*, (H. M. Blalock, ed.), Aldine:Chicago, IL 1971.

Sutherland, Roy A., (1982) "Home Banking: Electronic Money Invades the Living Room," *The Futurist*, V. 16, No. 2, April,1982.

Tate, Charles, ed., (1971) *Cable Television in the Cities: Community Control, Public Access, and Minority Ownership*, The Urban Institute:Washington, D.C., 1971.

Taylor, Thomas, (1981) "Telecommunications and Public Safety," *Telecommunications and Productivity*, (M. Moss, ed.), Addison-Wesley:Reading, MA, 1981.

Thompson, James D., (1967) *Organizations in Action*, McGraw-Hill:NY, 1967.

Thorndike, Robert M., (1978) *Correlational Procedures for Research*, Gardner Press:NY, NY, 1978.

Thorpe, Kenneth, (1985) "The Impact of Competing Technologies on Cable Television," *Video Media Competition* (E.M. Noam, ed.), Columbia University Press:New York, 1985.

Tracey, Michael, (1985) "Television and Cable Policy in Japan: An Essay," *Cable Television and the Future of Broadcasting* (R.M. Negrine, ed.), St. Martin's Press:New York, 1985.

Trounstine, Philip J., and Terry Christensen, (1982) *Movers and Shakers: The Study of Community Power*, St. Martin's Press:NY, NY, 1982.

Turk, Herman, (1977) "An Interorganizational View on Pluralism, Elitism, Conflict, and Policy Outputs in Large Communities," *Power, Paradigms and Community Research*, (Liebert & Imershein, eds.), Sage:Beverly Hills, CA, 1977.

United Cable Television Corporation, (1981) *Cablecasting and Public Access in the Eighties*, United Cable Television Corp.:Denver, Colorado, 1981.

U.S. Congress, (1992a) *Cable Television Consumer Protection and Competition Act of 1992: conference report*, U.S. Government Printing Office, 1992.

U.S. Congress, (1992b) *Cable Television Consumer Protection and Competition Act of 1992 report together with additional and dissenting views*, U.S. Government Printing Office:Washington, D.C., 1992.

U. S. Congress, (1992c) "Cable television regulation : hearings before the Subcommittee on Telecommunications and Finance of the Committee on Energy and Commerce," House of Representatives, 102nd Congress, 1st session, 1992.

U.S. Congress, (1992d) "Cable-instructional TV and S. 1200 Communications Competitiveness and Infrastructure Modernization Act of 1991: hearing before the Subcommittee on Communications of the Committee on Commerce, Science, and Transportation," United States Senate, 102nd Congress, 2nd session, February 28, 1992.

U.S. Congress, (1991) "Cable TV Consumer Protection Act of 1991 : hearing before the Subcommittee on Communications of the Committee on Commerce, Science, and Transportation," United States Senate, 102nd Congress, 1st session, March 14, 1991.

U.S. Congress, (1990) "Cable TV Consumer Protection Act of 1989 : hearings before the Subcommittee on Communications of the Committee on Commerce, Science, and Transportation, United States Senate, 101st Congress, 2nd session, March 29, and April 4, 1990.

U.S. Congress, (1989) "GAO cable rate survey : hearing before the Subcommittee on Telecommunications and Finance of the Committee on Energy and Commerce," House of Representatives, 101st Congress, 1st session, August 3, 1989.

U. S. Congress, (1982) "Cable Television Regulation: Hearings before the Committee on Commerce, Science and Transportation," United States Senate, 97th Congress, 2nd Session, January 18 and February 16, 1982.

U. S. Congress, (1976a) "Hearings before the Subcommittee on Communications of the Committee on Interstate and Foreign Commerce," United States House of Representatives, 94th Congress, 2nd Session, May 17-September 22, 1976.

U. S. Congress, (1976b) "Broadband Communications for Rural Development? Yes--But We Will Need a Marketing Concept," Office of Technology Assessment:Washington, D.C., November 15, 1976.

Van Valey, Thomas L., (1971) "On the Evaluation of Simple Models Containing Multiple Indicators of Unmeasured Variables," *Causal*

Models in the Social Sciences, (H. M. Blalock, ed.), Aldine:Chicago, IL, 1971.

Veith, Richard, (1976) *Talk-Back TV: Two Way Cable Television*, Tab Books:Blue Ridge Summit, PA, 1976.

Veljanovski, C.G., and W. D. Bishop, (1983) *Choice By Cable: The Economics of a New Era in Television*, Institute of Economic Affairs:London, U.K., 1983.

Verba, Sidney, and Norman Nie, (1972) *Participation in America*, Harper and Row:NY, 1972.

Waz, Joe, (1980) "Covering Community Concerns in the Cable TV Franchising Process," Address presented at the City-University Forum on Cable Television, Milwaukee, WI, July 24, 1980.

Webb, G. Kent, (1983) *The Economics of Cable Television*, Lexington Books, D.C. Heath & Co.:Lexington, Massachusetts, 1983.

Webster, James G., (1982) *The Impact of Cable and Pay Cable Television on Local Station Audiences*, National Association of Broadcasters:Washington, D.C., 1982.

Wenner, Lawrence A., (1975) "Cable TV Policy and Public Access," *Intellect*, V. 104, No. 2370, December, 1975.

Wessel, Harry, (1992) "'The Politics of Cable Regulation: A Federal, State and Local Perspective," paper presented at the annual National Conference of the Urban Affairs Association, Cleveland, Ohio, May 2, 1992.

White, Stephen, (1968) "Toward a Modest Experiment in Cable Television," *Public Interest*, No. 12, Summer, 1968.

Wicklein, John, (1980) "Two-Way Cable: Much Promise, Some Concern," *The Cable/Broadband Communications Book, Volume 2, 1980-81*, (M. L. Hollowell, ed.), knowledge Industry Press:White Plains, NY, 1980.

Wicks, Jr., David D., (1981) "Summary of CATV Industry in 1981 Based on 1980," *Current Developments in CATV*, (G. Shapiro, ed.), Practising Law Institute:NY, 1981.

Wiley, Richard E., and Richard M. Neustadt. (1982) "U.S. Communications Policy in the New Decade," *Journal of Communications*, V. 32, pp. 22-32, Spring, 1982.

Williams, Bruce A., (1979) "Beyond 'Incrementalism,' Organizational Theory and Public Policy," *Policy Studies Journal*, V. 7, No. 4, Summer, 1979.

Williams, Wendell W., (1955) "An Analysis of the Sustaining Local Public Service Programming of Selected Television Stations," dissertation, Indiana University, 1955.

Williamson, Oliver E., (1976) "Franchise Bidding for Natural Monopolies--in general and with respect to CATV," *Bell Journal of Economics*, V. &, No. 1, Spring, 1976.

Wines, Michael, (1981) "The Cable Revolution--tough choices for the industry and the government," *National Journal*, V. 13, pp. 1888-1895, October 24, 1981.

Wolf, Frank, (1972) *Television Programming for News and Public Affairs: A Quantitative Analysis of Networks and Stations*, Praeger:NY, 1972.

Wolfsohn, Tom, and Peg Kay, (1980) "Ascertainment of Community Needs: Proposing a Systems Approach," *The Cable/Broadband Communications Book: Volume 2, 1980-81*, (M. L. Hollowell, ed.), Knowledge Industry Publications:White Plains, NY, 1980.

Wurtzel, Alan, (1975) "Public Access Cagble TV Programming," *Journal of Communications*, V. 25, No. 3, 1975.

Yale Review of Law and Social Action, Editors, (1972) (Special Issue on Cable), Valume 2, No. 3, Spring, 1972.

Yates, R., N. Mahe, & J. Masson, (1990) *Fiber Optics and CATV Business Strategy*, Artech House Telecommunications, Inc.:Norwood, MA, 1990.

Yates, Douglas, (1976) "Political Innovation and Institution Building: The Experinece of Decentralization Experiments," *Theoretical Perspectives on Urban Politics*, (W. D. Hawley, ed.), Prentice-Hall:Englewood Cliffs, NJ, 1976.

Yin, Robert K., (1975) "Goals for Citizen Involvement: Some Possibilities and Some Evidence," Rand Paper No. P-5365, Rand Corp.:Santa Monica, CA, February, 1975.

Yin, Robert K., (1974) "Citizen Participation in Planning," *Cable Television: Franchising Considerations*, (Baer, et. al., eds.), Crane, Russak and Co.:NY, 1974.

Yin, Robert K., (1972) "Cable on the Public Mind," *Yale Review of Law and Social Action*, V. 2, No. 3, Spring, 1972.

Young, Elizabeth L., (1981) "Public Participation in Telecommunications: Who Will Have Control?" *Telecommunications and Productivity*, (M. Moss, ed.), Addison-Wesley:Reading, MA, 1981.

Younger, Mary Sue, (1979) *Handbook for linear regression*, Duxbury Press:North Scituate, MA, 1979.

Zeigler, Harmon, (1970) "The Communications Revolution and the Future of Interest Groups," *The Information Utilities and Social Choice*, (Sackman and Nie, eds.), AFIPS Press:Montvale, NJ, 1970.

Zoerner, Cyril Edward, (1966) "The Development of American Community Antenna Television," dissertation, University of Illinois, Urbana, IL, 1966.

Index